- THE MIND IN ANOTHER PLACE -

- THE MIND IN ANOTHER PLACE -

My Life as a Scholar

LUKE TIMOTHY JOHNSON

WILLIAM B. EERDMANS PUBLISHING COMPANY
GRAND RAPIDS, MICHIGAN

Wm. B. Eerdmans Publishing Co.
4035 Park East Court SE, Grand Rapids, Michigan 49546
www.eerdmans.com

28 27 26 25 24 23 22   1 2 3 4 5 6 7

ISBN 978-0-8028-8011-6

Library of Congress Cataloging-in-Publication Data

Names: Johnson, Luke Timothy, author.
Title: The mind in another place : my life as a scholar / Luke Timothy Johnson.
Description: Grand Rapids, Michigan : William B. Eerdmans Publishing Com-
     pany, [2022] | Includes bibliographical references and index. | Summary:
     "A memoir by Luke Timothy Johnson in which Johnson reflects on the life
     experiences that made him a scholar and on the general requirements of
     scholarship"—Provided by publisher.
Identifiers: LCCN 2021034644 | ISBN 9780802880116 (hardcover)
Subjects: LCSH: Johnson, Luke Timothy. | New Testament scholars—United
     States—Biography. | BISAC: BIOGRAPHY & AUTOBIOGRAPHY /
     Religious | RELIGION / Christian Theology / Ethics
Classification: LCC BS2351.J64 A3 2021 | DDC 220.609—dc23
LC record available at https://lccn.loc.gov/2021034644.

To Carl Holladay,
friend and colleague

Contents

Preface   ix

INTRODUCTION   Defining a Scholar   1

PART ONE. BECOMING A SCHOLAR

CHAPTER 1   Childhood (1943–1955)   19

CHAPTER 2   Adolescence (1955–1963)   35

CHAPTER 3   Monastic Life (1963–1971)   55

CHAPTER 4   Doctoral Studies (1971–1976)   75

PART TWO. BEING A SCHOLAR

CHAPTER 5   Yale Divinity School (1976–1982)   95

CHAPTER 6   Indiana University (1982–1992)   114

CHAPTER 7   Emory University (1992–2001)   134

CHAPTER 8   Emory University (2001–2016)   155

CHAPTER 9   Scholarship in Academic Retirement   174

CONTENTS

Part Three. A Scholar's Virtues

CHAPTER 10   Intellectual Virtues   187

CHAPTER 11   Moral Virtues   209

EPILOGUE   Looking Back and Forward   226

Notes   233

Index   253

Preface

Writing any sort of memoir is about the last thing I ever thought I would do. Let's face it: writing about one's own life smacks of immodesty, especially when one's life has not been notably noteworthy. I have been neither a Washington politico nor a Hollywood celebrity. I can shop at Walmart and Target without being recognized. So why have I taken the risk of revealing my inner narcissist? I can't be so deluded as to think that the world breathlessly awaits my memories. Indeed, I am not sure even my children, grandchildren, and great-grandchildren either know or care much how I have spent my life. And that's part of the rub.

I have come to realize that even the members of my family know little about me beyond the fact that I am overweight and occasionally humorous. They might be aware that I have retired, but retired from what? The best any of them could probably come up with is, "Well, from teaching." No more do my brothers and sisters have any real sense of my life as a scholar, who pretty much all the time had his "mind in another place." They have no idea about much of what I devoted my best energies to in my long working life. And realizing this, I realized as well how little most ordinary people know about the life of scholarship.

So I began thinking about a narrative that might tell others not only what I did but also what other people called scholars or academics do.

The more I pondered this, the more I came to see that the children and grandchildren, family and even friends, of other scholars might well be equally clueless concerning the scholar's life. And I pushed it one step further: even young people aspiring to the life of the mind, or scholars who have just begun their academic career, might have little notion of how much and how rapidly the scholarly life has changed in the past fifty years, or how uncertain the future of that way of life is.

Thus, I have set out this narrative of "Becoming a Scholar" (part 1) and "Being a Scholar" (part 2). It is not a complete autobiography or memoir. It tells my story with a focus entirely on my life as a scholar, with the goal of showing outsiders and would-be insiders alike some of the dimensions of the life of the mind as lived by one scholar for over fifty years. At the end (part 3), I discuss the intellectual and moral virtues necessary for excellent scholarship, in the hope of being helpful especially to younger scholars.

Throughout the narrative, I acknowledge the gifts that I received from family, teachers, colleagues, and students. In this spot, however, I really need to recognize the friendship and collegial support offered to me by Carl R. Holladay, to whom this book is dedicated. Many thanks to James Ernest of Eerdmans, who offered support and helpful feedback. And I gladly state my gratitude to my assistant, Elizabeth Arnold, who throughout the writing of this book has made everything easier and more pleasant.

Luke Timothy Johnson
February 26, 2021

Introduction

Defining a Scholar

*T*HE CARICATURE OF THE "ABSENT-MINDED PROFESSOR" IS ubiquitous and instantly recognizable. This is the guy—the cartoon is an ancient one, so the figure is usually male—who is loaded with obscure learning but is useless when it comes to domestic chores, basic bookkeeping, childcare, travel plans, or dozens of other things that normal people expect of themselves and other adults, like finding their own car keys.

The absent-minded professor is sometimes referred to as a "longhair." *Merriam-Webster's Dictionary*, in fact, makes "an impractical intellectual" its first definition of that word. Less neutrally, professors can be referred to as eggheads, dwellers of ivy-covered towers, fuzzy-headed intellectuals, even social parasites out of touch with the real world. Think of Cary Grant in the movie *Bringing Up Baby*, or Ryan O'Neal in *What's Up Doc?*, or the stock character in the satiric academic novels of Richard Russo (*Straight Man*), Jane Smiley (*Moo*), Kingsley Amis (*Lucky Jim*), Robert Parker (*Small Vices*), David Lodge (*Small World*), and Robertson Davies (*Rebel Angels*).

As with all widely diffused stereotypes, the "absent-minded professor" has some basis. There are any number of academicians who are not only unable to change a diaper or wash the dishes ("I need to do research in my study, dear") but are also imbecilic when it comes to their chosen vocation. In the nearly fifty years I labored in the academy, I observed many examples of professors who were so inept at even the simplest professional chores that they ended up enjoying lives of considerable leisure based entirely on their demonstrated incompetence: serve as a department chair? (please, no); take part in an important search? (obviously not); direct a dissertation? (only with assistance); construct a syllabus? (well, yes, so long as the same one could be used every year).

Perhaps predictably, these same academics are the ones who, after publishing the minimum required for tenure and promotion, combine scant research and dreary pedagogy. Every competent member of every university, college, or seminary department in the nation knows that some colleagues are helium-headed dullards, poseurs, charlatans. In their case, the term "absent-minded professor" really does capture the whole. There is just not a lot going on in the minds of those highly educated but strangely ineffectual drones.

This book is not about them.

It is, rather, about people who may display some of the symptoms of pure "absent-mindedness" but are, in fact, deeply and intensely engaged with an issue, question, problem, mystery, or conundrum that challenges their mind, and often their emotions and bodies as well—to such an extent that they can be said to have their mind in another place, not just momentarily but for extended periods of time. My subject matter is men and women who actually can change diapers and keep track of their car keys but who, even as they perform such quotidian tasks, are far more interested in something other than the diaper or the keys or the need for an oil change. It is the secret life of scholars with which I am concerned.

The term "scholar," however, demands further qualification. First, the phenomenon of "the mind in another place" is found also among a wide range of creative people who would not think of themselves, nor would others think of them, as scholars. Mathematicians and musicians, artists and architects, scientists and downhill skiers, novelists and playwrights can all display the same sort of detachment from everyday life caused by a compelling alternative passion.

Second, being a scholar is not the same thing as being an intellectual. The two realms often intersect, but not always. There are, indeed, probably as many true intellectuals among taxi drivers as among academicians. For the intellectual, the life of the mind takes priority over any other activity; reading is preferable to either food or drink. But the intellectual need not turn from reading to writing, need not ever turn a wide-ranging curiosity into genuine research.

As I use the term "scholarship" in this book, then, I mean an intellectual life that is both focused and productive.

By focused, I mean that the mind is not simply curious about any and every topic but that the mind actively seeks real knowledge about specific subjects and issues. By productive, I mean that such learning gained by the mind is communicated to others, or is applied to the solution of other problems, with an eye to eventual communication, through teaching, writing, or other medium. Scholarship, in short, is not dilettantism but is a disciplined process of discovery and disclosure.

Such scholarship requires both a community of other intellectuals engaged in the same or similar quests and the means of carrying out both discovery and disclosure. Thus, although the academy does not guarantee the presence of genuine scholarship, it is the natural home for scholars, because of its congregation of others whose minds are similarly bent, and because of its assemblage of resources, such as laboratories and libraries. Scholars can and do exist and thrive outside the halls of academe, but their task is made more difficult because of isolation and the lack of resources.

It is a bit like the relationship between sanctity and the church: as a human institution, the church is notoriously corrupt, falling short of its high calling in all sorts of ways, and it is certainly possible—it has been demonstrated—that humans can achieve holiness apart from participation in church life. But it is extraordinarily difficult to sustain so arduous a calling by oneself. The sacraments and practices of the community of faith whose whole point it is to make saints provide the context within which the Holy Spirit can touch some lives and transform them according to the mind of Christ, even though the majority of those self-designating as Christians show little awareness of, or ambition toward, that fundamental goal.

Similarly, despite all the corruption and mediocrity within the academy, despite the fact that much of the machinery of higher education is beside the point, despite the evidence that a majority of students and faculty care little about the life of the mind, despite the equally clear evidence of great intellectuals and artists who have contributed—and continue to contribute—to the world's growth in knowledge apart from any taint of academicism, it is very much the case that the structures and practices of the academy make it possible for those touched by the awareness of the intellectual life and fired by the ambition to put the mind in that other place, to achieve profound and lasting scholarship.

Genuine scholars—intellectuals whose minds are in another place in a focused and productive manner—appear moreover in many shapes and sizes, devote themselves to many and varied disciplines, engage their secret passions in diverse settings. Some work in laboratories, some in libraries, some in field research; some study present social and economic patterns, some seek understanding of analogous patterns in the past; some seek cures for pandemics that threaten the contemporary world, while others seek the causes for the collapse of previous worlds; some engage ancient languages, others the language of mathematical codes; some scramble frantically for funding from grants, while others relax into salaried sinecures.

Scholarship, in fact, is as diverse as those who practice it. In a very real sense, then, the treatment of "a scholar's life" can only be specific and particular: it must offer an invitation to the whole topic through the examination of a single case. In this book, I offer my own life as a single witness to the peculiar way of being human that is the scholar's.

I use the adjective "peculiar" advisedly. Only a small portion of humanity, for example, walks the lonely path that is the scholar's—and it is as lonely, in its own way, as is the path toward holiness. Even within the nominal "home" of the academy, the genuine scholar is often isolated precisely because the scholar so persistently has the mind in another place, thus failing to play the political games that gain academic recognition and reward. The true scholar is always marginal and a minority by the simple fact of having the mind in another place in a singular and passionate manner.

Genuine scholarship, furthermore, is difficult. Maintaining intellectual focus is hard enough; turning that focus into productive insight and argument is extraordinarily hard, a matter of heavy lifting for both the mind and the body. In terms of fatigue, scholarly writing is pretty much like digging ditches. With some important but rare exceptions, the scholarly life also carries with it a genteel poverty rather than wealth, obscurity rather than fame, impuissance rather than power. And for those scholars who also are teachers, it means a genuinely self-sacrificial life: grading ten thousand C papers with steadfast attention and rigor means experiencing something like a slow but steady brain drip.

So why do women and men choose to live this way? What is the positive attraction, the personal payoff, for those whose minds are always (or regularly) "in another place"? By offering an account of my own life as a scholar, I hope to make a little more intelligible the hardships and rewards that attach to this manner of life and to suggest how becoming a scholar involves some factors that are purposeful and some that seem, at least, to be accidental. Although this is certainly an account of my life (and therefore can be regarded as a kind of memoir), it is very much centered on my life "as a scholar" and can therefore be regarded as a kind of primer on the elements that go into the scholarly life.

I cannot, then, speak about the entire range of scholarship, but I hope to provide some insight into the way I became the kind of scholar I did and the way of life that scholarship involved. I was, until my retirement in 2016, an academic scholar. I was not a freelance entrepreneur or an employee of a for-profit corporation. My scholarship was practiced as a faculty member at Yale Divinity School (1976–1982), Indiana University (1982–1992), and Emory University (1992–2016). Within each of these institutions, membership in the faculty meant teaching at least four courses a year (undergraduate, professional, and graduate), publishing books and articles in peer-reviewed journals, and performing the diverse forms of service the academic institution requires of a faculty. I will have much to say about each of these dimensions of scholarship as I go along.[1]

In case you are wondering whether I am qualified to speak about becoming and being a scholar, I offer as crude evidence the publication of thirty-five books, over seventy-five scholarly articles, over one hundred popular articles, and over two hundred book reviews; the direction of twenty-seven PhD dissertations; and the presentation of over four hundred lectures to academic and ecclesiastical gatherings—plus some two hundred teaching videos. That's the production side, unusual only for the degree of popular or public engagement and (as I will discuss later) the number of scholarly controversies involved. As to the quality of all that production, others must speak, not I.

What about the focus? I worked under the rubric of Professor of New Testament and Christian Origins. This means that I labored within the broad field of the humanities rather than the sciences. More specifically, I studied religious, philosophical, and theological texts from the Mediterranean world spanning roughly 200 BCE to 300 CE, and even a bit beyond. Genuine scholarship in this area means working directly with texts written in Hebrew, Aramaic, Latin, and Greek. Ancillary disciplines include archaeology, epigraphy, text criticism, anthropology, sociology, history, philosophy, and religious phenomenology.

To be fully qualified as a scholar of the New Testament and Christian literature of the first four centuries CE, one must also command all of Jewish literature from the Bible to the Talmud and Greco-Roman literature from classical Athens to the philosophers of the early Roman Empire. To read the New Testament and early Christian literature adequately demands, in addition to a comprehensive knowledge of the religious and philosophical literature of antiquity, an understanding of the rise and growth of religious movements and a grasp of the nature of religious experience and practice. By "adequately," I mean, to be sure, adequately as a scholar, not as a religious person reading such texts for personal enlightenment or discernment. The two modes need not be disjoined, though in practice they often are.

Because genuine scholarship involves dialogue and dispute within a community of scholars—and the community of scholars engaged in the study of the New Testament and Christian origins is both vast and multinational—it is necessary to read and respond to scholars in contemporary languages as well. In my field, the sacred triad of scholarly languages has traditionally been English, French, and German. Those who know these languages and the literature written in them must pretend, to be sure, that nothing much has been said in languages other than these (I think it was Vico in *New Science* 127 who spoke of the "conceit of scholars" as the implicit identification of what they knew to what should be known).

The plan of this book is simple. Parts 1 and 2 are mainly an intellectual memoir, as I address "becoming" and then "being" a scholar. Part 3 turns more didactically to the virtues required of the excellent scholar. In the epilogue, I raise some questions concerning the prospects for such scholarship in the future.

I have two reasons for writing at this late point in my life—when my "career as a scholar" can universally be regarded as having concluded. The first reason is that I find that the life of scholarship, while deeply involving for its practitioners, remains difficult to grasp for those who do not live it. Even when ordinary folk reject the caricatures of lazy and fuzzy-headed drones that so delight legislatures and other despisers of critical thinking, they do not comprehend what scholars actually do or why they do it.

They know that it must mean something more than teaching a few classes and hanging out in the faculty lounge, but they have little idea of the range and depth of true scholarly research: the persistence and energy necessary to carry out the process of discovery and analysis, and the emotional and intellectual strength required to overcome the inevitable discouragement and depression that accompany writing, publication, and review. It is my hope that this personal account will make some of the mystery of the scholarly life more intelligible.

My second reason for writing now is that the kind of scholarship practiced by my generation (and previous generations) is changing so rapidly that in a very few years it may not even be recognizable, much less understood or appreciated. Some of these changes represent gains, some losses. Assessing which is which may be aided by having some sense of what scholarship is changing *from* as well as what it is changing *into*. I have in mind four main changes that began during my active scholarly life and have become ever more dominant. They are technological, sociological, ideological, and institutional changes.

Technological. The mode of scholarship I inherited and practiced was predigital. The typewriter was the most advanced form of "word processor" and the Xerox machine was in its most primitive form. Teachers reproduced materials for students by means of mimeograph and ditto machines, which used ink or chemicals to create (often messy and smelly) copies to be handed out in class. Handwriting was still demanded for taking notes in class, for research notes, and even for composition. Most of my New Testament commentaries, for example, were composed in longhand before being transferred to disk. Student papers were commented on and graded in longhand. Scholars corresponded with each other by letters (handwritten or typed) sent by "snail mail."

Above all, scholarship in my field involved finding, reading, and assimilating books. I remember the awe I felt at first entering the great nave of Yale's Sterling Library at the start of my doctoral studies and how I gasped at the huge card catalogs lining that nave. Those giant wooden cabinets (now removed) encased long drawers filled with index cards indicating the precise character and location of some two million books within the miles of shelves of that massive library. Manipulating such card catalogs was an art not unlike playing the accordion; with practice, one's fingers developed their own intelligence. Finding the rare books in the far reaches of Sterling (or in Yale's Beinecke Library) was an expedition as lonely and perilous as scaling a remote mountain. Even beginning a research project was physically demanding.

At the other end, after completing a manuscript, one sent it by mail to a publisher, received it back with corrections (inked in the margins), made the corrections (on the same paper pages), and had at last galley proofs before one's eyes. But the most mind numbing of all tasks still awaited: for my first twenty-five books, I compiled the multiple indices by hand, using (yes) index cards set in boxes, scanning each page of text and entering on the appropriate card every reference in longhand—this often involved as many as twenty boxes, thousands of cards, and tens of thousands of references, all of which then had to be typed up and sent physically by mail to the publisher.

My generation of scholars held in reverence compilers of concordances (like Moulton and Geden for the New Testament and Hatch and Redpath for the Septuagint) for the lonely labor they had expended on such detailed and invaluable work, made available now to anyone who could buy or borrow their volumes.[2] Perhaps even greater admiration was accorded lexicographers like Liddell and Scott (for all Greek literature), Lewis and Short (for Latin literature), and Arndt, Baur, Gingrich, and Danker (for New Testament and early Christian literature).[3] Lexicographers, compilers of concordances, and grammarians (such as Smyth; Blass, Debrunner, Funk; and Moule)[4] were admired not only for their industry but also for having made available a comprehensive base of impeccably accurate data to other scholars. We never referred to their titles. We knew them by name. They were our patriarchs, our progenitors, the ancestors who made possible our subsequent labors. We might quibble with them over some small point or other, but their authority was absolute in what mattered most, namely, the original meaning of the text.

Such scholarly tools were among the first purchases made by a young scholar, but the hunger for books containing primary texts from the ancient world made scholars haunt used bookstores for stray volumes of the Loeb Classical Library[5] or perhaps a volume of Scott's *Hermetica*.[6] The great collections of primary texts, such as Migne's *Patrologia Latina* and *Patrologia Graeca*,[7] or the multiple volumes containing the Oxyrhynchus Papyri,[8] to be sure, could be found only in libraries. One had to go to libraries to do real research in my field. But still, each scholar wanted above all to gather as many primary texts into a personal library as possible. Secondary literature was, well, secondary, even though not to be scorned, especially if written by a Schweitzer or a Bultmann, giants in the field.[9]

Books were the source of knowledge, the occasion for criticism, and the cause of pleasure. There was something sensuous about the touch, the smell, the sight of scholarly books, and something of ecstasy in working in a truly great library. The thought that one could add to the tradition of scholarly books and compose works that might be read and studied by future generations was an implicit fantasy, I think, of every young scholar in my field.

The technological revolution in biblical studies began in the early '80s with the introduction of the personal computer and then the Internet—the first edition of my *Writings of the New Testament* (1986) was based on a typescript produced in 1984 on the then sophisticated IBM Selectric typewriter with correction tape and replaceable type-heads. The full implications of the digital age have yet to unfold, to be sure, but its impact is already profound. The digital age has disrupted and reorganized the categories of time and space.

Teachers can now scan and print articles and books with ease, can construct dazzling PowerPoint presentations, can correct student essays and exams (submitted electronically) with marginal comments, returned electronically. Blogs and Vimeos are everyday instruments of instruction. "Distance learning" of every sort has diminished the necessity—if not the importance—of physical attendance at school.

Scholars communicate constantly through fax, e-mail, and electronic text, sometimes as well on a variety of social platforms. The publication of books and articles, be it noted, has scarcely ceased. There may well be more scholarly print floating around than at any previous time in history. Yet traditional publishing houses fight for survival. So vast has the world of scholarship become, and so interconnected electronically, that in my field, serious scholarly publication survives on subsistence rations, dependent on one side by the guaranteed purchase of every hefty volume and every periodical (however obscure) by the research libraries of universities, and on the other side by the income derived from the dissemination of lightweight best sellers of a popular character.[10]

How long scholarship will be defined in terms of actual (as distinct from digitally virtual) books is anyone's guess. In the meantime, the computer has changed virtually everything about the process of scholarly writing. Word processing enables an ease of composition (complete with autocorrect) that encourages speedy, if not necessarily thoughtful, output. No more card catalogs—the holdings of research libraries are all "online." Among other things, this means that bibliographies can be constructed without ever holding or reading the books and articles cited in footnotes. Most important, it means that scholars can confidently work from their office and home, with as much direct access to the world's learning as if they were in the research library. Those primary texts we formerly pined for and coveted? They are all available through the Internet. The Loeb Classical Library volumes that I scrimped to purchase are now totally accessible to those with access to Google.[11] To make the point dramatically: a college freshman today has more access to primary sources on a laptop than the great historians of the early twentieth century, like Adolf Harnack, had when they set out to write their works.[12]

Sociological. When I began serious scholarly work, I was a member of a Catholic religious order whose labors were supported by the church (as well as directed to the life of the church) and abetted by a celibate lifestyle that was free from domestic concerns. As I will recount, I myself quickly became a husband, a father, and eventually a grandfather, deeply enmeshed in such everyday joys and anxieties as offered by life in the world. My lay colleagues when I started were mostly men—there were already, to be sure, some important exceptions—whose wives adopted the conventional wifely roles of domestic management and support (even though many of them also held significant jobs). The increased admission of women to doctoral programs, and the concomitant decline of Catholic religious orders (the main supplier of celibate male scholars and, for that matter, scholarly nuns), meant a sea change in the composition of the scholarly community concerned with ancient religious texts. The number of female scholars and teachers in my field has multiplied many times over. And very few male scholars are any longer celibate members of religious orders, whose main concern is (or is professed to be) the upbuilding of the church. For both male and female scholars today, devotion to learning is relativized by the complexities presented by dual careers, by children, and (more often than not) by a late initiation into the world of scholarship.

When men and women fall in love with serious biblical scholarship only after a first career, or after advanced education in a completely different field, the effort to "catch up" within an abbreviated time span (and with one hand behind the back) leads inevitably and understandably to hyper-specialization. It is easier to become an "expert in Mark's Gospel" than to command all of ancient literature.

As I entered the academy, an even more profound sociological change had begun, as scholarship shifted its primary locus from the church (and its seminaries) to the university (and its departments of religion). Positions in universities immediately became more prestigious than those in seminaries, attracting the "best and brightest" to a form of scholarship carried out less in conversation with philosophy and theology and more in conversation with literature and the social sciences. Rather than a setting that sought above all for the ways in which the New Testament could be normative for the life of a believing community, the university offered the opportunity to approach ancient texts with an eye primarily to description and analysis. Catholic, Protestant, and Orthodox seminaries have not disappeared, but their importance within scholarship has greatly been diminished.

Ideological. I define ideology here as thought that arises from and is conformed to a set of convictions and practices. In that broad sense, New Testament scholarship was always "ideological," even when it was carried out within the framework of the church's canon and creed. What were formerly called "presuppositions" became evident, indeed, in the contradictory claims made on the basis of the New Testament by Catholic and Protestant apologists.

One of the compelling motivations for adopting a "scientific" model of biblical scholarship—one that based positions on evidence and logical argument—was to isolate and "bracket" such presuppositions (or ideological standpoints). Such was the Enlightenment ideal, embodied in what was universally designated as the "historical-critical method."

While partially successful in enabling a more ecumenical and collegial conversation concerning ancient texts, and while reaching considerable agreement on the relatively neutral areas of archaeological and linguistic research, traditional scholarship rarely managed to dislodge theological strongholds on points that really mattered to the respective parties.

The sociological shift in scholarship from the church to the academy (an increasingly secularly defined academy) also had major implications for the role of ideology. The first consequence was the abandonment of the ideological boundaries set by the Christian canon and creed. Scholars in secular academies seemed for a time to enjoy the "presuppositionless" scientific approach that post-Enlightenment thinkers had supposed would follow upon liberation from the church's constraints. And for a brief moment, the so-called historical-critical approach to ancient Christian and cognate literature genuinely appeared as a form of neutral description—although it was actually loaded with religious presuppositions of its own.[13]

But the void left by the removal of canon and creed was quickly filled by a variety of new ideological postures as new voices entered the scholarly arena: feminist, liberationist, postcolonial, and the like. Perhaps most problematic was the emergence of various forms of deconstructive criticism, which tended to reduce all texts to instruments of power needing to be purged of their oppressive force through "criticism." The animus toward ancient texts (defined as patriarchal, sexist, and imperialist) that was implicit in new ideological criticisms has become both more varied and more overt. Historical scholarship is at times viewed as a kind of therapeutic process designed to heal readers of the damages done them by ancient literature—above all as wielded by oppressive forces within contemporary society. Together with the sociological realities I have sketched, realities that encourage a hyperspecialization within the field, younger scholars now occasionally define themselves not only with respect to a small selection of texts but also with respect to a specific ideological posture, leading to such self-characterizations as "I am an Asian, feminist, postcolonial scholar in the Gospel of John."[14]

Institutional. About a decade before I started PhD work at Yale, the study of religion in state universities was legally allowed for the first time (previously, only privately funded schools could have such departments). The future for career opportunities seemed limitless. Soon, doctorates were being granted not only by the traditional elite universities in the East but also by public institutions across the country. The results were predictable. While the number of scholars increased exponentially, the number of available positions for them proved finite. I entered the job market precisely when it shifted from one in which a fresh Yale PhD would have the pick of four or five fine positions to one in which a Yale PhD had to compete with countless other young PhDs (in my case, three times unsuccessfully) for a dramatically reduced number of not-so-great positions. That situation has not improved but has rather gotten steadily worse as academics were relieved of retirement deadlines and tenured professors stayed in place long past their shelf life. Doctoral programs now scramble desperately to place their graduates in any sort of position, and many schools have radically curtailed or canceled programs of study altogether.

The growth in numbers of scholars in the study of ancient religion found expression in the expansion of learned societies. The Society of Biblical Literature (SBL), for example, went in my lifetime from being a group of male Ivy League scholars meeting in one large auditorium to an international association of thousands of men and women scholars who either teach at universities and seminaries or don't. Anyone who could win funding from their schools attended the yearly conference to hear or be heard, to sell or buy books, to hire or be hired. So important has the annual meeting of the SBL become that many scholars find their true home more in that company of associates than in what used to be called the *collegium* that is their particular context in church or academy. Finding a niche where one can present a paper in such congested and complex conferences, with panels and workshops devoted to every arcane (as well as banal) topic imaginable, naturally encourages the overspecialization of the field.

Scholarship in my field is today not in the least leisurely. It is, rather, fraught with anxiety. It is not merely a matter of would-be scholars getting into a program or finding a job. Universities themselves are being forced to justify—and sometimes jettison—courses of study that are not "successful" in the placement of graduates. Those young (or these days, not necessarily so young) scholars who find positions in universities or seminaries— there are very few ecclesial settings in which they could ply their craft—are then under tremendous pressure to produce publications, above all books or peer-reviewed articles, not only to secure tenure but also to win the meager financial rewards of promotion to associate and full professorship. Such pressure on young scholars (who fully understand that the quantity rather than the quality of their work is what really counts) encourages publications that do not reveal the fruit of long deliberation but are hasty concoctions of immature minds. Young scholars are expected to produce the tangible results of creative research while also learning how to develop classes, serve on endless committees, and, oh yes, manage to reserve some of their humanity for faith, family, and friends. The competitive character of contemporary academic life encourages careerism more than it does the slow cultivation of the mind and a scholarship that is wise as well as smart. It is far from an idyllic scene.

All these changes happened over the approximately fifty years I worked as a scholar, and, like everyone else in my generation, I had to find my way through a sometimes rapidly altering terrain. The account of each scholar's life over the past five decades would be worth considering, for the changes and challenges were seismic and scholars adapted (or failed to) in diverse ways.

Overall, however, I think I was perhaps less affected by these changes than I might otherwise have been, because by the time they occurred, I was already fully formed in my scholarly disposition and discipline. I certainly was fitted for scholarship by the usual measurements of aptitude and ambition. But in my case, scholarship was a concomitant of an earlier and deeper way in which my mind was in another place. My first and most persistent goal in life was to become a saint, and although scholarship was an aspect of the vocation I had chosen in order to pursue holiness (being a Benedictine monk), I fell into properly academic scholarship by accident.

It was as an intellectual who affirmed (and still to this day affirms) the faith into which I was born and baptized that I entered the realm of academia, and that fundamentally religious sense of my calling remains the first way in which *my* "mind is in another place." In my own stumbling and clumsy fashion, I find that I truly do seek the face of God. Scholarship, like all other human endeavors, has always seemed to me secondary to the serious business of becoming a certain kind of person; scholarship is a game that can be played, and must be played, seriously and intently, with the scholar never forgetting that it is only a game, whose stakes are not ultimate.

My ideas of how God makes one holy have certainly changed, but I have never had reason to disagree with Léon Bloy's dictum that "the only great tragedy in life is not to become a saint."[15] I need no reminding of how far short of that goal I have fallen, but I am steadfast in my conviction that it is the singular ambition that transcends all others.

For better or worse, then, my ideological approach to the texts of the New Testament is shaped by the Christian canon and creed, and the entire world of the Catholic tradition in which I was placed and in which I choose (with a strong sense of ambivalence) still to stand. I must depend on friendly critics and conversation partners to show me how my bias may distort my reading—this is the business, after all, of scholarly conversation: not that we all agree, but that we all engage in a spirit of generosity as well as of suspicion. In any case, my awareness of my primal commitment to having "my mind in another place" religiously was sharpened by spending most of my academic life in two Protestant seminaries and a state university.

When I received my PhD in New Testament from Yale University in 1976, I was told that the great scholar Nils Dahl had declared, "Well, Johnson has a Yale degree, but he is certainly not a Yale product." Although I am sure he did not mean it as a compliment—I was by no means a favorite of his—I recognize its truth. I learned so much—as I hope to show—from my Yale teachers and colleagues, but what I learned enriched rather than fundamentally shaped the sort of scholar I was.

My long life of reading and writing, I have always understood, was carried out *coram Deo* ("before God"). At the very least, this meant that, for me, the pertinent court of opinion concerning my work was less the opinion of other scholars than the judgment of God, who sees what is in our hearts. To understand how this was so, how my mind was as much in another place religiously (that is, in the implicit presence of God) as it was in another place intellectually (that is, in pursuit of some intellectual question), it is necessary to consider the story from the start, tracing the ways in which, to use Jean Le Clercq's lovely phrase, "the love of learning and the desire for God"[16] intertwined and grew together within me and found expression, I hope, in my life's work.

PART ONE

Becoming a Scholar

Chapter One

CHILDHOOD (1943–1955)

M Y FIRST ELEVEN YEARS WERE SPENT IN FIFIELD, Wisconsin, a tiny village of about four hundred people in the far north of that state, about sixty miles south of Lake Superior. It was always a hard place to get to, but in my boyhood, the Soo Line Railroad, whose tracks ran less than a hundred yards from our house, still carried passengers, newspapers, and mail from the big cities of Milwaukee and Chicago. Today, the railroad no longer carries passengers, and Fifield is even more remote, accessible only by the two state highways (13 and 70) that intersect it.

The biggest building in Fifield was the redbrick schoolhouse. In addition to a town hall, the village had two groceries, two churches (Roman Catholic and Congregational), three sets of gasoline pumps, and many taverns—one of them (The Northwoods) was, in regional parlance, a "supper club," which meant that it served food as well as the beer and brandy that the natives consumed in impressive quantities. The Northwoods—located about one hundred yards from our house—also had a small bowling alley that provided employment for teenage boys as pinsetters. Lying in bed at night, I could hear from one side the whistle of trains and, from the other side, the crash of bowling pins.

Apart from a tiny sawmill and a creamery, the town had no industry. The town of Park Falls (population ca. 2,500), four miles north of us, had a flourishing paper mill, which offered employment to many. Some younger men worked on the rails. Otherwise, the school bus delivered children, grades 1 through 12, from the hardscrabble farms scattered through the area. Once part of the great economic boom connected to the deforestation of the upper tier of the Midwest—my mother's father and brother still worked as loggers—Fifield, with the other villages dotting highway 13, remained economically mired in the Depression throughout my childhood, and in most respects still does. The many taverns, supper clubs, and rustic resorts on lakes reflected a desperate dependence on the wealthier folk from Milwaukee and Chicago who came up in the fall to hunt deer and in the summer to fish, and who spent some of their idle hours and extra cash in such establishments, drinking and telling tall tales. Lakes in the area were legendary in number and beauty. Equally legendary were the number and size of the mosquitoes that bred around them.

Even more beautiful than the spring-fed lakes was the Flambeau River, the south fork of which ran through the town and offered young people a place to skate in winter and swim (down by the footbridge) in summer.[1] During my childhood, winters were bitterly cold (I remember an absolute temperature one day of 40 below zero), but summers were mild and breezy. In the depth of winter, the Flambeau froze in spots a foot thick, and even in summer the briskness of the river was a challenge to the fainthearted.

Extremes of wealth and poverty were not on obvious display, although there were degrees of economic security within the overall poverty of the region. Managers at the paper mill and new car salesmen were well-off by local standards, while those we used to call hobos and bums (many of them alcoholic) were manifestly without means, needing help to get by.[2] Within that range, my family, even after the death of my father in 1944, which left my mother a widow with six children, could be considered moderately comfortable. We had a paid-for house, an (older) automobile, and the basic amenities of a 1940s' household: Maytag washer, oil heater, Singer sewing machine, plus the minor luxuries of an upright piano and a handsome combination radio-phonograph console.

Like everyone else, though, we wore hand-me-down clothes and socks that were darned more than once. Like everyone else, we relied in winter on the vegetables we had grown in our backyard garden, which our mother canned. The lack of iodine in local diets led to frequent cases of goiter or hyperthyroidism; chocolate-tasting iodine tablets were regularly distributed to grade school children as a preventative. For people without much cash or credit, barter was a common means of exchange: for doing a farmer's taxes, my mother could get a bushel of fresh corn; for helping make a tavern owner's insurance claim, she could receive several bottles of spirits.

Demographically, Fifield had a similar range of slight diversity within a predominantly European-based population. I never saw a person of color before I moved to Mississippi in 1955. The Native American Ojibwa reservation at nearby Lac de Flambeau made little impact on us in the days before the Chippewa established a casino there. But I well remember how ethnic and religious differences mattered to first-, second-, and third-generation European immigrants.[3] The epithets of "Canuck" and "Mick" and "Bohunk" and "Polack" were casually tossed about. Catholics were papists, and Lutherans were heretics. Since there were not many of them, Congregationalists were given a pass. In Park Falls, the Norwegian Lutheran church was despised for its laxity by the German Lutheran church.

A "mixed marriage" involving diverse European ethnicities was not quite as serious as one involving a Catholic and a Protestant (which needed a formal dispensation on the Catholic side), but it required careful consideration, nevertheless. Since my family drew from such a variety of European stock (French Canadian, Dutch, English, Scottish, Irish, German, and Nordic), we did not get caught up in such competition, although spiritually we all thought of ourselves as essentially Irish.

Family arrangements also were more diverse and sometimes casual than might be suspected for a small village in the late 1940s and early 1950s. My brother and I discovered just how diverse when we entered homes to collect payment for our paper route. Besides the sometimes bewildering and alien smells that enveloped us as we came out of the winter cold into porches and kitchens, we observed virtually every family arrangement now trumpeted as social advancement. One example: among my mother's good friends was a female transvestite named Fritzi who lived with a married couple and was possibly the partner of one of them. She dressed as a man, drank with the men, and did man's work. She was universally accepted, liked, and even admired. When money was low, she cut our hair in the kitchen. She was my first boss when I was maybe nine or ten: as she tended the town cemetery's lawn, I clipped the weeds around the tombstones.

MY FAMILY

My ancestry did not predict the emergence of a scholar from that little place on the map. There were no professors, lawyers, doctors, or other professional types among my forebears. We were, like others in the area, lower middle class, laborers and small business owners. My grandparents on both sides had grade school educations. My father, Merland Ferdinand Johnson, graduated from Fifield High School, sold insurance, ran a small service station, and served as town clerk. My mother, Bernice Nola Teeters, graduated from Park Falls High School and, after her husband's death, took over his insurance business and town clerkship while raising six children—the youngest of whom was me, born two months before my father's death and given the baptismal name of Timothy Robert Johnson.[4]

As I remember things, the lack of higher education among my elders did not mean a lack of intelligence, grammatical speech, or clear writing. Literacy was assumed, as was (especially in the days of war when sons were in the military) an avid interest in world affairs. The Milwaukee papers (*Journal* in the morning and *Sentinel* in the evening) were avidly read, as was the local news made available by the *Park Falls Herald*.[5] My father's side of the family contributed wit and laughter; my mother's side contributed drive and ambition.

Only two of my mother's seven siblings had a college education, one of them (Bernard) at West Point. The military was for us, as it was for many in small midwestern towns, one of the premier avenues of advancement for folk with such humble origins.[6] My mother's sister Laura made a career in the Women's Air Force. My oldest brother, Mickey, enlisted in the air force straight out of high school, served as radar technician in B-29 flights over North Korea, and used the GI Bill to get a BA from Millsaps College. Among my other siblings, my sister Nancy began training as a nurse, and when circumstances interrupted that, she also got a college degree later in life. My brother Pat received a PhD in clinical psychology from Catholic University. Clearly, my parents instilled in their children a hunger for education—and the circumstances of their children's lives turned out to stimulate that native drive, by giving them little option except to find their own way forward.

The Johnson family, as of November 20, 1943, consisted of my father and mother and six children. Mickey was thirteen, Mary Jane was twelve, Nancy was nine, Margaret was seven, Pat was three, and I was the newborn boy. Two hardworking parents, by all accounts passionately in love and popular members of the town,[7] and six hardy children, bright-eyed and (at least in their own eyes) good looking and smart. Life in the household seemed secure, and my older siblings tell me what a joyful time they had starting their lives in that time and place and with those parents. For gatherings of family and friends, my mother played tunes old and new on the piano, joining her lovely soprano voice to my father's fine baritone.

But then, one late fall day, my father went out in a snowstorm to help someone whose car was stuck in the snow. He got chilled, caught a fever, and, in the days when antibiotics were reserved for the military, quickly succumbed to an infection. Within weeks (January 31, 1944) he died of acute nephritis, at the age of thirty-six. My mother was left a widow with six children to raise and, somehow, a living to make.

I naturally do not myself remember how things went in those awful days when in the midst of her grief Mother needed to learn everything my father knew, take over what work of his she could, and hold the family together. I know that the older children helped. My brother Mickey got a special driver's permit at age thirteen to take my mother on her insurance calls; he kept the gas station going for some months and then went to work all through high school at my uncle Bill's garage in Park Falls. My twelve-year-old sister, Mary Jane, became, by all accounts, my chief and best surrogate mother. Until her death, she thought of me as "hers" in a special way. All I remember myself, sadly, is her singing me to sleep at naptime, lying next to me and crooning the tune "Baa Baa Black Sheep" with special emphasis on "one for the little boy who lives down the lane." By the time I started grade school at age five (we had no kindergarten), Mickey was in the air force and, shortly after, Mary Jane married Warren Fellinger, another member of the air force, who spent much of his military life doing secret electronic things in Albuquerque, New Mexico.

The family I personally remember, then, was reduced both in number and in resources. My sisters Nancy and Margaret were in high school, and my brother Pat and I were in grade school. Mother was the center of our lives and our guiding force. I know all sons think this, but I believe that it is fair to call my mother a remarkable woman. Even though she had to scramble to earn a living, using her brains in whatever way her neighbors' needs made available, she sent us off to school every day with oatmeal in our bellies and had a hot supper ready in the evening. On Saturdays she did the wash, cooked, and baked simultaneously—cookies, coffee cake, bread. In the days before frozen food, everything was "from scratch," including wonderful birthday cakes made to order for each child. Even with all her children helping at this chore or that (ironing clothes, scrubbing the kitchen floor, pounding dust out of rugs on the clothesline, changing window screens for storm windows and back again according to season), she would rub her arms and state distractedly, "I have so much to do I don't know where to start."[8]

Despite never seeming to have a spare moment, certainly not for herself, Mother somehow managed to gift each of us with a sense of very special and individual significance in her eyes, and in God's eyes. She had the ability to combine seriousness, and at times severity, with an attitude of complete trust in her children. We enjoyed a kind of freedom—of thought, of movement, of enterprise—that seems no longer possible for today's youth. When I sat in the elm tree across the driveway from our house reading *Tom Sawyer*, I recognized even at nine how his Hannibal adventures paralleled what we experienced growing up in Fifield.

The sibling who unquestionably had the biggest influence on me in the years between my first and sixth grades in school was my brother Pat, three years older than I. Like most big brothers, he was both mentor and tormentor, but since this is a book about becoming a scholar, I want to stress the way in which he was my first and, in many ways, best teacher. In those years, I was pretty much an appendage to this skinny version of the all-American boy. Everywhere he went, I went. This meant not only that I swam and skated with the older kids, and played sandlot baseball with them, but that I participated (and sometimes was chief collaborator) in Pat's astonishing range of interests and activities. He was yang to my yin, who dragged me along on all his many adventures. And as he went, he explained. He had (and has) a remarkable gift for clear exposition, and he poured all of what he was learning into me. Or at least he tried.

Pat and I put on plays in the garage for the neighboring kids; we had an army club (complete with authentic patches donated by our military kin) that actually went into battle with another group of "armed" kids; we had a construction company that hauled dirt and tried to build a cabin in the woods. Pat and I delivered papers both morning and evening throughout the town—dividing it between us: we snipped open the wire-bound stacks of papers when they had been tossed out of the train, folded them together, divided them into paper-boy bags, and set out to bring the news of the world to our fellow townspeople. On his own, Pat was a Boy Scout avid for merit badges (I was the victim who was bandaged again and again so he and his friends could win a "life-saver" merit badge); he collected stamps; he built birdhouses and a lumber lift for our wagon.

I will turn to reading in a bit, but I should say here that it was Pat who devoured first the pages of *Boys' Life* and *Mad* magazine, and who had first dibs on the sports pages of the *Milwaukee Journal*—the Boston Braves' move to Milwaukee in 1953 was for all of us a transforming event, gluing us to the broadcast of every game by Earl Gillespie and Blaine Walsh—and what we then called "the funnies," above all, *Pogo* (my mother's favorite), *Li'l Abner*, the *Katzenjammer Kids*, and *Out Our Way*. It was Pat who involved me in reading dozens and dozens of comic books (GI Joe and Superman the favorites) and trading stacks of them with other kids in town; it was Pat who initiated our practice of crouching on the floor in stores and reading all the magazines they stocked.

A perfect illustration of Pat's entrepreneurial spirit was the publication of the *Fifield News* by the Johnson brothers, aged twelve and nine. Pat had received a small printing press for Christmas, with paper, ink, slots for type, rubber type, and a tool to fit the slots into the wheel that could be turned under the ink pad. Many boys would have spent a week fooling with the thing. Not Pat. He became publisher and printer of a new commercial venture, for which I was "reporter and typesetter." We printed some twenty issues of the paper (about six small pages an issue), and, yes, we sold it around town. Naturally, it sold well, because most of the news it contained was about the comings and goings (and pregnancies and births) in the Johnson family. The grown-up newspaper at the county seat, the *Philips Bee*, heard about our doings, sent a reporter to our house, and printed an article about these two boys with an enterprising spirit, complete with a photograph of Pat and me setting type out of egg crates. It was actually hard and unglamorous work, from which I derived mostly the ability to read backward and upside down (necessary when setting type by hand). I also grasped early on the connection between research (reporting), writing, and publication.

Family Traits

These, then, were the people I lived with for my first eleven years, with my active memory embracing around six or seven of those years. Looking back some seventy years later, I am able to discern four distinct traits of my family that were obvious to me then and seem even more significant now, as I ask how I became the kind of scholar I became. By no means do I claim that any of these characteristics were unique to us, but in combination, they made a distinctive context for my most formative years.

Religious faith. The church easily dominated the school in terms of organizing our lives and influencing our perceptions. Although our ancestors were Protestant, grandmothers on both sides were Roman Catholics. I suspect that we became Catholic on my mother's side through the Quebecois heritage of my mother's mother, Mary Amo. On my father's side, my grandmother Lucy Katon was Irish Catholic. I did not learn how recently we had become Catholic until my brother Pat (in a later-life enterprise) did a complete family genealogy. I could not imagine being anything else.

We were not nominal Catholics; we were *practicing* Catholics, and in the post-Tridentine church of the forties and fifties that meant the complete structuring of life by faith. Because we attended public rather than parochial school, we were taught our catechism on Saturday mornings by nuns from Saint Anthony's parish in Park Falls. Instruction included the basics of the Baltimore Catechism—"Who made you?" "God made me." "Why did God make you?" "He made me to know, love, and serve Him in this life, and be happy with Him forever"—and rewritten Bible stories. But those rudiments, plus memorizing such odd esoterica as the Nine Choirs of Angels, did not shape us as Catholics nearly as much as the way in which everything we did somehow connected to life before God. We willingly gave ourselves to a set of moral convictions that were so bedrock that it would be difficult to distinguish what was being a "Catholic" from what was just being a "Johnson."

The church of Saint Francis of Assisi in Fifield—closer to a chapel than a full-grown church—had as its pastor Father Otto Weber, a Passionist priest whose youth had been spent in the Black Forest of Bavaria. He was a regular and welcome visitor to our house. My sisters Nancy and Margaret constituted much of the choir, at times all of it. Nancy played the foot-pedal organ, and Margaret harmonized Latin and English hymns (there were a few, even then). Similarly, Pat and I made up half the altar boy cohort, which meant that we served Mass, together or apart, every Sunday and most weekdays of our childhood. I started memorizing the Latin responses (without understanding them) by the time I was eight or nine, and still remember most of them.

I vividly remember tripping over a too-large cassock (mine always had to be belted, I was so tiny) the first time I served at the Lenten Stations of the Cross, and how Pat and I would lead Father Weber (all of us dressed in vestments) through the town, ringing the altar bell before him, as he brought communion to the sick and the elderly. As with delivering papers, such intimate access brought me a very early awareness of states of poverty and physical distress. Louise Grassel, I recall, had cerebral palsy, and her involuntary contortions made giving her communion a challenge.[9]

It was a matter of course that we went to confession on Saturday afternoon, fasted from midnight before receiving communion on Sunday, observed the days of fasting and abstinence during Lent, and made midnight Mass the center of our Christmas celebration. One of my very earliest memories is waking up in my brother Mickey's arms on the walk home from midnight Mass, to see the soft drifting fall of snow shining in the light under which we were passing. The movies we were given permission to see were those approved by the Catholic censorship instrument, the Legion of Decency, which sometimes led to odd cognitive dissonances. *Samson and Delilah* was fine, despite the seductiveness of Hedy Lamarr, because it was biblical. But *Joan of Arc*, about a bona fide saint, was off bounds because Ingrid Bergman had committed adultery! Despite these strict boundaries, I grew up without any trace of the mythical Irish Catholic guilt.

We prayed as we woke in the morning, before we ate meals, and when we went to bed. Short prayers throughout the day (called, unfortunately, "ejaculations") were encouraged. My mother, for example, said many times over a version of what is known as the Jesus Prayer, "Lord Jesus Christ, have mercy on me, a sinner." Her real and intense piety—without doubt deepened by her sorrow and anxiety—communicated itself to the children. For some of us, that faith stuck; for others, it slipped away.

On me, the impact of my mother's faith was immediate and lasting. I have no question that my basic trust in creation, and my sense of God's presence, leached from her to me in a manner so subtle and pervasive that it has defined much of my subsequent life. A short dialogue: I said to her as she was bathing me on Saturday night, because I did not like the tickling on my feet as she scrubbed them, "Why do we need to clean our feet?

I will be wearing shoes at Mass. Nobody will see my feet." She said to me, "God will see your feet. God sees everything." That simple, and for me, that convincing.

But my mother was also complex in her spirituality. On one side, her favorite prayer was "Saint Teresa's Bookmark," a set of statements ascribed to Teresa of Ávila and inscribed on the prayer book my mother gave me on my eleventh birthday, three months before her death: "Let nothing disturb thee, let nothing affright thee; all things are passing; God alone is changeless; Patient endurance gaineth all things; he who has God wanteth nothing; God alone sufficeth."

On the other side, she was a serious student of astrology and read tea leaves for her friends. She was, as my sister Nancy noted, a bit "fey," which in Irish parlance suggests an otherworldliness—she would perhaps these days be called a spiritual searcher. With this difference: all her exploration into the mystical and mysterious was not in rejection of her strict version of Catholic observance but in longing for what she had so suddenly and devastatingly lost. It took me many years to appreciate that for her, the years of my childhood were not only years of great effort but also years of great sorrow.

I was confused, for example, when, sitting at her side as she played the piano and sang Stephen Foster's "Beautiful Dreamer," she broke down in tears and could not go on—not knowing either that this was one of her and Daddy's favorite songs or that he was the beautiful dreamer that she wished would "wake unto her." Often during the year we all would visit my father's grave to pray and place flowers; these short pilgrimages gave me all I knew personally about my daddy—that I lived in a family that was bound to him forever in love and prayer.

Music. All my memories of my Fifield childhood are intertwined with memories of music. Music was a constant in my family. My mother and my sisters Nancy and Margaret played the piano, and all of us sang, while washing dishes, while riding in the car (a separate repertoire for that setting), while playing cards or Monopoly, while doing any of our outdoor chores. We sang songs learned from our parents from the Civil War era ("The boys in blue were fighting," "She had a dark and a roving eye"), the twenties ("For it was Mary, long before the fashion changed"), and the Depression ("I'm a broken down man without money or friends"). My mother taught all of us "Froggie went a-courtin'" and "The owl and the pussycat went to sea." We played and sang to popular sheet music, and we had a handsome volume containing the complete songs of Stephen Foster. Our singing was always most fun when Margaret provided her natural gift for harmonization in her distinctive alto voice.

We also listened to music of every sort on the radio and phonograph. Sunday afternoons, the Longines-Wittnauer broadcast of its *Symphony of the Air* was mandatory background to paging through the rotogravure section of the paper or taking a nap. One of the benefits of Mother's business barter with tavern owners was a steady flow of 45 rpm records that had outlasted jukebox use. We naturally knew everything that ranked in the weekly radio show *Hit Parade*, but we were indiscriminate lovers of every sort of music: classical (Chopin's Ballade in G Minor never ceases to draw me into an intense nostalgia for that time and place), pop (it was the age of great crooners), Broadway musicals (Ezio Pinza singing "One Enchanted Evening" from *South Pacific*), and country western. It was a time when Ezio Pinza and Mario Lanza; Louis Armstrong, Perry Como, Frank Sinatra, Frankie Laine, and Bing Crosby; Patti Page, Ella Fitzgerald, and Doris Day; the Ink Spots, Nat King Cole, the Weavers, Woody Guthrie, and Hank Williams did not inhabit separate spheres but were all "popular."

The music we heard was singable. It was also lyrically memorable. Even the nonsense songs ("Mairzy Doats" and "The Doggie in the Window") were cleverly written. Musicals gave us the lyrics of Oscar Hammerstein and Cole Porter. Music was for me the most memorable way of experiencing poetry, and the most intoxicating way of enhancing the experience of life itself. Songs also invited a child in a remote little town to imagine a much larger world; whether they included "Pyramids along the Nile" or "Climb the highest mountain" or "Mona Lisa," songs evoked a rich imaginative world. Think what images were evoked in a little boy by lyrics like these: "If you've got the money, honey, I've got the time," or "There's a pawnshop on the corner in Pittsburgh, Pennsylvania, and I walk up and down 'neath its clock," or "Shrimp boats are a-coming, their sails are in sight," or "Good-bye, Joe, me gotta go row the pirogue down the bayou." The effect of such constant and early immersion in music, and the seductive attraction of music, was not an insignificant factor in shaping my subsequent life. I am not anything like a musician. But singing is probably the thing I like most to do, because, both physically and spiritually, singing enlarges the self, and, when done with others, creates communion that, while implicit, is powerful and real.

Wit and Humor. When not singing or reading, we talked. A lot. Loudly. Everyone in the family was highly verbal and highly opinionated. Cross-talk, correction of fact or grammar, intermittent comment, and topping each other's lines were constant, especially at the dinner table. The more introverted (and probably more thoughtful) included Mother, Mary Jane, and Margaret, but each of them was also capable of a devastating comment and unfailingly provided an audience for those of us who got drunk on talk and laughter. We seldom told jokes. We practiced what the French call *esprit,* a combination of intelligence, wit, and verbal combat. This love of language and laughter was a clear inheritance from my father's family. All the Johnson relatives were bright, and simply funny. Humor was never meant to hurt, and I think it seldom did. It was a matter of high spirits and intellectual engagement.

The continuous interplay of verbal acrobatics had to be shushed every evening at dinner by mother, who would say, "Hush now, Gabriel Heatter is coming on." This was the nightly fifteen minutes of national news that came over the radio on the Mutual Broadcasting System. Between that brief reportage and the consumption of the daily newspaper (and *Life* magazine, when available), we all had a pretty good grasp of what was happening in the world outside our village. I had my first political debate in 1948 during the Truman-Dewey presidential campaign (I was for Truman, of course, because my family was deep-blue working-class Democrat), on what we called the "Teeter-Totters" in the school playground with another first-grader. When I was ten, I explained the significance of Stalin's death in 1953 and the ascension of Malenkov in the Soviet Politboro to an adult in-law who had not had the advantage of our kind of upbringing.

I will have occasion to speak again later about my natural instinct to be in-dependent, contrarian, and even polemical, as a scholar. And I will note later intellectual influences that encouraged rather than suppressed that instinct. But it started very early, around the dinner table with my brothers and sisters, all of whom were smart, literate, opinionated, and funny. They still are.

Reading. This family trait had the most direct influence on my later life as a scholar. I grew up in a family whose members all read widely and pretty much indiscriminately. Once more, the influence came from Mother, who was a serious reader, especially of poetry and drama. I have mentioned all the ephemera we kids read in comics and magazines. But it was the reading of books that I remember best. Books were borrowed from the Park Falls Library, and often from its bookmobile that stopped outside our house. But the most current books came from my aunt Laura, who sent Mother boxes of books that she had acquired and read. The same freedom that marked our conversation and movements held for reading. No one ever censored what we read from the many books scattered about the house. Books enlarged still further our imagination concerning the world that lay outside our town.

The love of reading, of words, of poetry, was instilled in Pat and me directly through our mother reading aloud to us as we sat on her knees as she rocked before the heater. We were the youngest, and she probably had the leisure to give us this attention. Over the course of several years, before her illness made it no longer possible, Mother read to us all of the Grimm brothers' and Andersen's fairy tales,[10] *Alice in Wonderland,* and *Alice through the Looking-Glass.* A particular favorite of mine was T. H. White's brilliant recasting of the Lilliputian tale in *Mistress Masham's Repose.*[11] Mother read through the entire anthology *The Best-Loved Poetry of the American People*—although, for boys eight and five, "Casey at the Bat" required more repetition than most other poems.[12] There is no question in my mind that my mother's practice of reading aloud to us, and my siblings' habits of reading for hours on end (usually head down in a chair with legs draped over the back), profoundly affected my later life as a scholar. Reading for me has never been an imposed chore. It has always been a mental liberation. Reading indiscriminately in all genres and at all levels has never seemed to me an impediment to a well-ordered mind. Instead, it has always seemed the natural way to feed the mind.

School

I attended Fifield grade school from the ages of five to eleven. I was not an impressive student. I begged my mother not to send me to school, and on the first day of first grade, somehow got confused and missed the line marching to the lunchroom, went outside on the playground, and refused to move from the swings when Pat came out to plead for my return. In my eyes, that one mistake had sealed my academic career. Pat had to run home and get Mother, who took my hand and led me down to where everyone was eating lunch.[13]

Each grade school classroom contained two classes. Through the day, teachers rotated instruction to one side with "homework" for the other side. Consequently, all work was pretty much done during school hours. I had none of the burden of homework such as our contemporary child laborers must carry.[14] Reading, writing (spelling), arithmetic, and recitation were the standards: we did fairly impressive amounts of memorization, and we were intensely patriotic. We sang a lot together. The *Weekly Reader* was distributed to everyone and informed us of historical, geographical, political, and even scientific news. A helpful reminder of the changing face of science: I remember vividly a headline, "The Miracle Fiber," with the accompanying article extolling the wondrous way asbestos made everyone safer in their homes and schools!

For me, as for most of my peers, grade school was mainly about recess. For a small-town boy, this meant genuine free time (nothing was organized) to play with boys—the girls mainly did their own things—of my own age, and we played with great enthusiasm: building snow forts and waging snowball battles, icing down the long walkway up to the school and sliding, hunched on our heels or (more daringly) standing upright, at what seemed great speed.[15] In the fall and spring, we played tag and hide-and-seek and all the other group things we could not do when isolated on our farms or with the other three boys our age in the whole village. In one such adventure, when two other boys and I in the fifth grade were playing cowboys, our "bonfire" made of autumn leaves quickly set fire to the woods behind the school; fortunately, it was doused by "the big guys" (seventh and eighth graders), who were playing baseball nearby. That day I was banished to sit (it seemed forever) on a chair in the kitchen. That was also the day I learned the word "arsonist."

During my sixth-grade year (I was eleven), two actual academic events stand out. I narrowly won a "reading report contest" run by Miss Wilson, in which Lee Newman and I were finalists. We would quickly read a book from the bookshelf in the back of the room, run to her desk, do an oral report, and then read another. I forget the number of books we each read, but I remember the prize was a real baseball. I somehow also won the local forensics competition, and so was sent with other kids from the county by school bus to the city of Superior to compete in the Regional Forensics Competition. I was on a panel that was to argue the pro side of the proposition "The Saint Lawrence Seaway should be constructed." I naturally knew nothing about it, was overawed by the older kids who seemed to know everything, needed to be coached up to speak at all, and brought no glory to our side.

Also in the sixth grade, I got my first glasses to correct myopia and astigmatism. No wonder I could never see what the teacher wrote on the board! While the glasses enabled me to see at a distance, the fact of their necessity also reinforced my tendency to deal with what lay close to hand, above all, books.

The best part about school was that it encouraged and enabled wide reading beyond textbooks, complementing perfectly the freedom for reading everything that came my way at home. Simply to suggest how serious some of my reading was, and how, at least intellectually, it prepared me for a harder and more evil world than the one I had yet experienced, I can name three books that I read before I was twelve. The first was *Pictorial History of the Second World War*, in which the pages devoted to the discovery of the Holocaust victims at Dachau and Buchenwald mesmerized me. I stared with uncomprehending wonder at the piles of corpses in the camps and—worse!—the skeletal figures of the survivors in their barracks. The second was Richard Wright's *Uncle Tom's Children*, a set of novellas set in the segregated South.[16] As he states in his introduction to *Native Son*,[17] Wright regretted writing the book, but it left an indelible impression on a boy who had never yet even seen a Black American. In these stories I learned about Jim Crow, lynching, raping, and every form of violence caused by racist dispositions and laws. The third book was John Hersey's *Hiroshima*, which recounted, in novelistic fashion (it was a pioneer of the so-called new journalism later practiced by Mailer and Wolfe), the horrors of the atomic explosion as experienced through the witness of a handful of survivors.[18] Books such as these not only taught me about a larger world outside my home and town, but they also taught me that the larger world can be unspeakably cruel, and even that worlds can collapse and disappear. I was being made ready for my own world to do just that.

The End of Childhood

Mother had a series of seizures in early 1954. Margaret, Pat, and I were the only children at home by this point. Mickey was in Mississippi with his new wife, LaNelle, and a new son; Mary Jane was in New Mexico with her husband, Warren, and a new daughter. Nancy was training to be a nurse in Milwaukee. The severity of the attacks led to consultation at the hospital in Marshfield, and then referral to the Mayo Brothers' Clinic in Minnesota. Mother's aggressive brain tumor was removed surgically at Rochester in May, but she was left badly disabled, and the surgeons predicted that she would die in a year. They missed by two months. This marvelously verbal and insightful woman spent her remaining days aphasic and unable to care for the children she had so nurtured.

After her surgery, Nancy (who by default became Mother's chief care-giver because of her training—at the age of nineteen!) flew with mother to Jackson, Mississippi, to do radiation treatments. The decision was made to move all of us there. We spent a hot and miserable summer in the Battlefield Apartments—it was the summer of the *Brown v. Board of Education* decision and the Army-McCarthy Hearings—nine people in a two-bedroom apartment, until Aunt Laura intervened and Mother, Nancy, Margaret, Pat, and I returned to Fifield, to school and work, and something like normalcy—given the fact (known to all the children but Pat and me) that our mother was dying even as we went about our lives. She died February 2, 1955, the day after her forty-fifth birthday.

Now, we were fully orphans and truly on our own. The sibling family entered its diaspora existence. After the school year ended, Pat and I took the Greyhound bus back to Jackson, Mississippi, where we were to live with Mickey and LaNelle (and their now two children). My long loneliness had begun.

Chapter Two

ADOLESCENCE (1955–1963)

Y ADOLESCENT YEARS WERE SPENT IN TWO OVER-
lapping settings. For two years (1955–1957), my brother Pat and I, now definitively orphaned and transported to a totally alien environment, lived
with my oldest brother, Mickey, and his wife, Lanelle (with their two and
eventually five children), in Jackson, Mississippi—a place that, in those
years, was truly a different world from my childhood home in Wisconsin.
In 1957, I entered the seminary in Covington, Louisiana, to study for the
priesthood under the auspices of the Diocese of Natchez-Jackson. Over
the next six years (1957–1963), though, I returned to Jackson for summer
vacations. My experience of Mississippi was therefore extended in various
ways for eight years. After finishing high school in Jackson, Pat also came to
the seminary and spent three years there with me. I will try to trace some of
my developing intellectual instincts first in the sustained Mississippi period,
and then in the six-year seminary period.

JACKSON IN THE 1950S

The day in mid-July of 1955 that Pat and I stepped out of the frigid air of
a Greyhound bus into the heat and humidity of Jackson, I felt that a wet
blanket had been thrown over my head. The sense of constricted breath-
ing did not soon lift. These were evil days in the Deep South, above all
in Mississippi. The month after we arrived in Jackson, Emmett Till was
lynched. As a perfect bracket, the day I left for the monastery in 1963, Med-

gar Evers had just been assassinated. We had unwittingly entered the place where segregation and Jim Crow were going into their death throes, and that death was not pretty. As we stepped off the bus, we could plainly see the separate water fountains for "Whites Only" and "Colored Only." These were the days of Governor Ross Barnett, of the White Citizens Council (or the Klan); when, on the local Channel 3 news, Bob Neblett could regularly refer (always in crime reports) to "Nigras." In short, Mississippi conformed precisely to the violent images I had encountered in Richard Wright's *Uncle Tom's Children*.

Everything about this world was alien and alienating to Pat and me. The weather was just the most obvious, if also the most oppressive, element. Never before had we experienced such heat, such violent thunderstorms, such shirt-sopping humidity. The Mississippi summer sapped energy and enthusiasm. Survival meant moving from one air-conditioned spot to another. Equally strange was the language. People in Jackson did not talk the way they did in Wisconsin: Black and white alike used different locutions, different word emphases, and an entirely different pace and tone of speech than the ones to which we had been accustomed.[1] Classmates teased us for our Wisconsin accents, and what they considered our peculiar dialect.

Hardest of all was coming to grips with the strange and elaborate social codes of the segregated South. I learned quickly that young people were to say "Sir" and "Ma'am" to their elders. That was easy enough. But I got into trouble when I called Black men and women "Sir" and "Ma'am." Similarly, I was corrected when (as a young boy would) I sought a seat in the back of a city bus. Both Black and white riders gently steered me to my proper place. And although I learned eventually how to adapt my behavior (what choice was there?), I never accepted the validity of putting mayonnaise on hamburgers or of eating okra without camouflaging it in a gumbo.

Pat and I entered this world within six months of our mother's death. Adjustment to such a strange new world was made more difficult by the fact that adjustment was required while we were in a state of grief, which nobody really acknowledged—what use would it be? The shock of such violent immersion in a foreign culture—with, truly, a foreign language— was added to the impact of a sorrow (loss of mother, loss of family, loss of home) that was silent and without validation.

Adolescence (1955–1963)

LIFE IN A NEW FAMILY

I shall always be grateful that Mickey did what my mother asked of him, taking Pat and me into his household. It was certainly not easy for him and LaNelle, the thoroughly southern woman from Ludlow, Mississippi, who grew up as a "hard-shell" Baptist and whose parents did not know what to think about her converting to Catholicism.[2] Mickey and LaNelle were in their midtwenties and already had two small children (eighteen months and four months old, respectively). Both worked full time. Mickey worked nights at Dixie Rent-a-Car on South Lamar Street while he was finishing college at Millsaps. He then began his career in electronic business machines—eventually becoming a high-level executive at Burroughs Corporation. LaNelle held a steady stream of office positions.

Taking two boys into this already complex mix was inevitably difficult. The way was not made easier for them by their perilous financial situation; they were barely getting by before two hungry boys showed up. The first small house they managed to get into—because Pat and I were arriving—had no air-conditioning. It was "cooled" only by a highly ineffective attic fan. Especially in those first years, Pat and I were not so much assimilated into a new family as we were resident aliens within a chaotically forming family.

The transition was not easy for Pat and me, either. Mickey and LaNelle were virtual strangers, especially to me. At best, I think, they could be characterized as distracted surrogate parents. They got better at parenting over time, judging by the deep affection in which (at the ages of ninety-three and ninety) they are held by their own children, all of whom turned out just fine. But they were not good at it in those early days.

Pat and I consequently bonded even more closely. The good part of this was that we each had an ally who shared the same story. The bad part was that my dependence on Pat grew greater, as did his tendency to dominate me. I think Pat, who was starting his sophomore year in high school, adapted to the new setting better than I did. Pat was quickly old enough to get jobs outside the house. But I was the designated babysitter (I learned to change diapers, and give bottles and burp the baby) and the yard boy. Pushing a power mower through the septic tank seepage at the end of the yard is a distinctive memory of the two years I spent full time with Mickey and LaNelle.

I was, in truth, a thoroughly miserable boy. Only at the distance given by the passage of sixty-five years can I recognize, and accept, that I was also an angry boy. For much of our first year in Mississippi, I begged Pat to manage an escape to Wisconsin. Pat cunningly colluded in planning while simultaneously postponing. He knew that eventually even my resistance to our situation would ease. It did, but only temporarily. Eventually, I managed my own escape.

Temporary solace was afforded in the summers when Pat and I rode a Greyhound for thirty-six hours through the middle of the country to spend weeks with our sisters back in Wisconsin. As we rode, we smoked cigarillos and thought ourselves suave. Another oasis was a Thanksgiving weekend we spent with our aunt Laura in Waco, Texas, where she was head of the officers' club at the air force base—she had reached the rank of lieutenant colonel in the women's air force, and it was a thrill to see the male soldiers salute her. In Aunt Laura's well-appointed flat, we played Louis Armstrong's version of "Blueberry Hill" and insisted to her that Fats Domino's version was much superior—naturally, she had never heard of Fats Domino.

Another pleasant experience in my second Jackson summer was the chance to play Little League baseball (for Jennings Air Conditioning). My eyesight allowed me to play only pitcher or catcher, but I did well enough to make the all-star team . . . my only moment of athletic distinction. Overall, though, I saw my experience of those two years in the heat and humidity of Jackson as standing in stark contrast to the life I lived before my mother's death. And though grief for my mother was buried somewhere, only to be retrieved many years later, grief over my changed circumstances was immediate and real.

In contrast to our former life centered on the church with an all-pervasive sense of religious faith structuring our lives in the home, Mickey and LaNelle were Sunday Mass Catholics.[3] We attended Mass for a time at Saint Mary's, and then when Saint Theresa's parish was established in our suburb, we gathered for worship in the dusty section of the school building that served as sanctuary. Pat and I naturally served as acolytes and, I am not sure how, found ourselves under the obligation of cleaning that uncleanable space every Saturday afternoon, without remuneration—or, I wonder now, was this part of us paying off the tuition for Catholic school? In any case, if my religious life was to be fed, it would be at school, not at home.

In contrast to a home in which music was constant and varied, we now lived in one in which music was heard but not much produced. Pat and I still sang together while doing the dishes or driving in the car, but Mickey apparently knew only one song ("Give me some men, some stouthearted men") that he sang when we were driving, and I don't believe I have ever heard LaNelle sing. There was no piano. Eventually, there was a phonograph and a handful of records, but mostly our musical fare came by way of AM radio. This was not all bad, for we heard firsthand the earliest efforts of the Mississippi phenom Elvis Presley, and we were attuned to Little Richard, Fats Domino, Bill Haley and the Comets, and the Big Bopper.[4]

In contrast to a house where the give-and-take of speech was standard and laughter was frequent, we now inhabited a space where most of the talking came from the black and white television, and its laughter was canned. In my memory, Pat became increasingly taciturn over these years; his speech with me became even more didactic and directive. Mickey and LaNelle frequently fussed and feuded, something I had never heard from adults before. Of wit or the playful turning of language there was little.

Although this was eventually to change, the house we now occupied was completely without books. Some of Mickey's Millsaps yearbooks supplied my earliest lunchtime reading. Otherwise, the public library (and bookmobile) supplied us with books to read. Mickey was always an avid reader of the newspaper, and both he and LaNelle later read in the way we used to in Wisconsin. But not at the beginning. With the exceptions I will note later, nothing I read in this two-year period sticks with me,[5] a lacuna that perhaps suggests best of all the sort of fog through which I was passing.

THE GIFT OF CATHOLIC SCHOOL

The greatest gift Mickey and LaNelle gave us was enrolling us in Catholic schools in downtown Jackson. Pat attended Saint Joseph High School, and I attended seventh and eighth grade at the adjacent Saint Peter's Grade School. Both schools sat on the same property with a convent of Sisters of Mercy and Saint Peter's Cathedral. The residence of Bishop Gerow was across the street. I don't know how our schooling was funded; were we supported by the bishop? Was our church cleaning part of the deal? I don't know. In any case, Mickey dropped us off at school every weekday morning, and after school we rode a rickety bus out to a spot about a mile from our house, walking the rest of the way home.

Catholic school provided me with the sense of structure, stability, and sanity that I desperately needed. In that sense, it was a saving gift. The grade-school kids attended Mass every day before classes. The Mass was still in Latin, with the celebrant facing the altar. Some of us were selected to read aloud from the new Saint Joseph Missal to provide a simultaneous English version. Depending on the speed of the priest's Latin, this could pose a challenge. Auxiliary Bishop Brunini ripped so rapidly through what was then called "the last gospel" at the end of Mass (John 1:1–18), that the effort to keep pace sometimes resembled a drag race more than worship. I can't say that I derived any deep religious insight from this rote exercise, but what it gave me was what I needed most: the comfort of familiar ritual in the presence of a beautiful and well-ordered place.

I was singularly blessed by having two outstanding female teachers in seventh and eighth grade. Joanne Boone was a tiny woman with a sharp intelligence, wide knowledge of the world, and firm moral convictions. I was astounded at her statement after the class had read a section of a textbook devoted to the history of Mississippi: the textbook had extolled the deeds of Senator Theodore Bilbo, a noted racist.[6] Ms. Boone said crisply, "The book is wrong. Segregation is evil." The book is wrong! This was the first time I had experienced an intellectual and moral judgment that stood against the culturally approved version, and I was both shocked and thrilled. Ms. Boone also opened her house one afternoon a year to her rowdy classes, so that they could experience something of the gracious side of Mississippi life.

The teacher who influenced me the most, however, was Sister Paulinus Oakes. She was a young Sister of Mercy from Vicksburg, who combined astounding energy, crisp intelligence, and a moral authority that commanded respect. She was my basketball and football coach as well as classroom teacher. Later in life she worked tirelessly in hospital chaplaincy, ministering especially to the victims of AIDS. On the side, she wrote a substantial history of the Sisters of Mercy.[7] Sister Paulinus put the lie to all the caricatures of nuns peddled by movies and comedians. She passionately committed herself to the good of every student she ever taught.

She brooked no foolishness, either. One example: There was some cheating going on when I was in the eighth grade. She called me up to her desk. She said, "I have been told that Lance Drane copied some math answers from you. Is this true?" Now, to appreciate this, you have to understand that I am (and always have been) a dunce in math. I don't know why I was in an advanced class. I also do not know why Lance, who went on to become an engineer at NASA, would want to copy *my* answers, above all. It was a onetime thing. I distinctly remember his panic at not having done his homework and us crouching in the hallway so he could get my answers. He probably got a C! Anyway, I confessed, and Sister Paulinus allowed that, as it happened only once, and that I gave the answers rather than received them, she would not have to call Mickey in for a conference. The lesson took. This was my last academic malfeasance.

Another example: In my ebullience at recess, I had organized a Peter Pan Club that consisted mainly of five eleven-year-old boys running around, pretending to be pirates. Paulinus called me in and gently pointed out that I had, in my recruitment, excluded one boy in the class. I was shamed, to be sure, but I fear my tendency to seek like-minded lovers of fun as friends has, in later life, not always escaped the same blindness to exclusion.

Sister Paulinus apparently saw something more in me than a cheater and a former of cliques. She saw in me a future priest, and she began a campaign of recruitment. She had me read and make a class presentation on Cardinal Wiseman's five-hundred-page 1854 novel, *Fabiola; or, The Church of the Catacombs*. As she no doubt anticipated, this tale of lurid persecutions, heroic witness, and noble martyrdom fired my religious zeal. This was followed at some point by a book that intrigued me even more, called *This Is the Seminary*, in which the seminary appeared much like a year-round summer camp for enthusiastic young men.[8] Paulinus also alerted my pastor to the possibility that Timmy Johnson might have "a vocation." Slowly, over the course of the eighth grade and the summer, the possibility moved closer to being a probability, and then became a concrete option.

Some readers may quail at the thought of such "grooming" of a susceptible twelve-year-old boy, but it is important to recognize the historical context. First, Mississippi had only about a 1 percent Catholic population in the 1950s and was a "missionary territory" served mainly by Irish priests;[9] establishing a native clergy was considered a paramount good. Second, in contrast to the present day, the priesthood in America enjoyed unparalleled esteem among both Catholics and non-Catholics; remember the afterglow of the Bing Crosby movies *Going My Way* and *The Bells of St. Mary's*. Third, most Catholic families then considered it a blessing and honor to have one of their number a priest or religious; this was a call to a higher way of life, and one that was universally honored rather than reprobated. Fourth, entering seminary at a very young age was standard in the pre–Vatican Council church. No doubt it was thought that recruiting prepubescent boys, keeping them isolated from women until ordination, and all along the way training them up in asceticism would make them good celibate priests.

In any case, I was willing to be so groomed. I had only the vaguest notion about what it meant to be a priest, but I was full of fire to be a saint of some sort. Most of all, I wanted no longer to be acted on but to act. I wanted to be in a structured environment that made more sense to me than the Jackson family. I needed to be away from Pat and to claim my independence. I spoke above of "managing my own escape," and this was it. Going to the seminary at the age of thirteen was, surely, more a flight from than a flight toward, but, and this is the essential thing, it was *my* flight. Despite the doubts and entreaties of Mickey, I seized hold of my own life and pointed it in a direction that would lead to places I could not then imagine.

LIFE AT SEMINARY

In the fall of 1957, Mickey and LaNelle drove me to Saint Joseph Seminary in Covington, Louisiana, where Bishop Richard Gerow (1885–1977) sent Mississippi students to begin their studies toward the priesthood. Louisiana was as hot as Mississippi, and even wetter. Covington is set directly across Lake Pontchartrain from New Orleans. It was joined to the city by a single span of causeway (twenty-two miles in length) across the huge lake.[10] In 1957, Covington was a sleepy small town. The Sunday we arrived, the annual appearance of the "love bugs" had a plague-like quality, covering car windshields, needing to be swept away from the face as one walked through the intense heat and humidity. The seminary itself was located on the River Road, which ran along the Bogue Falaya, and had its own post office designation as Saint Benedict, Louisiana. It was known to all as "Saint Ben's."[11]

Saint Ben's was a minor seminary in the post-Tridentine structure of priestly education, with instruction through four years of high school and two years of junior college. It was administered by, and drew the bulk of its faculty from, the Benedictine monastery of Saint Joseph. Major seminary (for us, Notre Dame Seminary on Carrollton Avenue in New Orleans) included two years of the study of philosophy (with the awarding of a BA degree) and four years of theological study (ending with an MDiv degree).

Before the construction of its new buildings in 1960, the nearly four hundred seminarians at Saint Ben's occupied one wing of the three-story redbrick monastery building, where classrooms, dormitories, and library were located. Additional buildings included a student refectory (dining hall) adjacent to the monastic refectory (joined by a common kitchen), a Quonset hut housing overflow senior students, a gymnasium, a snack bar, a swimming pool (yea!), and Benet Hall, a dilapidated old wooden firetrap of an auditorium, which hosted student concerts, plays, and assemblies of every sort. Two small ponds equipped with rowboats provided the venue for fierce sea battles. There were handball courts and extensive playing fields for baseball and flagball—our stand-in for football. The grounds were completely flat (this was southern Louisiana) and were surrounded on every side by many acres of piney woods, which allowed ample space for hiking, squirrel trapping, and snake hunting among the younger boys.

At Saint Ben's, I encountered quite a different cultural mix from the one in Mississippi. Southern Louisiana was predominantly and self-confidently Catholic. The monastery still had some older monks of German heritage, who had come from the abbey's motherhouse in Indiana, Saint Meinrad Archabbey. The younger monks were of a more mixed ethnicity. My fellow seminarians were drawn from Mississippi, from New Orleans—many of them with an Italian or French background—and from the bayou country west and south of New Orleans. The kids from the bayou country carried a distinctively Cajun accent (some had only learned English as a second language when they went to school). Students from New Orleans tended to be middle-class and relatively sophisticated; students from the bayous tended to be poorer and less worldly. Once more, my Wisconsin accent was both novel and exotic to the Louisiana students. In turn, I was fascinated by all the new varieties of accent and vocabulary they offered, and quickly adopted some of their idioms as my own.

I thrived in the highly structured life of the minor seminary. Every day was pretty much like every other day, and its predictable patterns comforted a boy who had recently experienced the collapse of his world. We woke early, washed up in cold water, and gathered in the study hall for morning prayer and fifteen minutes of meditation. Meditation was led by a monastic prefect (every class had one) who was responsible for discipline and this sort of instruction. The prefect would read aloud from a classic like Saint Francis de Sales's *Introduction to the Devout Life*.

Breakfast in the refectory would be followed by four hours of class; students stayed in the same room, with teachers coming and going. Then all students attended High Mass in the monastic church. The church was Romanesque in style, its interior adorned with murals painted by the Swiss monk Dom Gregory de Witt. At meals, students ate at tables seating twelve, served by a corps of fellow students who ate after them. The school rector and two other prefects sat at a table on a slightly raised dais, with a podium beside it. After opening prayer, the meals were lively and noisy— imagine nearly four hundred adolescent boys in a big barn-like dining hall. At the end of lunch, a student would read from the podium a passage from Thomas à Kempis's *Imitation of Christ*.

Lunch was followed by the long afternoon recreation. Students had free rein to pursue sports and whatever freelance fun their imaginations could conjure. Study hall ran from that long recreation to dinner. Students sat at lift-top desks seating two, so one always had a desk mate. Unruly behavior at meals or study hall led to the punishment of kneeling in the open space between the rows of desks and in front of the prefect's podium, and in more severe cases, "flying," which was kneeling with arms extended (sometimes loaded with a book in each hand). Such highly visible punishment did not bring shame. Just the opposite. Egregious miscreants laughed at being so singled out. A more severe discipline was Saturday afternoon "detention hall," during which we copied out the *Student Handbook*, with particular attention to the passages describing "the Christian gentleman." I spent many hours there, for although I relished the structure of this life, I was also naturally high-spirited and mischievous.

Dinner always ended with a student reading from Pius Parsch's commentary on the liturgy of the day.[12] The evening study hall was lengthy, and attention had to be given first to required homework. But those with good grades could spent the last hour of study time reading whatever they chose from the library. The evening ended with another reading by the prefect (usually the life of a saint),[13] who then led the students in prayer (usually a litany).[14] And then to bed.

Except for the fifth and sixth classes, all the seminarians slept in one dormitory that was jammed with bunk beds and lockers. Down the long hall leading to the dorm was the "night jakes" intended for nocturnal relief. It was lit by a single bulb hanging from the ceiling. In my first two years at Saint Ben's, I spent many nighttime hours there, reading Sherlock Holmes stories and then, with intense fascination, G. K. Chesterton's complete collection of Father Brown mysteries. I cannot remember the reasons for my insomnia. But I am grateful I had such good companions with me in my wakeful hours.

The weekends differed mainly because on Saturday and Sunday we not only shared the celebration of Mass with the monks but also attended vespers, followed by Benediction of the Blessed Sacrament. Saturday afternoon, when all of us had taken our weekly shower (waiting in long lines to enter the wooden stalls) and had shined our shoes while we sat beneath the music room window listening to classical music, we marched in ranks (everywhere we marched in ranks) to the church with shiny faces, wet hair, and clean clothes. The two upper classes wore their cassocks and surplices. Especially in the late fall and winter, this evening service had a magical quality to me: the solemn procession of the monks with their profound bows, the aroma of incense pervading the air, the beauty of the Gregorian chant, the splendor of the church and of the ritual of benediction—all these accompanied by the full-throated singing of four hundred young men.

Seminarians at Saint Ben's met the Benedictine monks at many levels. The monks were our teachers, prefects, coaches, confessors, and spiritual directors. Above all, the students shared in the rich liturgical heritage of the Benedictines. I have already mentioned daily Mass and weekend vespers. I have a vivid memory of joining the monks on All Souls' Day, chanting in procession to the cemetery—the peaceful place where my late wife, Joy, now lies buried, and where I one day will lie as well—to pray in the presence of all the monks whose procession through life had led them to this spot. We would process with the monks as well on Ember Days,[15] marching with them through the monastery and seminary grounds, singing litanies in Latin call-and-response: "Sancta Maria, Ora pro nobis . . . omnes martyres et confessores, orate pro nobis."[16]

Such practices made it impossible not to think of one's own life as part of the communion of saints. Sharing the monastic life of worship was most intense during the annual retreat in the last three days of Holy Week. We spent the Sacred Triduum in absolute silence, apart from our immersion in the liturgical acts that made us participants in the death and resurrection of Christ: Maundy Thursday, with the abbot washing the feet of the youngest students; Good Friday, with the Lamentations from Jeremiah being chanted in Latin as we approached to kiss the cross; the fathomless silence of Holy Saturday, as we symbolically waited at the tomb; then, in an explosion of light and music, the midnight celebration of new life in the Easter Vigil, with the glorious singing of the Exultet.

During my adolescence at Saint Ben's, I was enveloped once more in the world of beautiful music. The seminary did not allow listening to pop music—don't worry, we got plenty of that in summer vacations—and made available a considerable collection of classical music; music appreciation classes helped adolescent boys understand the complex interconnections and hidden treasures of that tradition. Even more important, seminarians were able to participate in the making of great music. The severe beauties of Gregorian chant showed us how, for long centuries before us, the Latin texts of Scripture and the liturgy had been elaborated and interpreted though the stark melodies in the diatonic scale. It was a great privilege to be invited, as I was, to join the Schola Cantorum, an elite group of students who joined the monks every day in singing the antiphons and graduals of the Mass.

Not just the acknowledged masterpieces of Gregorian chant (the Exultet, the Christus Factus Est, the Dies Irae) but also the everyday chanting of petitions and praise slowly seeped into the hearts of seminarians. There was also a choir that sang polyphonic motets (like those of Palestrina), which I joined as a boy soprano in my first year; when my voice changed, I moved over to the bass/baritone sections. Talented musicians among the seminarians also played in the student orchestra, and the organists among them joined the ranks of monk-organists in providing a menu of the world's greatest organ composers. Every day, before and after Mass, students heard the masterworks of Bach, Buxtehude, and Vidor. The greatest learning at Saint Ben's, in fact, came through the liturgy.

This was fortunate, because actual classroom instruction was unexceptional, at times even mediocre. In their first four years, students took a mix of English, history, religion, and social studies, with a minimum of mathematics (algebra and geometry). There was much of the same mix in the last two years, with college math and chemistry added to courses in literature and European and American history. Most distinctive in the curriculum was the emphasis on language; we took six years of Latin, two years of French, and two years of Greek.[17]

I was not a particularly good classroom student. I received mostly Bs, with consistent Cs in math and science classes. To some extent, this was because my "mind was in another place." I found that classes were predictable and largely boring, so I spent as much time as possible reading on my own. I began a lifelong habit of haunting libraries, following my nose to books that I wanted and needed to read. I was constantly surprised and delighted at the things I discovered simply by browsing the stacks. The library became preeminently the space that allowed my mind to be in another place. It was a haven of secret delight.

Although I was wretchedly inept at the math and lab work demanded by biology and chemistry, I was interested in the theoretical aspects of science; I remember, for example, reading books on atomic theory and on genetics. I was also big on intellectual self-improvement, reading books on building a broader vocabulary (based on the knowledge of etymologies—Latin and Greek were pertinent, after all!) and books on building memory skills. This last connected to a special training course several of us underwent (under the direction of Fr. Pius) in brute memorization. I also enjoyed the paracurricular program in reading skills, and by my fourth year I could read thousands of words a minute with good comprehension (the GRE, here I come!).

It would be difficult to overstate the advantage that such training in rapid reading and in retention gave me in my later life as a scholar. Some things, surely, should not be speed-read. Poetry, philosophy, and theology need to be read slowly and reflectively. But so much of secondary literature is boilerplate, with original contributions representing a tiny portion of most books and articles. Speeding over the dross is entirely appropriate—indeed, the inability to read quickly and with comprehension is a serious liability for anyone seeking the life of scholarship.

My reading in this period was wide and spontaneous but also serious—apart from the lifelong love affair I began with the great British humorist

P. G. Wodehouse. I moved from Chesterton's short stories to his novels,[18] and from there to his many collections of essays, and from there to his autobiography, and from there to his masterworks, above all *Heretics* (1905) and *Orthodoxy* (1908). Chesterton seduced me with his style, but he also stunned me with his thought. His imprint was a lasting one. I naturally read his friend and polemical ally, Hilaire Belloc, as well.[19] I particularly reveled in the verses written by Chesterton and Belloc.[20] I discovered on my own as well the poetry of Charles Péguy—which had a lasting influence on my entire view of life[21]—and Dylan Thomas; the latter because of being bewitched by his reading of "A Child's Christmas in Wales." Only in my fifth and sixth years did I pay attention to T. S. Eliot, whose "Love Song of J. Alfred Prufrock" and *The Wasteland* moved me in ways I did not fully understand but helped stimulate the desire to write poetry, which quickly turned to the effort to write poetry, an urge that has issued in a large body of verses that blessedly has remained private. Before and after my life of real scholarship, though, poetry has been an important way in which my mind has occupied another place.

During my high school days, Chesterton helped me grasp what thinking might mean, so I was eager to learn philosophy. My accidental discovery in the library of the Modern Library Edition of Epictetus and Marcus Aurelius riveted me: here was language that gripped me as much as Scripture did: these ancient philosophers were not at all antique. They spoke to the human condition in every age. They certainly spoke to me, and they still do. On my own, but inevitably, given the context, I began to read theology and spirituality in a serious way. Augustine's *Confessions* offered me the mantra that has guided me through the vicissitudes of my subsequent life: "You have made us for yourself, O Lord, and our hearts are restless until they rest in thee."[22] Much later, I wrote an autobiographically framed essay based on that statement of Augustine's, which was called "Happiness and the Restless Heart: An Augustinian Perspective."[23] But that was far in the future.

Thomas Merton's *Seven Storey Mountain* likewise made a lasting impact and impelled me to read—as it was published—everything written by this contemporary Augustine; certainly, such persistent reading of Merton did nothing to redirect my nascent attraction to the monastic life. I was also deeply influenced—as my many quotations from his work in my journals attest—by the Cistercian Eugene Boylan's *This Tremendous Lover*. During retreats, I would read Teresa's *Way of Perfection* and John of the Cross's *Ascent of Mt. Carmel*. None of this was systematic. I read as I browsed, one book or author leading me to another.

By no means did I neglect fiction. Another of my self-improvement projects was to read through the list of the ten greatest novels, according to Mortimer Adler.[24] So I dove into *Huckleberry Finn, Pride and Prejudice, Jane Eyre*, and the like. As soon as they were available to me (the library imposed age limits), I read through the great Catholic novelists of the Continent (Georges Bernanos, François Mauriac), of England (Graham Greene), and of the USA (J. F. Powers, Edwin O'Connell). From there, I moved into the expansive realm of great fiction generally, reading through all that was available to me of Hemingway, Fitzgerald, Faulkner, and the rest. Given my experience of segregation in Mississippi, it is small wonder that I was especially drawn in by the two novels of Alan Paton's dealing with apartheid in South Africa, *Cry the Beloved Country* (1948) and *Too Late the Phalarope* (1953).

I must emphasize that all this reading and mental self-improvement was entirely under the radar. No one at all knew that, as I went about the daily rounds, my mind was fairly constantly "in another place." That situation changed dramatically one day in my third year (1959–1960). Father Hugh Baumann, my English teacher, announced in class one day that he wanted, for the next session, a list of all the books we had read so far in the first two months of the semester. I handed in a list of sixty books, including Chesterton, Belloc, Mauriac, Greene, and a two-volume history of the Supreme Court. Two things resulted. First, Fr. Hugh spread the word of this prodigy (!) to the other faculty, so that the perception of me changed overnight—and all my grades went up, with no change of effort on my part. Second, Fr. Hugh began to give me special reading and writing assignments, for example, to write an essay on the murals in the abbey church. Suddenly, this unprepossessing and slightly raggedy boy discovered a way of being in the world: I was, and could be, an intellectual. What I had been all along under the surface was now revealed and—even more exciting—validated.

Being an intellectual, however, as I noted in my introduction, is not yet being a scholar. My intellectual energies were strong, but they were also scattered in every direction. Because everything available to me was excellent, I did not, in my reading, feel the need to discriminate among all these goods; everything was fresh and new and of equal importance. Only the term papers written for history and English classes in my fourth and fifth year pushed me to anything like research. One such paper was on the divorce of Henry VIII, and my sources were utterly predictable: all Catholic, all popularizations. A bit more ambitious was a term paper that traced ideas of politics through Western history, a paper based entirely on the index of *The Great Books* (again, Mortimer Adler), but which led me through fascinating byways from Plato and Aristotle to Rabelais and Rousseau.

Apart from these intellectual alarms and excursions, which I could not have foreseen, the book I had read when at Saint Peter's Grade School on the seminary was not far off the mark when it came to describing the delights of free time available to four hundred adolescent boys in the piney woods of Louisiana: digging caves in the clay banks of the Bogue Falaya, trapping flying squirrels and a variety of snakes for pets (I had a large speckled king snake named Freddie), and sports of every sort: swimming, basketball (I was a semiblind point guard), flagball (semiblind halfback), and baseball (semiblind catcher). I was best at handball, because I was slow of foot but had quick reflexes, and I could actually see what was happening on the small court.

The all-boy school gave everyone willing the chance to play or sing in concerts, to compete in speech contests, and to perform in various dramas. In my time, I appeared in at least two one-act plays (one of them *Hope Is the Thing with Feathers*), in addition to *No Time for Sergeants* (I played the sergeant), and, for our sixth class major production, Eliot's *Murder in the Cathedral* (I was one of the murderous knights). We watched movies every other Saturday. The drama players from Catholic University came every year to present a play by Shakespeare.

Occasional lecturers livened the scene: most notably, Jimmy Woods and I hosted Dorothy Day as a lecturer and ate lunch with her after her talk. Jimmy was, with Mike Haddad, my best friend in minor seminary. He came from a radical Irish Catholic family on Magazine Street in New Orleans, and it was through him that I learned about Dorothy Day. When I read her autobiography, *The Long Loneliness*, I began reading the *Catholic Worker* and admired the hands-on dedication to the poor shown by her and her mentor, Peter Maurin. Jimmy introduced me as well to the early examples of folk music, in recordings of Woody Guthrie, Burl Ives, and the Weavers. In various ways, seminarians were kept aware of what was happening in the larger world. I remember listening on radio to the Kennedy-Nixon debates in 1960, for example, as well as to Kennedy's inaugural speech. This, to be sure, was exceptional—Kennedy was a Catholic!

Leadership roles were also available. Seminarians were selected to read those passages from Thomas à Kempis and Pius Parsch at meals. Some were appointed as student prefects for younger students, monitoring their study halls and reading an edifying book to them before their evening prayers. I served as class president my two final years at Saint Ben's and as chair of the student council. Most significant for my future life as a writer, my first real published article, on the election of John XXIII, appeared as a winner of the student essay contest in 1958 sponsored by the New Orleans newspaper the *Times Picayune*. I began writing for the student paper, *Entre Nous*—a serious enterprise—in my sophomore year. I became part of the editorial board in my senior year of high school, and in my sixth year, was editor in chief. This small-bore experience of journalism taught me a lot about deadlines and clear writing. Like publishing the *Fifield News* with my brother Pat, it helped encourage my sense that writing and publishing were the natural fruits of research and thought.

Perhaps the best part of seminary life—apart from the liturgy and my own wildly discursive reading—was the cheerful badinage I experienced with the other young boys. This aspect of my younger life in Wisconsin was restored to me with a vengeance. My freshman class at Saint Ben's was exceptionally bright and verbal. We were not good athletes; I don't think we ever had a winning season in any sport, regularly losing even to lower classmen. But we had in our group a lot of really smart kids. Many of them, to be sure, never made it to the priesthood. Some of them, indeed, may have been a little sociopathic. But who said that sociopaths can't have fun? And a major component of that fun was humor, often at the expense of another. Not meanness, but sharpness. The ability to top another's line, to "score" verbally, was widely admired. And for someone who entered the school bespectacled at four feet nine inches tall, it was an excellent survival tool.

Summers Back Home

Seminarians went home for summer vacations. For me and for my brother Pat—who had followed me to seminary when he finished high school—this was decidedly a mixed blessing. On the positive side, it meant being able to listen to rock and roll music on the radio and to sneak cigarettes. On the negative side, it meant entering again into all the complexities of life in Jackson that I had tried to flee. Mickey and LaNelle soon had a much nicer house in north Jackson, and we began to worship at the new Saint Richard's parish. The pastor of Saint Richard's was exceptional on two counts. First, Msgr. Josiah Chatham was a home-grown Mississippian, not an Irish missionary; second, he was a bona fide intellectual, with a kind of urbane demeanor I had not before met in Catholic clergy. Especially in the years after I joined the monastery, Pat became very attached to Msgr. Chatham and joined him in his active stance against racism (Pat even became a member of the Congress of Racial Equality [CORE]). Another Chatham disciple was Bernard Law, another member of Saint Richard's, who had graduated from Saint Ben's and had been recently ordained. He visited Saint Ben's frequently over the years. We had no idea then that a meteoric rise in the hierarchy awaited him, or that he would ultimately be the poster boy of clergy criminality when his cover-up of the crimes of pedophile priests in Boston was exposed.

I think that when Pat came to Saint Ben's, he anticipated that our former leader-follower relationship would be reestablished. But it was broken forever. Summers were difficult precisely because Pat continued in his didactic/repressive mode, and I was increasingly restive in response. The intensity was occasionally relieved when we traveled to see our sisters in Wisconsin, or by our working separately as camp counselors at one of the abbey's summer camps. But when we were together in Jackson, my passive resistance to Pat's desire to control every situation he (or we) was in made the tension palpable.

My own attitude was not helped by the expectation every summer that I would work as the family maid and babysitter, without remuneration; this was a money-saving move—the regular maid, Lilly Mae, would be let go when we were home on vacation—what in the world did her family do without her meager wages?[25] In contrast, Pat was able to drive and find work outside the house.

During these summer stints, I was consequently even more reliant on Pat for money, for transportation, and for whatever excursions outside the house could be managed (such as a run to the A&W Drive-In). Such minimum-security captivity did not raise my spirits between the ages of fourteen and nineteen. It made me even more eager to be completely and finally free and on my own. On the plus side, once more I learned the domestic skills that would prove invaluable in my later life; and the sheer boredom of life locked up with three children in the dismally hot suburbs meant that I had a lot of opportunity to read. In this case, the public library near Saint Richard's church was regularly raided as I continued my assault on American literature.

When Pat completed three years at Saint Ben's, he went to the pontifical seminary in Worthington, Ohio, for major seminary. He spent six years there. He left ministerial training only shortly before ordination to the priesthood. He went to do doctoral work in psychology at Catholic University on a Veterans Affairs (VA) scholarship, and after completing his PhD and clinical internship in a VA hospital, he set up his own practice as a clinical psychologist. At fifty-five, he retired, and at the age of eighty is still as interested in the world as he was when a boy: he bikes, kayaks, sculpts, and is generally (having early on become a dedicated atheist) enjoying the heaven that he is convinced is available only here and now. I continue to be amazed that brothers who were so close when young are now so far apart in their views of the world.

Once I broke the psychological hold Pat had over me (in my leaving at thirteen and going on my own to the seminary), I simply had to endure the episodic flare-ups of disagreement that occurred, knowing that my life was, and is, my own.[26] I am grateful that in later years we were able, with considerable effort, to sort through the damages of those days of youth, and we can now respect and like each other just as we are in our separate universes. It is clear to me, however, that the strong contrarian strain that runs through much of my scholarship owes not a little to my early and primal need to assert independence from a very smart and very dominant presence to whom I was indebted for so much.

THE DECISION FOR SCHOLARSHIP

As I have already noted, when I went to the seminary at thirteen, it was as much a flight from than a flight toward. Going to Saint Ben's was not my choice. It was Bishop Gerow who sent me there (and paid my tuition), because that is where he sent his minor seminarians. Depending on one's perspective, my landing at Saint Ben's can be considered an accident or chance. I prefer to regard it as divine providence. Saint Ben's turned out to be the perfect place for me to navigate adolescence. It restored to my world all the values I had treasured in my Wisconsin family: pervasive religious faith, wonderful music, wit and humor (mostly from other students), and the freedom to do wide reading. More than restored; Saint Ben's elevated all these values to a new level. I experienced there the liturgy as I never had before, was schooled in great music, and, even as I enjoyed having friends again who made me laugh and whom I made laugh, was allowed to exercise my intellectual gifts in a deeper way.

I surely was still far from being a scholar. But I was on the way. I recognized that I was an intellectual increasingly desirous of serious thought and study. And I knew that further growth would not come through taking classes alone; it would require a passionate and solitary quest within a structure that would allow such a lonely path of inquiry.

When I graduated at the age of nineteen, then, I had a real choice that I alone could make. I could continue as a student for the Natchez-Jackson diocese, go to the major seminary the bishop sent me to, and become a parish priest. Or I could join the Benedictine monastery and, in effect, continue the life that I had in some way already begun. The more I contemplated it, the more I realized that being a parish priest had no appeal. The active life, I concluded, was not for me; I did not trust my capacity to stay faithful in the world without the kind of support the monastery provided. The monastic life offered me the possibility of pursuing both sanctity and scholarship.

In my final semester, then, I petitioned the bishop and Msgr. Chatham to be allowed to switch tracks and enter the monastic life. Generously, they both supported me. I sought leave from Abbot David to become a postulant in the monastery in the summer of 1963, and he agreed. As a departing gift at graduation, my Greek teacher, Fr. Marion Larmann, handed me the *Rule of Benedict*, writing on the flyleaf that this book would guide my future life. And so it did, for the next ten years.

Chapter Three

Monastic Life (1963–1971)

HEN I ENTERED THE NOVITIATE AT SAINT JO-
seph's Abbey in late summer of 1963, I thought I was walking into a tranquil
and unchanging world. The community was of medium size for Benedictine monasteries, with a total of about sixty monks. Some were assigned to
parishes in the area. Others served in a foundation recently established at
Esquipulas, Guatemala. On hand was a still-robust body of monks, garbed
in the distinctive Benedictine habit: a simple black tunic with a leather
belt around the waist, over which was a scapular with cowl, or hood. The
abbot during my whole time as a monk was David Melançon, from Donald-
sonville, Louisiana—a symbol of the increased proportion of monks with
French origins. He had been my Latin teacher for one year in the minor
seminary. He was a very bad Latin teacher; he was an excellent abbot.

Changing Times

In 1963, all of the *Opus Dei* (Divine Office) was chanted in Latin, as it had
been for 1,500 years; the daily Eucharist was also in Latin. The monks' main
work was administering and teaching in the adjacent minor seminary from
which I had so recently graduated. But the common life demanded that
all the monks play a variety of roles (cantor, organist, mechanic, tailor,
barber, etc.). The community consisted of choir monks and lay brothers.
Choir monks were solemnly professed and were either ordained as priests
or in training for such ordination. Lay brothers made simple vows, said a

shortened version of the Office in English, and performed the bulk of the practical work required in a large community of men.

The monks lived a radically communal life, in which all possessions were shared and "no one called anything his own." The practice of a community of goods expressed the virtues of obedience and humility. All this was standard and had been for centuries, going back to the motherhouse in Indiana, Saint Meinrad, and the grandmother house in Einsiedeln, Switzerland, and probably back to Saint Benedict's sixth-century foundation at Monte Cassino in Italy.

Appearances, however, deceived. As I began this new life, forces of turmoil and dramatic change were already at work below the surface. Pope John XXIII had announced the Second Vatican Council in 1959, and the Council met in four sessions between October of 1962 and December of 1965. It issued its first constitution, on the liturgy, in 1963. As I entered, then, the reforming ferment of the Council was already stirring. In 1965, Mass was celebrated in English for the first time at the abbey. In 1968, the Divine Office began to be chanted in English rather than Latin.

Debate over monastic reform, indeed, characterized my entire time as a religious. Sometimes the tensions were extremely strong. At stake on one hand was the value of a way of life 1,500 years old, based on one of history's handful of brilliant constitutional compositions, *The Rule of Benedict* (ca. 640). At stake on the other hand was *aggiornamento*: the desire of the church to be relevant to the needs of the twentieth century.

The internal reform of the Catholic Church, in turn, coincided with America's entering a period of violent turmoil, which affected the monks as it did others. President John F. Kennedy was assassinated in 1963, the year I entered the monastery. The Vietnam War was expanded under President Johnson, and in the late '60s the war generated opposition even among otherwise docile young seminarians. The emergence of the hippies in the "Summer of Love" (1967) presaged generations of experiments in music, drugs, and social arrangement.

Martin Luther King and other civil rights leaders were ever more persistent in pressing the rights of Blacks. But the civil rights movement also fragmented into rival factions, some of them espousing violence. King was assassinated in April of 1968, and Robert Kennedy in June of the same year. All these events spun the nation into cultural and political confusion and made the monastic life seem only a passive, if empathic, observer.

This was also a time of great cultural upheaval around issues of sexuality. A flood of books appeared that challenged the validity or value of celibacy on psychosexual grounds. Much emphasis was placed on personal fulfill-ment, and the celibate life was an easy target, especially when it had been practiced in a rigid and moralistic fashion. Monastic life could seem, even to some of its adherents, out of touch, even otiose, in a religion that was rapidly privileging the active over the contemplative life and saw witness in terms of engagement with, rather than flight from, the secular world. The most influential theological book in the USA was Harvey Cox's 1965 publication, *The Secular City*, which unabashedly celebrated the desacral-ization of society.

During my ten years as a monk, the effect of all these upheavals was the disaffection and then the departure of many monks. The radical depletion of Catholic religious orders had begun. The summer I entered, two of my fa-vorite teachers (and I had hoped, future colleagues) left the community, and many more followed. Perhaps as an indication of the monastic lean years that were to come, I was the only novice to enter Saint Joseph's Abbey in 1963.

THE MONASTIC LIFE

Benedictine monasticism centers on prayer and work, with the lives of the monks being formed most pervasively by liturgy. The structure of every day is basically the same, with prayer a fundamental element in the routine. Every year is also essentially the same, with days and seasons marked, not by the secular calendar, but by two overlapping liturgical calendars: The first and most important is the temporal cycle, which follows the story of salvation in Scripture: the year begins with Advent, which prepares for the Christmas season. A period of Ordinary Time then leads to the forty days of Lent, which prepare for Holy Week, the Sacred Triduum, and Easter. The Easter season climaxes with Pentecost and Trinity Sunday. Another period of Ordinary Time bridges the seasons.

The second liturgical cycle is the sanctoral; it celebrates all the saints in the history of the church. Each day has one saint or another to honor. The climax of this cycle comes on November 1 and 2, with the feast of All Saints and All Souls (when prayer is offered for the dead). The memory of older monks even today is triggered not by connection to events occurring in the news but by connection to a liturgical season or feast.

The daily regimen was constant (with a few minor variations) during my entire time as a monk. We woke up to the summons of a church bell (rung by a younger monk) at 5:30 a.m. and splashed water on our faces. Lauds at 6:00 a.m. was the first segment of the *Opus Dei*. It consisted of the chanting of psalms and other prayers (at Lauds, the Canticle of Zachary). Lauds was followed by a time of contemplative prayer and *lectio divina* (meditative reading). Before the liturgical reform, priest-monks used this time to say individual masses at side altars lining the nave of the abbey church; younger monks would precede them to the altar, cruets and lit taper in their hands. During that segment of time, a murmur of prayer arose from every part of the darkened nave, which was lit only by the flickering candles on the altars.

Breakfast at 7:00 was in silence. Silence, in fact, was the norm for the entire day, with necessary words only to be spoken while at work and conversation at recreation being the exceptions. At lunch and dinner, the silence was broken by public reading. As the monks ate and listened, they signaled their needs to each other by a simple set of hand signals—scratch one finger, salt; two fingers, pepper. Those who first finished eating bussed the dishes and cutlery of the others. Service at table was expected of all on a regular basis.

After breakfast, the monastic workday began, with students studying, teachers teaching, and bakers baking. At midmorning, work was interrupted for the common recitation of the "little hours" (prime, terce, sext, and none = first, third, sixth, and ninth hours) in the chapter room.[1] Work continued until 11:00 a.m., when High Mass (attended by all monks and students) was celebrated.[2] Lunch was at noon. The books read at the two main meals were always substantial. I remember, for example, plowing through all eight volumes of Daniel-Rops's history of the church, Xavier-Rynne's letters from the Vatican Council, and Dee Brown's *Bury My Heart at Wounded Knee.*

A short period of recreation (with time for a short walk and conversation) led to the daily siesta—a wonderful inheritance from European monks. After siesta, more work, followed by a period of contemplative prayer. Vespers was at 5:00 p.m. and was followed immediately by dinner at 6:00; more reading from the podium at dinner, with the meal closing with the reading of a chapter of the Rule. A longer recreation period after dinner led to the largest block of the *Opus Dei*, the hour called Matins. As the name suggests, it was formerly chanted in the early hours of the morning, but the custom among American monks was to hold it in the evening. Matins consisted of the chanting of the longest psalms, the reading of Scripture *seriatim*, readings from patristic authors (Augustine, Jerome, Leo, and especially Gregory the Great), and prayers. All in Latin, to be sure.

Matins was followed by a period of silent reading in the monk's cell. The day ended with the praying of Compline at 9:00. Then began the Great Silence, when absolute silence reigned and monks remained in their cells. In sum, monks daily spent about six hours in public prayer (the Office and Mass), two hours in silent prayer, and four to six hours in work. As this simple sketch indicates, a monk's life was immersed in the imaginative world of Scripture: all 150 psalms were chanted each week, some many times over. Filled with the words of these ancient poems and prayers, the monk inescapably thought of God as a living presence and power.[3]

MY NOVITIATE YEAR

The novitiate is a yearlong process of discernment, during which the candidate sees how he fits within the monastic life and the community sees whether he has an aptitude for this distinctive and difficult path of discipleship. If the mutual discernment proves positive, the novice makes a three-year simple vow of obedience, stability, and conversion of life. At the end of that three-year period, the monk makes solemn vows, which are binding for life.

The novice's main task is to learn the way of life through a full participation in every activity and through regular conferences with the novice master. I was very fortunate to have as my novice master Father Andrew Becnel, who combined an utterly simple spirit with deceptively wide learning. He was extraordinarily well read, and he encouraged me in turn to browse widely in Scripture, patristics, and monastic literature. Father Andrew taught and exemplified the monastic virtues of humility, hospitality, and kindness.

My work assignment as a novice was twofold. First, I was to provide caregiving assistance to two elderly monks, Fr. Fintan and Fr. Adalbert. Fr. Fintan was easy; I simply had to bring him trays of food at meals.

Fr. Adalbert was a more complicated case, altogether. A tough old Texan (one of the surviving monks from the time of the abbey's founding), he had terrible varicose veins that had opened up as suppurating sores on his legs. So, after my breakfast, I would go to his cell, clean his soiled bed and body, and help him with his own meal. Then I would sit him up and treat his legs. A thick crust of several centimeters of dead skin covered his legs around the open sores. Using baby oil, I patiently softened the crust and bit by bit (over the course of the year) got his legs clean. Then I applied Neosporin to the sores and bandaged them. My background in changing diapers and feeding children helped in what was not an easy chore.

That done, I could get to my other assignment, which was to clean the entire monastic building. This meant running an oil mop on all three floors, sweeping the three flights of stairs, and above all, cleaning the communal jakes, each of which had three urinals, three commodes, three sinks, and two showers, and, being communal, were constantly in need of cleaning. Once again, my domestic duties in Jackson made such janitorial work easier than it would otherwise have been. I had almost infinite energy in those days and considerable physical strength. I basically did not think any task was beyond me. I vividly remember walking a huge cypress armoire (taller, wider, and heavier than me) up three flights and down a long hallway, by myself.

Apart from this work in the morning hours, and participating in the daily round of monastic observances, the novitiate year allowed me the indulgence of reading whatever I desired, without being fettered by class assignments or exams. What a luxury! I quickly discovered that the freedom to read widely and deeply could be exercised especially during the Great Silence. In the periods of silent prayer during the day, reading was properly for purposes of personal transformation. Thus, I then devoted myself to the ancient classics of monastic literature (the *Apophthegmata Patrum*, the *Institutes* and *Conferences* of John Cassian, Gregory the Great's *Life of Benedict*) and important modern authorities (Dom Columba Marmion, Hubert van Zeller, and [of course] all of Thomas Merton). I began once more to keep a journal, or notebook, large parts of which consisted of striking passages I wanted to remember. In the night, however, reading of a more discursive character was possible. I learned to stretch the night for two or three hours after the last time of prayer.

In addition to reading theology (Matthias Scheeben, Robert Gleason, Henri de Lubac, Yves Congar, Pierre Teilhard de Chardin, Odo Casel),[4] I found myself discovering a love for the close reading of Scripture. I began to read the handful of volumes of the Anchor Bible that had come out, both in the Old Testament and New, as well as volumes by the new generation of Catholic scholars who had come to prominence since Pius XII's encyclical *Divino afflante Spiritu* in 1943:[5] Lucien Cerfaux, Jacques Dupont, Bruce Vawter, John McKenzie, Ceslas Spicq, Roland Murphy, and Barnabas Ahern.[6] I was especially concerned to rehabilitate my Greek, which I had learned only superficially in seminary. So, I pored over my Vulgate/ Greek edition of the New Testament and began working through Lightfoot's commentary on Philippians, Taylor's commentary on Mark, and Spicq's two-volume French commentary on Hebrews. It was Ceslas Spicq on Hebrews and Jacques Dupont on Paul who above all gave me a sense of what broad and deep biblical scholarship looked like. At nineteen, I was getting a glimpse of the sort of life of the mind that most drew me, but I was still far from being a scholar. I was still only a (slightly more focused and intent) intellectual.

Two Years of Philosophy

On making simple vows in 1964, I took the name Luke, partly because it was biblical and partly because it was short and difficult to twist by the clever young boys I thought I would someday teach. Thus, my authorial name, Luke Timothy Johnson. Holding to my monk name is deliberate. The mark of monasticism on me is permanent, and the name reminds me that, in addition to my baptism into the faith, I also carry with me the effects of another initiation into a special form of discipleship. By my vows, I also signed onto the system of preparation for the ordained priesthood as prescribed by canon law. This meant that my next years would be spent in the formal study of philosophy (two years) and theology (four years).

The young monks at Saint Ben's studied philosophy at Notre Dame Seminary, located on Carrollton Avenue in New Orleans. Every school day, five or six of us would pile into an abbey station wagon and cross Lake Pontchartrain, silent all the way there and chattering all the way back. We drove across the then two-lane, twenty-three-mile bridge, which in conditions of fog and storm was a perilous undertaking: pile-ups and traffic jams were frequent occurrences. Notre Dame was staffed by members of the Marist order and offered the full six-year curriculum of major seminaries. The other young monks traveling with me, in fact, were all in theology classes. I was the sole philosophy student from the abbey.

In 1964, the classic curriculum of philosophy classes remained unchanged. Lectures were in Latin, and exams were, too! Students moved progressively through the categories of philosophy that date all the way back to Diogenes Laertius in the third century. The framework was the form of scholastic philosophy that had been dominant within Catholicism since the time of Leo XIII, namely, neo-Thomism. Thomas Aquinas was the unsurpassed authority and the abiding spirit. Students began with logic, Aristotelian logic, to be sure; then they moved to epistemology (theories of knowledge), cosmology (the natural world from a supernatural perspective), metaphysics (above all, inquiring into the distinction between *essentia* and *esse*, which is at the heart of Thomism), and ethics (how being issues in consistent action, on the premise that *agere sequitur esse*). Although the schema is rigid, I was deeply grateful for learning it, first, because Thomas's philosophy is a remarkably sound and sane perspective on reality, and second, because this framework allowed me space to explore all other philosophical voices without confusion.

To supplement my classes, I used the library to good advantage. I focused first on contemporary neo-Thomists, reading as much as I could of Jacques Maritain, Étienne Gilson, Yves Simon, Dietrich von Hildebrand, and Ananda Coomaraswamy. All were profitable in the way they engaged other philosophies, politics, and culture through a Thomist lens. Most helpful, not surprisingly, was G. K. Chesterton's *Saint Thomas Aquinas: The Dumb Ox*, which captured as well as anything I have ever read what it means to think of Thomas as an *existential* thinker.

Because the work of a monk-student was to study, I was free, apart from the regular round of prayer, meals, and recreation, to indulge as never before my passion for wide reading. Actual work on classes took little time. Instead, I went on a spree of freelance reading in philosophy. Given a frame of reference by Frederick Copleston's monumental eight-volume *History of Philosophy*, I indiscriminately and without any sense of sequence read

A. J. Ayer, David Hume, Bertrand Russell, Henri Bergson, G. W. F. Hegel, Maurice Merleau-Ponty, Pierre-Joseph Proudhon, Karl Marx (only the *Manifesto*), José Ortega y Gasset, Miguel de Unamuno, Nikolai Berdyaev, Jean-Paul Sartre, Albert Camus, Blaise Pascal, Ernst Cassirer, and Martin Heidegger.[7] I read only a snippet of Kant, because I found him dull beyond words. I did not read Nietzsche until, at the age of fifty-eight, I wrote *The Creed: What Christians Believe and Why It Matters*, and wanted him to be my implied conversation partner.[8] A scan of this list indicates that, with some notable exceptions (Hegel, Ayer, Russell), I was drawn to thinkers who might be called existentialist in orientation and whose approach was concrete and phenomenological. Human experience as the object of thought and the shaper of thought summoned my attention, and would continue to do so for the rest of my life as a scholar.

The two thinkers who influenced me the most were Søren Kierkegaard and Gabriel Marcel. I cannot remember how I found either, but once found, they galvanized my mind. I started on Kierkegaard with his journals (only portions of which were then available) and went on to *Either/Or* (1843), *Fear and Trembling* (1843), *The Sickness unto Death* (1849), *The Concept of Anxiety* (1844), *Philosophical Fragments* (1844), and *Concluding Unscientific Postscript* (1846). Kierkegaard thrilled me first because of the sheer brilliance of his writing and the daring character of the dialectic he was working out through his use of pseudonymous authorship, but also because he thought directly on the face of existence. I was probably led to Gabriel Marcel through Bergson—and to Bergson in the first place through Maritain!—and found in him the thinker whose impress continues to this day. His willingness to tease out the implications of lived experience and his refusal ever to escape to abstraction seemed to me to be enduringly right. I ripped through *The Philosophy of Existence* (1948), *Being and Having* (1948), *The Mystery of Being* (1951), *Man against Mass Society* (1962), *Homo Viator* (1962), and *Creative Fidelity* (1964). In Marcel, I found a French Catholic existentialist philosopher who would be an intellectual companion for life.

As earlier, my voracious reading went completely unnoticed by either fellow monks or seminary professors. Nobody seemed to have any clue that I was engaged in such a passionate pursuit. But what was I was pursuing? "Truth" is much too large an answer, for I was not interested in a "truth" that was other than the one within which I lived. I think I was truly hungry to read the words written by great minds. By no means did I wish to become a Kierkegaardian or a disciple of Marcel. Why I valued them, I think, was that in them I began to learn how to think in a way I had not before. Philosophy, I understood, was not about dogma, it was about a process of reflection on reality. It was about thinking, concretely, clearly, and without deception, on human existence in all its manifestations.

At the end of these two years immersed in philosophy, I came to two conclusions. The first is that I really had learned what thinking was about, and that I had started to think for myself in response to all these thinkers. This gave me a great boost of self-confidence. The second is that whatever thinking I would do in my subsequent life, it would be based not on abstractions but on contact with and reflection on actual human experience. I would not be a student of texts alone, but of texts as transparent to existence in the world.

Thus, in combination with this self-directed course of philosophical inquiry, I continued to read avidly in the fields of psychology, sociology, and anthropology. And, naturally, I remained in thrall to great fiction, which I read at an even greater pace. If my own existence remained highly local and circumscribed, I was able to vicariously experience the widest variety of human behavior, beautiful and ugly, simple and complex, through novels, short stories, and poetry.

An odd event intersected my course of reading during this period. Abbot David directed me to serve as the midwife for a fellow monk's laboring doctoral dissertation that could not come to term. Father Anthony Tassin was working toward a PhD in English literature from Tulane University. His dissertation was on Faulkner's fictional Yoknapatawpha County in Mississippi. Anthony was approaching the task through the lens of the New Criticism associated especially with Cleanth Brooks, Robert Penn Warren, Allen Tate, and John Crowe Ransom. He had gathered lots of notes but had then broken down and could not move forward. The abbot wanted me to pick up the pieces and bring it to conclusion. I succeeded in doing so, and in the process discovered an entirely new area of inquiry (literary criticism), with its own domains and debates, that would in the course of time be important to me.

Four Years of Theology

Abbot David chose to send me to Saint Meinrad School of Theology for my theological studies, rather than have me continue at Notre Dame. This was, for me, a singular blessing. It continued to provide a context of pervasive religious faith, monastic discipline, excellent music, good fellowship, and wide reading. I can see now that my time at Saint Meinrad, an archabbey and seminary set on a high hill in southern Indiana, and at the time one of the best theologates in the country, set me firmly on the path to become a scholar.

My own community—still only edging out of the bricks-and-mortar stage of development—lacked the substantial tradition of serious scholarship of its considerably older and much larger parent institution. The monastic library at Saint Meinrad (which was accessible to students) had a splendid collection, with particularly rich resources in primary sources. During my time there, I was able to share fully in the monastic life as a visitor who had no other obligation except to study. The main way I contributed to the Saint Meinrad community was by singing in their Schola Cantorum and occasionally helping out, as I was increasingly doing in my own monastery, as assistant cantor (leader of song).

During the four years I spent there, the monastery and school of theology struggled with a number of tensions. First, the decrees of Vatican II pressed all religious communities to decide individually how reforms were to be embodied. At Saint Meinrad, a deep rift developed between older monks (largely conservative) and younger monks (largely liberal). The liberals argued for change on the basis of history, arguing, for example, that patristic-era eucharistic formulae clearly antedated and were superior to the Tridentine version, while the conservatives stood on the basis of tradition. Sadly, ideological differences mingled with personal animosity, forcing one to pick sides.

A second tension involved the question how to teach theology, now that the traditional scholastic handbooks had been abandoned. That question proved difficult to answer. Students still learned doctrine and morals and canon law, but in a much more ad hoc and diverse manner. The third tension was caused by the school of theology having to deal with a swollen student body; because the theologate of the Passionist order in Louisville had closed, Passionist seminarians lodged and studied at Saint Meinrad. My entering class, consequently, had almost seventy members, including candidates for the diocesan priesthood, monks from various abbeys, and the Passionists.

I entered the school of theology at the point when its faculty had made two clear decisions. The first concerned rigor. The basic grade was to be a C; students had to demonstrate that they deserved Bs or As. During my time in the theologate, that standard was fairly well maintained. The second decision concerned the curricular framework: not scholasticism but history was to hold the learning of theology together. Thus, church history was required—I should mention that all through seminary education, electives were rare and often nonexistent—every semester of the four years. History, moreover, was to be based as much as possible on the study of primary more than secondary sources. The Second Vatican Council had been preceded by a century of reform-minded Catholic scholars "returning to the sources," and this spirit animated the program at Saint Meinrad.

My first year at Saint Meinrad was particularly memorable. The class in early Christianity was taught by the young Aidan Kavanagh, who would become a universally recognized authority in the study of liturgy, and Polycarp Sherwood, who had published a pioneering and authoritative work on Maximus the Confessor.[9] Classes were demonstrations of superb scholarship, with specific attention to the sources (as much as possible in the original languages). Aidan led us from Jewish synagogue services through the early Christian church orders, which displayed the variety of early eucharistic prayers that shortly would, on the Council's decree, stand alongside and relativize the Tridentine Latin Mass.

Polycarp dealt with the development of doctrine in complex and rambling lectures that students called "Sherwood's Forest," but occasionally he would exegete passages from patristic writers (in Latin and Greek) with great delicacy and precision. Learning from scholars such as these was a feast. It was also tough. We were assigned short papers, which were strictly research projects; thus, I wrote one paper on the sources available for Montanism and another on Marcionism. The point was to move from secondary sources (encyclopedias, articles, monographs) to the primary sources, and then to sort out the most reliable primary sources, and the critical editions available. The very tough and bright teaching associates (Ephraim Carr and Matthias Newman, who both also became noteworthy scholars) splashed red ink all over these efforts. But we learned. One's grade in this class depended on these assignments, but most of all on a single final exam. Weeks before the exam, a sheet with twenty-eight separate topics was distributed to students. At the three-hour exam, three of these topics were assigned by the professors to each student, at random. To pass, one had to control all twenty-eight topics!

Another brilliant professor was the youthful Colman Grabert, whose command of the theology of Karl Rahner and Hans Urs von Balthasar was breathtaking, and whose presentations in doctrinal theology were dense and closely argued. I vividly remember how, in teaching the subject of grace, Colman led the class through Paul's argument in Romans 5 (again, in Greek). Not all classes were as scintillating as his, but the standard was high. The monks were learned men, and they poured their scholarship more into teaching than into publication.

I became friends with two monks from Saint Meinrad who were in my class, and I discovered for the first time the thrill of a positive competition for excellence. Both Nathan Mitchell and Raymond Studzinski went on to become professors: Nathan at the University of Notre Dame (in liturgy) and Raymond at Catholic University and Fordham (in ethics). The three of us, together with Colman, would in the evening walk the road around and around the monastery, discussing and arguing over every imaginable theological topic.

The demanding character of classes did not slow in the least my outside reading, which now became more focused and intense. My status as a visitor gave me even more time to read than I had enjoyed at Saint Ben's. To be sure, I continued to read fiction and poetry, but I focused on theology, Scripture, and psychology. In theology, I still read French Catholic authors like Yves Congar, Henri de Lubac, Louis Bouyer, and Jean Daniélou,[10] but now expanded to include a predominantly German cohort. I read Karl Rahner's *Inspiration in the Bible* and *On the Theology of Death*,[11] as well as the first eleven volumes of his *Theological Investigations*.[12] I read the early works of Balthasar, as well as Piet Schoonenberg, Edward Schillebeeckx, Bernard Haring, and Louis Monden.[13] For recreation, I read the first twenty issues of the international theological journal *Concilium*.[14] I was also able to make some initial forays into Protestant theology.[15]

In Scripture, I was fortunate to have excellent classes in Luke-Acts and Hebrews given by the Passionist Barnabas Ahern, and another on the Gospel of John by Aelred Cody (giving me a chance to read Raymond Brown's commentary).[16] Although I still favored more conservative scholars like Oscar Cullmann and Joachim Jeremias,[17] I made forays into Rudolf Bultmann's commentary on John and fought vigorously with his *Theology of the New Testament*.

In psychology, I continued along the path blazed for me by Viktor Frankl's *Man's Search for Meaning* (1959), finding particularly appealing Erik Erikson, Adrian van Kaam, and the brilliant William Lynch, whose *Images of Hope: Imagination as Healer of the Hopeless* (1965) affected me profoundly.[18] I was also intrigued by the marriage of psychology and spirituality in Henri Nouwen's earliest books, *Intimacy* (1969) and *Creative Ministry* (1971).

Three moments from my time at Saint Meinrad stand out as significant for my becoming a scholar. The first was a Jewish-Christian dialogue between the Conservative rabbi Arthur Hertzberg and the German Catholic theologian Johannes Baptist Metz (a student of Rahner), who represented the new "political theology" that deliberately engaged Marxist theory and praxis. The entire student body and monastery attended the lengthy, multiday sessions, attending to the carefully prepared presentations and then the give-and-take between these two renowned and deeply committed persons. It was my first real experience of public theology—and on such an important issue, in light of Vatican II's declaration on the Jews—and it left me with the sense that such public intellectual activity was eminently worthwhile.

The second was the chance to work for an MA in religious studies at Indiana University in Bloomington. The School of Theology and the Department of Religious Studies at IU made it possible for those of us who qualified (the GREs were taken cold, with no preparation!) to take a semester of classes on campus, then write a thesis, and so receive the MA virtually simultaneously with the MDiv from Saint Meinrad. We lived in the graduate residence, Eigenmann Hall, mingled with all the other students, and participated fully in a normal graduate program. This was the first time I had mingled with, much less partied with, women of any age, since grade school. Given that this was 1969, when "Hey Jude" and "The

Age of Aquarius" blared in the student lounge, when a malcontent set fire to the university library, and when the "Free University" held classes in the meadow, the atmosphere was heady for one who thought of himself as otherworldly. Heady, and invigorating, but not yet destabilizing.

The classes at IU stimulated me to do my best work. I piggybacked Wayne Meeks's lecture class on Paul to undergraduates. Meeks was a superb lecturer, able to make sense of even the most complex questions. I had the chance to write a paper for him on the rabbinic background to Romans 5 (thus finding my way around the Talmud and *Shi'ur Komah* speculation), and another on Ignatius of Antioch as a Paulinist. My final paper was an extensive analysis of temple imagery in Ephesians 2, enabling me to work my way into other Jewish material, this time apocalyptic texts and Qumran. I also had a seminar on Gnostic myth with Meeks (Nathan also took it), which tested the then prominent theory that there was a pre-Christian "redeemed redeemer myth." I was assigned to write on the *Poimandres*, and it delighted me to bury myself in the close analysis of the text and the (then) finite literature on it. A third class was on rabbinic thought with the great Jewish scholar Henry Fischel, a pioneer in establishing the connections between rabbinic literature and Hellenistic philosophy. Fischel allowed me to pursue the issue of rabbinic mysticism, enabling me to discover Gershom Scholem and the wonders of *merkabah* mysticism. All these courses were demanding but well within my ideological wheelhouse.

The most mind-opening class was William May's course on religion and culture. We began by examining some of the classic texts in religious phenomenology (Otto, van der Leeuw, Eliade),[19] and then began to apply its categories to cultural phenomena—such as the burgeoning student movement. The books that most challenged me were Peter Berger and Thomas Luckman's *Social Construction of Reality* and Peter Berger's *Sacred Canopy*.[20] As I had with my first reading of Bultmann, I fought Berger page by page, but I ended up completely accepting his argument. I fully understood that, for the first time, I had thereby stepped out of the monastic world by which I had defined myself. I grasped that the monastic culture, and indeed, Catholicism itself, was but one of many "plausibility structures" by which humans secure identity. And, remarkably, I was less afraid than exhilarated. For May, I wrote a long paper using Eliade, van der Leeuw, and Émile Durkheim[21] as a lens for examining what might be called religious patterns in Leo Tolstoy's novella *The Death of Ivan Ilych*. When I returned to Saint Meinrad the next semester, I completed my thesis, "Norms for True and False Prophecy in First Corinthians." I thought it would be the first step in my future work on prophecy in the New Testament.

The final event came about by accident. When we returned to Saint Meinrad from IU, we discovered that the new instructor for the first-year history class (the class that had so impressed me) was on leave in order to complete his dissertation at the University of Chicago. Nathan, Raymond, and I were recruited to teach the class. Nathan dealt with liturgy, Raymond with moral issues, and I lectured on doctrinal development. Naturally, I had to do a deeper dive into this material than had been required when I took the class, had to genuinely examine each of the patristic authors and all the conciliar texts in the original language in order to construct some fifteen lectures extending from the second-century apologists to Chalcedon. This grueling but also exhilarating exercise stood me in good stead in later years. I was confident in my control of early Christian literature after the New Testament. That same year, I also gave a lecture to first-year theologians in the sacramental theology class, on the Eucharist according to Thomas Aquinas, using both the *Summa theologiae* and Thomas's *Commentary on the Gospel of John*. I found both the work of preparation and the discipline of lecturing to be deeply satisfying.

In addition, I took the first steps toward the habit of publication. My paper for Henry Fischel on Jewish Gnosticism was published in the Saint Meinrad scholarly journal, *Resonance*, as was a paper I wrote for my final class in church history, "The Natural Knowledge of God according to Vatican I's *Dei Filius*"; both articles were redolent with footnotes based on the primary sources. Saint Meinrad's influence was clear. As soon as my thesis for IU was accepted, I submitted it in revised form to the *American Benedictine Review*, a genuine peer-reviewed journal. Within months, it, too, was published.

Through all of this study, my life as a monk continued apace and became more complicated, as I went through the process leading to ordination. I passed through the ritual induction into all the "minor" and "major" orders, and I was ordained to the priesthood in the late spring of 1970. Already as a deacon, and even more as a priest, I had begun to preach regularly to the college students and the monastic community. I was struck, though, by how different the act of preaching seemed to me from the act of teaching. In teaching, I could stand aside and point to the text; in preaching, I stood under the authority of the text. This awareness made preaching always an activity that caused me considerable anguish. Being under the Word is not a comfortable place. Increasingly, I was also asked to give retreats and days of recollection.

Back to Saint Ben's

I spent the entire year of 1970–1971 back in my home monastery in Louisiana. Apart from one session of summer school in Indiana, I had, in fact, spent three months of each year in my own community. During these summer sojourns I participated fully in the routine of my monastic home. My work assignments were enjoyable precisely because they involved the kind of hard physical labor that encouraged contemplation: hauling garbage to the dump in a monster army surplus truck; mucking out the holding barn at the dairy; lifting 100-pound bags of insulation from a boxcar and transferring them first to a storage shed and then, when needed, to the two-thousand-foot ditch we dug for water pipes; and always, cutting back the growth that threatened to overwhelm the grounds: driving a bush hog, pulling chain-mowers, and pushing hand mowers in the brutal Louisiana heat. Apart from those assignments, though, I was free to spend many hours reading in the monastic music room.

But when I returned full time (as I thought) to my community, I was considerably changed from the young man I had been as a novice. I noticed that, unconsciously, I had allowed the alternating pattern of stays at Saint Meinrad and Saint Ben's to camouflage deeper personal issues. I realized that, however satisfying the studies at Saint Meinrad, I would each year grow more and more critical of the tensions within that large community. "Things were better at home," I would tell myself, as I eagerly awaited the summer. And each summer, it would at first seem as though they were. Yet, by late August, I was always itchy to get back to Saint Meinrad.

One cause of irritation at Saint Meinrad was the constant conflict between the younger, reformist monks (with whom I gladly if unreflectively aligned myself) and the older, traditionalist monks. It was all too easy for we young theological blackshirts to caricature and despise the clingers (as we saw them) to old ways. After all, we had history on our side. We were right! We wanted revolution now. And we got it. Reforms were so drastic that all the old forms of piety were discarded. The Latin texts that had sustained monks for 1,500 years were literally thrashed. The Gregorian chant was replaced by ersatz compositions of little worth.

Worst of all, we had no concern for the stories that might have been told by the older monks, about what those forms of piety had meant to them, about what the cost of radical change might be. We may have been right on the issues, but we were certainly not righteous in our dispositions. A decade later, I looked back at this frenzied period and felt a great weight of guilt at our (and specifically my) behavior, and I began a lifelong project of thinking how communities might discern righteously through the recognition of God's activity among all God's people.

The atmosphere was certainly better at my own community. We did not experience such hostile divisions. Charity continued to reign. The problem lay, surely, not with the community but, as I was increasingly aware, with me. Certain fundamental things had shifted within me, making me begin to wonder if I was truly fit for life as a monk. At the most overt level, I was deeply troubled, as many Catholic theologians were at that time, by the encyclical *Humanae vitae* promulgated by Pope Paul VI in 1968. I considered his argument supporting the prohibition of artificial means of birth control both formally and materially in error, and I was not sure how I could deal, as a priest, with penitents who confessed such practice as a sin.

More covertly, I was increasingly aware of the tension within me between an awakening desire for intimacy and my punctilious observance of the rules. In light of Paul's letter to the Romans, I felt deeply convicted of a "works righteousness" in my rigid (one might even call it obsessive-compulsive) adherence to rules. Finally, my experience at Saint Meinrad and at Indiana University gave me a much greater confidence in my intellectual abilities, as well as an openness to "the world" from which I had turned when becoming a monk. By dint of a habit of intellectualization and a knack for compartmentalization, I had suppressed desires that I could not name even to myself. But I was a tinderbox, ready to be lit.

A big factor in lighting that fuse was the Catholic charismatic movement. It had begun at Duquesne University in 1967 and spread to Ann Arbor in 1970 and Notre Dame in 1971. There were also charismatic communities in New Orleans and in many other locations. This movement, which emphasized the gift of the Spirit as an actual and present power in lives, which could be expressed by speaking in tongues, prophecy, and healings, spread rapidly among Catholics who were, in light of the Council, eager for renewal by God and not just by ecclesiastical decrees.

As it happened, a charismatic group began in Covington, Louisiana, and met in the seminary for its prayer meetings. Along with Father Benedict Songy, an attractive, vivacious thirty-six-year-old local woman with six children was part of the leadership team. Her name was Joy Barnett, and she attended Mass daily at the abbey church. She and her husband enjoyed considerable wealth, and they lived at Oak Hill Farm outside Covington in a nine-thousand-square-foot modern/rustic house. When I arrived back at the abbey with a thesis on the norms for true and false prophecy in 1 Corinthians, it was seized upon and reproduced by the group, which then asked me to be a participant in the prayer meetings and provide scriptural teachings. I agreed and began to attend regularly, as many other monks did as well.

My monastic assignment for that year was to be a lecturer to seminarians in Saint Joseph's College (the old seminary system had been rejiggered over the intervening years). In the fall I taught Old Testament—with an emphasis on Israel's writings emerging from the experience of God—and the history of liturgy. In this latter class, I began with the analysis of body language, moved to anthropological theories of play and ritual (Johan Huizinga),[22] and then began to build the history of Christian worship from the synagogue all the way to the contemporary renewal. In the spring semester, I taught New Testament—with an emphasis on the experience of the resurrection and the Holy Spirit as the key to the production of these texts—and comparative religion, which demanded that I read widely in traditions I had formerly had at best a nodding acquaintance. The experience of teaching a full load convinced me that I could hold my own in this trade, and I was eager to take the next step.

My life became more complicated when Joy Barnett's spiritual director insisted that she take the class on comparative religion with me. Meeting her in this context led to a friendship that would eventually explode my life and reshape it.

In the course of the year, I applied, with Abbot David's permission, to three American universities for doctoral work. I did not want to go the usual

Roman route taken by most Catholic religious. I considered that I had learned already what I could from the best in Catholic scholarship, and I wanted to be challenged by another setting. I knew little to nothing about graduate programs. Even though I would have liked to work in Old Testament, my Hebrew was at best paltry, whereas my languages were just fine for the New Testament, and I was quite willing to work that side of the canon.

I applied to the University of Iowa and was summarily rejected. I was accepted by the Graduate Theological Union at Berkeley but really could not picture myself on the West Coast. I applied to Yale because my favorite Indiana teacher, Wayne Meeks, had just joined their faculty, and I wanted more of him. Undoubtedly because Meeks had had me in class, Yale overlooked my monkishness and accepted me. Not only me; in a spasm of ecumenism, they also accepted into their doctoral program the Jesuit priest William S. Kurz.

My life was about to undergo changes I could never have anticipated. I entered doctoral work as a monk and ended it as a husband with a child and six stepchildren. I began at Yale as an intellectual with scholarly leanings and some scholarly ability, and I left Yale with the focus and desire to produce that mark the mature scholar.

The summer before leaving for New Haven, then, I worked hard to get my Hebrew at least to the intermediate stage and began to slog away at German, knowing that this language, in addition to my French, would be examined in the course of my first two years. I was eager to meet this new challenge, thinking that it would equip me to return to the abbey and serve it through my scholarship. Things didn't turn out as planned.

Chapter Four

DOCTORAL STUDIES (1971–1976)

*T*HE PROCESS OF BEING ADMITTED TO A TOP-RANKED PHD program in the early '70s was much simpler than it is now. Today, students are avidly recruited, submit impressive portfolios (with résumés, essays, and extensive statements concerning their "philosophy of teaching"), are given campus tours and on-site interviews, and are offered lucrative scholarships and stipends. When I applied to Yale in 1970, I sent in my GRE scores and a half-page statement that said in effect, "I like the New Testament and hope to teach it to seminarians," together with letters from my IU teachers, Wayne Meeks and William May, plus a Saint Meinrad professor, whose name, sadly, I no longer recall. That was it.

Eventually, I received a short note to the effect that I was accepted, and that I should show up on a certain day. I received a Yale University Fellowship, which covered tuition. My other expenses were to be covered by the monastery. The Jesuit priest Bill Kurz and I were selected from about sixty applicants, and we had no idea why. We had never met the faculty, and the faculty (except in my case, Meeks) had never met us. It was like being picked up with calipers by a divine power and transported to a new existence, without any sense of what qualities in oneself merited that election. Such apparently random grace can exhilarate, to be sure, but it can also mystify.

When I arrived in New Haven in the fall of 1971, I knew nothing of New Haven, nothing of the university, nothing of the New Testament department, nothing of the demands of doctoral work, nothing of the place where I was to live. I quickly learned much about each.

New Haven

Yale University as I imagined it was nestled in a charming New England town set high on a cliff above the crashing waves of the Atlantic Ocean. New Haven was far from a charming town, and it sat on no cliff. It squatted, rather, on the torpid Long Island Sound, one of the many small cities strung between New York and Boston, a graceless sprawl linked by the Boston Post Road and by Interstate 95. Mayor Richard C. Lee had just left office in 1970, after sixteen years trying to make New Haven the poster child of 1960s-style urban renewal. Inspired by the redoubtable Robert Moses and assisted by heaps of money from the Kennedy and Johnson administrations, Lee had overseen the construction of the Oak Street Connector (a spur off I-95) that forced the evacuation of hundreds of families living in a "slum" (read: neighborhood) and their relocation to "projects" intended to represent a cleaner, safer, and more prosperous life. In place of the offensive neighborhoods, Lee erected a great parking garage, coliseum, and shopping center abutting the lovely and ancient New Haven Green. By the time I arrived in the fall of 1971, the consequences of such social engineering were beginning to appear, though it would take several more decades for the full scale of social disorder to be realized, as the monuments slowly crumpled and the dreams more quickly faded.

Ethnic tensions had long been a feature of New Haven life. The largely WASP faculty of Yale hunkered down in the few safe neighborhoods, hoping for the best. The "renewal" of downtown was intended above all to provide the university a more salubrious environment. Working-class Italians (who formed a large portion of the unions that kept town-gown relations at a boil) struggled with and against a fast-growing Hispanic and African American population. Poverty and crime stalked the projects. Racial tensions flared with the trial for murder in 1970 of Bobby Seale, cofounder of the Black Panther Party. When I arrived, student protestors of various stripes camped out on the New Haven Green. Black Panthers in full regalia patrolled Broadway in front of the Yale Co-op. Over the eleven years I spent in the city, the urban spiral continued downward, so that the green increasingly became dotted with the homeless and the hopeless, and certain streets (like Chapel Street and Dixwell Avenue) were decidedly unsafe for students to travel.

My lodging for my first year and a half in New Haven was the rectory of Saint Boniface Church, located on desolate State Street. This old German national church claimed only a few hundred members and had just lost both its school and its nuns. The pastor, Hock O'Mara, was battling cancer and paid attention mostly to golf. I picked up the slack on what few pastoral responsibilities there were, mainly saying Mass on weekdays and Sundays, teaching Bible to a circle of elderly women (mostly ex-schoolteachers), and working with what few young people remained in the congregation. The pastor's and my only real meal of the day was prepared by a young woman from the Culinary Institute of America, which was then situated in New Haven. Otherwise, we ate at random as bachelors do.

The rectory was comfortable and quiet, conducive to sustained study. The main interruptions during the day were pleas for help from solitary homeless folk who rang the doorbell. We always answered with sandwiches and milk. Walking from Saint Boniface to campus gave me a good view of the shabby and splendid sides of New Haven. In addition to my priestly responsibilities in the parish, I joined the Yale charismatic community that met in the basement of the Catholic center. As in Louisiana, I served as something of a participant-observer, becoming ever more convinced that God's Holy Spirit was, through this grassroots movement, powerfully at work among God's people.

YALE

One reason why New Haven struggled financially was that its entire center was occupied by a tax-exempt university with a several billion dollar endowment, whose magnificent buildings on the edge of the green and extending in every direction stood as a constant point of comparison to the financially distressed workers of the city. And, no question about it, the Yale campus was truly magnificent. Its residential colleges were built around courtyards and displayed architectural styles ranging from the Gothic (Branford) to the modern (Stiles). At the center of the university was the Gothic tower of Sterling Library; the jewel-like Beinecke Rare Book and Manuscript Library, with its translucent marble walls and its permanent display of the Gutenberg Bible; and the underground "cross-campus" library holding the undergraduate collection.

The liberal icon Kingman Brewster was still president of the university, and he had initiated the induction of female undergraduates in 1969. Unlike Harvard, which privileged its graduate programs, Yale prided itself on its undergraduate education, with world-class scholars lecturing to the brilliant students recruited from across the country. One of the glories of Yale in those days, and one of the keys to its superb program in religious studies, was its strength in disciplines ancillary to the study of early Christianity; ancient history, classics, ancient Near Eastern languages, and philosophy all offered resources for research and instruction.

The Religious Studies Department at Yale was brand-new. It had just recently severed from Yale Divinity School (YDS), and the separation was not altogether painless. Some faculty members belonged to the graduate school, some to the divinity school. Some divinity school faulty formerly important to graduate students (like the great Paul Minear in New Testament) found themselves marginalized by an arrangement that privileged the faculty in the department. But although the department's official home was in a house downtown, all classes continued to be taught in divinity school classrooms, and the impressive YDS theological library was an indispensable resource for faculty and graduate students alike.

When I began work at Yale on my PhD, the New Testament faculty was arguably the finest in the nation, equal if not superior to those of Harvard and Chicago. The senior professor was Nils Dahl, who had studied under Rudolf Bultmann; Dahl was deeply learned in Jewish literature, and his essays were models of clarity and incisive insight.[1] Unfortunately, he was not a good teacher nor a terribly efficient director of dissertations. Wayne Meeks was himself a graduate of the Yale program and had studied (together with J. Z. Smith) under the great pioneer in the study of Hellenistic Judaism, E. R. Goodenough. He had recently arrived from Indiana University and had published his classic dissertation on the prophet-king in the Gospel of John; in 1972, his seminal study on the sectarian character of that gospel would appear.[2] He was just beginning his lengthy investigation of the social world of early Christianity, which would find expression in his influential study of Paul, *The First Urban Christians* (1981). Meeks represented a combination of theoretical daring and exegetical precision.

Abraham Malherbe was also a newly arrived member of the faculty. A student of Arthur Darby Nock at Harvard, he had been, with Everett Ferguson, one of the moving spirits shaping the Church of Christ's embrace

of the historical-critical method. Malherbe brought to the Yale program
a vast knowledge of Hellenistic literature, with a particular emphasis on
moral philosophy.[3] His crisp South African accent and severe demeanor
camouflaged a genuine pastoral concern for students. The junior member
of the team was Rowan Greer, another graduate of Yale, who brought the
distinctive perspective of the Anglican tradition and who (fittingly) kept
one foot—it was eventually both feet—in patristic studies.

As I have mentioned, William Kurz and I were classmates. Senior to us
was a group of young scholars that was outstanding in terms of intelligence
and drive: Mary Rose D'Angelo, Terry Callan, Reuven Kimmelman, Alan
Segal, Don Juel, David Balch, Bruce Schein, and Ronald Hock all went on
to productive scholarly careers and provided Kurz and me stiff competition
for excellence. Responding to a mind as supple and learned as Alan Segal's
was no easy thing! When we migrated to Near Eastern Languages to study
rabbinic texts, Kurz and I profited from the great learning and generous
sharing of the young Jewish scholars Alan Cooper and Bruce Zukerman.

As I started the program at Yale, I was able to assess my weaknesses and
strengths. It was immediately clear to me that I lagged far behind my colleagues in languages (Kurz, for example, had a masters in classics). My Hebrew was, well, elementary. I therefore spent a whole year studying intermediate Hebrew with Brevard Childs and brought my skill to the point where I
could profitably spend the entire second year studying midrash with Judah
Goldin using the unpointed Hebrew text: in the first semester, we read the
Avot of Rabbi Nathan, and in the second semester, the Sifre on Deuteronomy.
Goldin was a splendid example of the strengths offered to New Testament
students at Yale by departments such as Near Eastern Languages. He was an
internationally renowned scholar of Judaica, and his seminars were displays of
erudition and pedagogical finesse. His pedagogical method was as ancient as
midrash itself: we sat around a long table, with Goldin sitting at the head and
occasionally jumping up with excitement; each of us read aloud in turn from
the Hebrew and then provided a translation and interpretation; Goldin would
then lead the group into further discussion. He was very hard on the Jewish
students who had grown up in the language, but he was endlessly kind and
patient with goyim like Bill and I who dared to participate in such a daunting
yet thrilling exercise. Every seminar session was memorable.

My German was even more rudimentary than my Hebrew. I said to
Malherbe when seeing the first assignment in the history of interpretation

seminar, Hans von Campenhausen's long monograph, *Die Entstehung der christlichen Bibel*,[4] "Mr. Malherbe, I don't think my German is good enough to read this." Malherbe to me: "By the time you finish the book, it will be." Speaking of German monographs, my discovery of Erich Fascher's 1927 study *Prophētēs* quickly persuaded me that the dream I had before entering Yale of writing a definitive study of prophecy in the New Testament was not needed. So much for that.

I also saw, however, that I brought distinctive gifts to the conversation: I had an unparalleled background in philosophy and theology; I had acquired a distinctive literary-critical approach to complement or challenge the regnant historical-critical paradigm; and I had an indefatigable work ethic. On this basis, I was willing to enter the fray.

But it was not easy. I had to spend untold hours during my entire first year toiling over Hebrew (and Campenhausen!). I grew deeply discouraged when I compared myself to the brilliant people in Malherbe's Hellenistic Moralists seminar. Halfway through the first semester, in fact, I made an appointment with him and confessed that I felt completely inadequate to this level of academic life, as shown by the brilliance of my seminar colleagues whose performance, I thought, put me in the shade. I considered that perhaps I ought to go back to the monastery. Malherbe's pastoral response is one I have passed on to many subsequent graduate students feeling the same inadequacy that I did then. He said, in effect, "Your colleagues in this seminar are talking out of what they learned last year"—I was the only newbie in the seminar—"that's why you feel overwhelmed. Trust me, next year, you will be impressing first-year students in the same way." Whether or not that turned out to be the case, it was the right shot of encouragement.

In addition to Hebrew and the seminars on midrash, I took three exegesis classes (one on 1 Corinthians, one on John, and one on Mark). The class on 1 Corinthians, with the visiting professor Frederick Wisse—an expert in the Nag Hammadi writings—was especially useful on two counts. First, since Kurz and I were the only students, it gave me a chance to learn and appreciate this bright and modest man, who not only was a fellow religious (Jesuit) but also was, like me, a native of Wisconsin—a Midwesterner in whom there was no guile. Second, Wisse demanded that we submit full-fledged exegesis papers each week, to be read aloud; more important, he also prepared his own written exegesis and shared it with us. It was a true experience of collegiality. With generous and critical feedback from both Kurz and Wisse, I made significant progress in the art of exegesis. The classes on John and Mark were with Dahl, and not memorable.

The New Testament faculty team-taught the seminar on the history of interpretation through the patristic period. As generally in those days, medieval interpretation was bypassed, and the history of modern criticism was covered by means of a reading course. Directed reading courses, with short papers submitted throughout, in Greco-Roman background and Jewish background to the New Testament prepared students for final examinations on those subjects.

Two classes were especially fruitful for my later work as a scholar. In my first year, as I have mentioned, I took two semesters of "Hellenistic Moralists and the New Testament" with Malherbe. In the first semester, I chose to pursue the topic of how sophists and philosophers used polemic against each other. I read and annotated all of Lucian of Samosata, Plutarch, Epictetus, and Dio Chrysostom, as well as parts of Aelius Aristides and Seneca; I compiled a huge body of notes on this rhetoric, and my typed class presentation ran to some thirty pages. In the second semester, under Malherbe's direction, I applied all this analysis to a major paper (some forty pages long) on the polemic of the Pastoral Letters. I argued that the recent judgment on this topic by Robert Karris of Harvard was wrong, and that the polemic served, not to establish Paul's authority (as Karris argued), but as a foil for Paul's positive *protrepsis* (exhortation) of his delegates, Timothy and Titus. This immersion in the rhetoric of Greco-Roman philosophers has paid many dividends over the years. Malherbe persuaded a student who had come to the program convinced that the Jewish context of nascent Christianity was all-important, that the Greco-Roman world was at least as significant, even if he carried this to a humorous extreme: in an advising session, he asked why in the world I was spending so much time on Hebrew: "All you need to do is read the Septuagint" (the ancient Greek translation of the Hebrew Bible).

The second seminar (with Wayne Meeks) developed further my interest in the social analysis of ancient communities, which had begun at Indiana with my reading of Durkheim and Berger. Meeks was then still at an early stage of his own pursuit of a sociological method. Our questions in the seminar focused primarily on the manifest and latent functions of philosophical and religious texts—following the lead of Robert Merton. We read rabbinic material, Pythagorean and Epicurean texts, and the Qumran writings. Kurz and I did all the research (exhaustive research), and Meeks provided all the right questions. Once more, I compiled a priceless collection of primary data.

My paper for this class was a close analysis of the community of possessions at Qumran, in which I argued that the practice was a function of the ideology of holiness in that sectarian version of Judaism. As a monk who had lived in a community of possessions, this topic was particularly attractive, especially since monastic literature consistently connected this practice to an imitation of the apostolic church (as described in Acts 2:42–47 and 4:32–37). This same interest led me to write my final paper for Judah Goldin on the use of possessions in the rabbinic tradition, which steadfastly rejected any notion of community property in favor of organized almsgiving. I began to see the way forward to a dissertation on Luke-Acts, in conversation with these disparate ancient accounts.

My interest in Luke-Acts, I discovered, was shared by Kurz and by several other doctoral students (Dennis Hamm, Jerome Neyrey, and Halvor Moxnes). We began to meet weekly to read Luke-Acts together in Greek. No higher criticism was allowed; we simply followed the narrative as it developed. This was one of the best of my experiences in doctoral work: a congregation of equals, all lovers of the text as it stood, all committed to the religious pertinence of the text, all open to the give-and-take of honest exchange. I treasure the memory of those nighttime meetings at the Orange Street house of Jesuits.

Joy

A totally unexpected force entered my life in the fall of my first year at Yale. I mentioned Joy Barnett in the previous chapter, and how my friendship with her grew through sharing in the work of the charismatic movement and through her taking a class with me. During the summer of my preparation for Yale, that friendship grew, but neither of us realized how much it had grown or how it had changed into something greater than friendship. In late September, however, Joy visited me in New Haven, and I accompanied her on a trip to visit her daughter at a prep school in Lenox, Massachusetts.

By the end of that intense though thoroughly platonic weekend, we both knew that we were more comfortable with each other than we had ever been with anyone else before, and that we needed to come to grips with this new and powerful thing. Was it a temptation from the devil? Was it a gift of God's Holy Spirit? In searching and candid phone calls and letters over the next months, we tried as best we could to face the truth, wherever it may lead us.

It is impossible adequately to describe the woman who so fundamentally reshaped my life. She was beautiful, and she dressed with a great sense of individuality and flair. She had dropped out of high school, yet she had an astonishingly wide vocabulary and a stunning ability to put words to paper. She was intellectually avid, reading philosophy, psychology, theology, and literature and thinking about what she read. She was self-analytical, with a keen sense of discernment. She was a gourmet cook; she rode horses; she was a superb home stylist. She saw beauty everywhere in nature. She loved every form of music. Above all, she had a robust and infectious sense of humor. She was simply fun to be with. As Kris Kristofferson's song puts it, "Loving her was easier than anything I'll ever do again." No matter what the trials and tribulations that subsequently were to befall us, I never for a moment regretted entrusting my heart to her.

This was, however, scarcely a "boy meets girl, girl marries boy" scenario. At thirty-seven, Joy was nine and a half years my senior. She had been married twenty years, and she had six children, ages nineteen to nine. Although she struggled with a marriage that had grown cold in many ways, she took her vow seriously. She had been a daily communicant since childhood. She was a leader in the national charismatic movement; she was known and respected by my fellow monks and the abbot. She was, in all respects, a thoroughly virtuous, prudent, and careful person. How could she let this happen?

To top it off, she had suffered from childhood with a strange, periodic-chronic condition that is now recognized as an autoimmune disease, somewhere in the spectrum of familial Mediterranean fever (she was Sicilian and French) and other similar inflammatory conditions. How could she inflict herself, her children, and her illness—we knew it would never be substantially better—on a young man with (she thought) a great ministry to fulfill? The sickness was vicious when it hit. Indeed, she had only shortly before we met spent six months in the hospital, some of it in intensive care, with pericarditis (many side symptoms occurred mysteriously). She had experienced a remission of that condition when she prayed to God to give her the strength to meet what she needed to meet in her life, and she regarded her healing as a call to bring truth to her life. But as a cradle Catholic, she never conceived of divorce as a possibility she might have to face.

My situation was not so complex as Joy's, but it was equally daunting. I was a solemnly professed monk and a priest. I, too, had been a daily communicant since my adolescence. I was increasingly known in Louisiana and Mississippi as a preacher and retreat leader. My leaving the monastery— breaking my vows—and marrying a divorced woman seemed equally impossible to me. Yet, what were we to do with what was apparently a gift from God, given without our asking, given, in fact, despite our greatest fears?

Interspersed with my short stints back at the monastery, the flow of long letters and equally lengthy phone calls continued between 1971 and 1973. We tried to work out how we could be faithful to God and honor what (we were increasingly convinced) God had given us, and not do damage to those to whom we were committed. In the winter of 1972–1973, I left the rectory and moved to a one-room apartment on Chapel Street. I set to work on papers petitioning for a dispensation from my vows. My petition was rejected; leaving the monastery meant, in effect, to be excommunicated. Joy's husband had already separated from her, and the process of divorce (on the grounds of abandonment) began. She petitioned the church for an annulment, and that petition likewise was rejected. We were on our own.

Cut off from the tradition that had sustained each of us throughout our lives, we depended even more on each other to make our way forward in darkness rather than light, in ambiguity rather than certainty. In June of 1973, I drove Joy and three of the youngest children to New Haven, where we leased a house near the divinity school on Edgehill Avenue. We began to try to create a life together, because each of our past lives was lost forever. We each would have to figure out how to seek sanctity divorced from the contexts that had formerly given shape to that most fundamental of quests.

To call all of this a distraction would be much too dismissive. The gift of Joy's love was the most important thing in my life, and it remained the most important element of my life for forty-seven years until Joy died in 2017. Joy was, and remained to the end, not only the singular symbol of God's grace in my life but the embodiment of that grace. She was for me "the love of God poured into our hearts through the Holy Spirit." She taught me what grace was simply by being who she was. It was not an affectation when I would later declare that everything I knew about grace I learned from Joy. There is a reason why I dedicated the great majority of my books to her.

Not a distraction. But this new and powerful reality shattered the certainties of my former existence and meant that, from the very start of doctoral work, I labored at scholarship with one figurative hand behind my back. The other hand was always busy trying to stir and discern emotional tea leaves, and trying to deal with the human damage that illicit love (even if holy) can leave in its wake. Joy and I married in early 1974, and our daughter Tiffany was born later that year. I was now a new creation: a husband, a stepfather of six children (three of them full time in the household), and the father of one. I had not finished my PhD, and I was still a long way from having a job that could support this venture.

Finishing Doctoral Work

The way to doctoral candidacy at Yale was largely through examinations. During course work, competence in reading French and German and Hebrew had to be certified. In the second year, a more comprehensive examination in Greek was administered, which included translating a patristic author, a Hellenistic author, and the New Testament (my assigned passage was from Hebrews). At the end of the second year, comprehensive examinations were taken in the Greco-Roman and Jewish backgrounds to the New Testament. Finally, there was an exegetical exam: a New Testament passage was assigned by the faculty, and the candidate had three hours to write a coherent and possibly interesting interpretation of the passage. This was followed by an oral examination based on that written exam, at which the entire faculty was present.

I got through the earlier qualifying examinations fairly handily, and my exegesis exam was well within my range, being on Acts 4:32–37. By this time, I had built up a fair head of steam about this passage, and I held forth with vigor. All good. But at the oral examination—the night before which I had absolutely no sleep—Nils Dahl spotted the one great deficiency in my paper, which was its total neglect of the textual variants in the passage.

The reader will remember that Dahl and I had only a distant relationship, at best. In front of the entire New Testament faculty, Dahl submitted me to a merciless forty-five-minute interrogation about the textual apparatus. I responded feebly but somehow was allowed to pass. The experience set my own resolution concerning the way I would conduct examinations—if ever I had the opportunity to do so. It is all too easy to expose what students do not know and to humiliate them. A better approach is to probe at the students' strengths and see if they can expand on what they have written.

In May of 1973, I offered my dissertation proposal to the faculty. Building on the interest I had formed in Meeks's seminar on ideology and practice, and taking advantage of the substantial research (and writing!) I had done in rabbinic Judaism, Qumran, and Greco-Roman schools, I proposed doing a comparative study of early Christianity (the key text being Acts) and these other intentional communities, with respect to their practices concerning possessions. The entire faculty considered the proposal and quizzed me on it. Although they had misgivings because of the ambition of the project, they gave the go-ahead.

A larger question, however, had imposed itself at the beginning of that last semester: How was I to live? I had left my own monastic community of possessions and had only about a thousand dollars to my name as I faced the future. With my apartment costing $145 a month, this sum would not last long, even if I ate only scraps. As so often in my life, Meeks came through as my benefactor. He wrote in my support for a Kent Fellowship. Now defunct, this was an ancillary of the Danforth fellowships that was directed specifically at those writing dissertations. If I won it (and the competition was understandably fierce), it would pay my tuition and fees as well as provide me a living stipend for three years. I made it to the round of personal interviews. The tweed-coated, leather-on-the-elbows, pipe-smoking, and wonderfully condescending professor from Wellesley asked concerning my stated interest in the literary features of Luke-Acts, "But don't you agree with Nietzsche that the New Testament is only a vulgar production with no literary value?" I responded that Nietzsche and he would just have to count me among the vulgarians. Despite this exchange, I won the fellowship, which provided me at least a baseline support, whatever happened with Joy and me.

Meeks also lined me up for teaching assistant positions (one with him in his undergraduate class, then one each for Malherbe and Greer at the divinity school), and he arranged that, for a small stipend, I edit a book on teaching undergraduates published by the Society for Values in Higher Education, called *Teaching Religion to Undergraduates: Some Approaches and Ideas from Teachers to Teachers.* Meeks never flagged in his support of me, all during my subsequent career. A markedly reserved and undemonstrative man, Meeks is also a profoundly good and generous man, to whom I remain deeply grateful.

Meeks also made the contacts that helped me secure a summer position teaching New Testament at Gonzaga University in Spokane. So, shortly after—indeed, immediately after—getting Joy and the children to the house on Edgehill Road, I flew to Washington State for five weeks of teaching undergraduates and nuns the letters of Paul. Despite an aching loneliness that was only exacerbated by my isolated and spartan student room, I enjoyed the actual teaching, which again confirmed me in the conviction that, even if I was not much of a scholar—on the Dahl-Malherbe-Meeks scale—I was nonetheless a good teacher. It was impossible to miss how lights went on in blasé students' eyes when a passage of Paul became clear to them, or how students who took the class only to get the requirement out of the way became enthusiasts.

I got seriously to work on my dissertation when I returned to New Haven. Joy had secured an apartment for me (we were not yet married), but the night I arrived from Spokane, I stayed with her and the children. During the night we experienced a home invasion: when we discovered that the phone lines had been cut, Joy and I herded the children into one bedroom and shoved a heavy dresser against the door. When the thieves left, I went to a phone booth and called the New Haven police. We put bars on the basement windows, but I stayed in the house from that point forward. I wrote in a little cubby in the attic.

Starting with Luke-Acts, and working on that composition into the spring of 1974, I discovered that a straightforward social analysis of the description of community possessions in Acts 2 and 4 was not possible without taking the rhetoric of the entire narrative into account. The difficulty was that Luke consistently spoke of the use of possessions, but he did not speak of the use of possessions consistently. Something other than simple reportage or straightforward command was at work in his narrative. Trying to figure out what this could be led me to write over eighty pages simply on the literary context of the key passage. When I showed it to Meeks, he said I would either have to cut this material down to thirty pages or make it the basis of a new kind of dissertation. To do that, though, I would have to write a new proposal on "the literary function of possessions in Luke-Acts," convene the faculty, and hold a new colloquy.

In the late spring of 1974 (a year after my first proposal defense), then, I cobbled together a new proposal. I say "cobbled" because not even I knew what exactly I would find through a literary analysis, or of what use it would be. I was following my nose. The faculty met at the end of the spring semester to consider the new proposal. They were not welcoming. To understand the resistance they manifested, it is important to remember just how dominant the historical-critical paradigm was in those years, how seemingly unassailable. When Walter Wink's *The Bible in Human Transformation* appeared in 1971, arguing that the historical-critical method was "bankrupt," the faculty and graduate students at Yale dismissed it scornfully.

My 1973 proposal was by no means a frontal attack on historical criticism. But by approaching the narrative of Luke-Acts in strictly literary terms, I was joining a tiny handful of scholars (Luis Alonso Schökel and William Beardslee, for example) who argued for such an approach. I was not then or ever particularly interested in "method" as such, but I did want to solve a problem, and it seemed to me that a literary analysis would lead me there. My committee was extremely reluctant to agree. The discussion became so heated that I finally declared, "Well, it is my job to write a dissertation, and your job to read it," and walked out of the room. The faculty grudgingly accepted the proposal. Meeks would direct, but since Meeks knew far less about literary criticism than I did, he would direct with a light hand, which is what I needed.

This inauspicious event colored the next two years, which I count among the hardest of my scholarly life. The period of dissertation writing is difficult for all graduate students; they are no longer, as "good students," responding to the ideas of professors but are on their own to make an "original contribution" to scholarship. They are much like swimmers who have trained endlessly by swimming laps with coaches shouting encouragement but are now expected to swim the English Channel alone. Discouragement, depression, and self-loathing are the common lot of dissertation writers. Not only was I not exempt from these, I experienced them in an intense fashion, to the point that I seriously contemplated dropping out and becoming a prep school teacher.

The rejection of my petition for dispensation from Rome; the finalization of Joy's divorce; the commotion of marrying before a justice of the peace, and then again informally with Kurz and the children as witnesses; the constant adjustments required of a new stepfather whose credentials were in the eyes of the children nonexistent—all of these made work on a project that only I seemed interested in very difficult indeed. So, like many writers of dissertations, I did little writing. When Tiffany was born in October, and Joy's health—both physical and emotional—was in the balance (she began a five-year period of clinical depression), and all domestic duties fell on me, I discovered, to my horror, that I had experienced some sort of breakdown myself. I found that I could not read Greek, and that I had lost pretty much all my scholarly memory. It was a devastating realization.

At this point, recognizing that I needed to pull myself together, write the dissertation, and get a teaching position so that I could support my family (the proceeds of the sale of her house that came to Joy through the divorce settlement would elapse in a few short years), I began a deliberate program of recovery. I began by activating vocabulary and the memory of words. For the first time in my life, I worked crossword puzzles endlessly, trying to kick-start my memory. From there, I began to read, not serious fiction, but mystery novels, learning again how to follow a plot. Slowly, the self-therapy worked. Slowly, I found that I could read and remember. Slowly, I was able to read the Greek of the New Testament again.

But this experience left a deep and abiding mark on me. First, I knew that great chunks of my memory bank were gone, possibly forever. Second, I was aware ever afterward how fragile my mind was, and how I needed to be strong physically and emotionally if my mind was to operate effectively.

The acute sense of isolation that Joy and I felt—we were both cut off from family, both cut off from the communities of faith that had defined our lives—was partially eased for me by my teaching assistant duties. Leading discussion groups reassured me that I was not entirely lacking in pedagogical ability. Otherwise, my overriding sense of isolation led to a self-excommunication from the life of the graduate school. I felt that I was a scandal and a reproach because of my halting start to the dissertation, because of my irregular ecclesial and marital status, and because I was making no progress on the dissertation—and I was already in my fourth year. I had only one year of funding from the Kent Fellowship left, and time seemed to move both infinitely slowly (as depressions do) and infinitely quickly (as deadlines inexorably approached).

The only other exception to my isolation that I can now recall is when I was recruited to respond from the side of Yale to Harvard professor Helmut Koester's programmatic paper on his new introduction to the New Testament. The Yale-Harvard meeting was an annual event, but I cannot remember a time previously when a Yale graduate student was assigned to answer the senior scholar from Harvard. Worse, Koester failed to provide me a copy of his paper ahead of time. My response therefore had to be completely *ex tempore*. But whatever anxieties I might have felt, by this time in doctoral work my alienation was such that I simply let fly with a critique that was, in the circumstances, audacious. It was, naturally, greeted largely by silence.

The most important part of my recovery (besides taking care of Joy and the baby as well as the other children) was energetically attacking the dissertation. Now, the chaotic household and the hundreds of domestic obligations focused rather than distracted me. I learned once and for all the habit of scholarly compartmentalization. I was able, in a word, to put my mind in another place, even when my body was present to the place where it was needed. I remember, for example, lying on the floor of the dining room, writing part of my dissertation with my right hand while rocking the infant Tiffany in her cradle with my left hand.

Coming out of my personal cognitive crisis, I was finally able to grasp conceptually the dominant literary pattern of Luke-Acts, which I abbreviated as the story of the prophet and the people. Luke wrote to show gentile believers how God had proven faithful to his promises to Israel by sending the prophet Jesus as "the prophet like Moses," and then, after the resurrection of Jesus, sending the apostles and other "men of the Spirit" as prophets with the liberating good news first announced and enacted by Jesus. Corresponding to God's sending of the prophets was the response of the people to God's prophetic emissaries, either positive (in faith) or negative (in rejection). Once I had hold of this, I was able to see that Luke's "inconsistent consistent" language about possessions served a literary function, namely, to symbolize those responses of faith and rejection. The upshot of my analysis is that Luke's two-volume composition is literarily unified and coherent, and that any effort to interpret Luke must come to grips with the narrative character of the work.

I submitted the dissertation in the spring of 1976, and it was accepted by the committee. Yale did not have a dissertation defense, only readers' reports that were kept by the graduate school. Despite all the disruptions and divagations, I had managed to complete the doctoral program in five years, which was pretty much standard at that time.

FINDING WORK

My naïveté about the world of academia persisted throughout my time in doctoral work. I had gone to Yale in the first place because of the desire to study with Meeks, completely unaware of its distinguished place in the constellation of great universities. And I remained largely ignorant. I remember being both impressed and intimidated by the ease with which my seniors in the program—such as Ron Hock, Don Juel, and David Balch—would discourse about faculty positions in various universities: they plotted the movement of professors like astronomers the stars. Severed from the monastery, afloat in the bubble of my isolated family, I remained clueless about how to enter that alien world.

A sign of my innocence was my writing a batch of letters to colleges in the Northeast, asking if they had any positions open and offering my services. A kind colleague informed me that this direct approach would not work. I needed, he said, to attend the annual Society of Biblical Literature (SBL) meeting and put myself through the meat grinder of interviews that provided one of the main attractions of the conference. I attended a conference in the fall of 1994 and washed out completely, failing to get a second look from schools such as the University of Detroit (to teach Greek!) and North Carolina State University. The next year, acting on a tip from Terry Callan, I crashed the interviews being carried out by Georgetown University, told them my application was in the mail (false), that I was an ex-priest (true), and that I was the best teacher in America (well . . .). Such brashness apparently attracted them, and they brought me to campus in DC to give a lecture and interview. All went well, and several months later Georgetown offered me a tenure-track position in New Testament.

But then, the specter of my excommunicated status started to work on the administration of Georgetown, as they were processing my hire. The apostolic delegate of the Roman Catholic Church resided in DC, and he was intensely interested in the activities of the theology department at Georgetown. I received a phone call from the department chair, saying that my hire had hit a snag. The university was fearful of the repercussions of hiring an ex-priest, especially one now married to a divorced woman. Would I be willing, he asked, to reapply for a dispensation from my vows? Perhaps if I cleaned up my canonical status, I could be hired. I refused to do so, and the Georgetown position evaporated.

In the late spring of 1976, then, I had no job and no prospects of a job. But when I was in upstate New York, picking up my daughter Mary from Ithaca College, I received a call from Joy. She said Abe Malherbe was trying to reach me. When I called Abe, he said he had heard about the commotion with Georgetown and that I should not worry. He said that Yale Divinity School had been intending to hire me all along (they were very good at keeping some secrets)! On my return to New Haven, I went through a whirlwind day of *pro forma* interviews and was offered the position as assistant professor of New Testament, a term appointment good potentially for eight years. Naturally, I leaped at the offer. I loved being at Yale. The position stabilized one part of our life so that we could work at all the other aspects (children, sickness, depression). I knew and liked the students at Yale Divinity School. This was, quite literally, a gift from God.

- PART TWO -

Being a Scholar

Chapter Five

YALE DIVINITY SCHOOL (1976–1982)

*F*OR THE SAKE OF NEATNESS, I HAVE DIVIDED MY NARRATIVE into two parts: becoming a scholar and being a scholar. The distinction, to be sure, is an artificial one. True scholarship is always "becoming," in the sense that it is constantly growing and maturing. This is true especially in the humanities. In mathematics and music, so I understand, one must make one's mark quickly if one is to make a mark at all. But not in my field. Even though at the age of thirty-three I had all the tools of scholarship, I was incapable of writing at that age what I could write when I was sixty-three. The growth is not in intelligence or technique but in a steadily greater knowledge, and above all, a cultivation of better judgment. In the humanities, the very best scholarship manifests itself in a kind of wisdom.

At thirty-three, I could claim to "be" a scholar in the sense that I had passed through a long period of formation and I was now in a certified academic position. But for me, and I am sure most other academic scholars at the same stage, there was much more "becoming" still ahead. Each faculty position I held over the next forty years held its own challenges, and each offered opportunities to sharpen and deepen my skills. Such was certainly the case with my first real academic job at Yale Divinity School—for tidiness' sake passing over the semester I had lectured at Saint Meinrad, or the year I served as a full-time faculty member at Saint Joseph Seminary, or the summer I had taught undergraduates at Gonzaga.

THE POSITION

The junior faculty position to which I was hired was a placement peculiar to Yale. A young scholar was given three years at the assistant level, then, if proven worthy, would be granted another five years at the associate level. Eight years maximum with, it was firmly stressed, no chance of tenure, no chance at all. With this instrument, Yale was able to infuse new life into its faculty while not committing itself to the young scholars thus circulating through.

From one perspective, it was a highly exploitative situation: Yale gained the benefit of extraordinary talent and energy while risking nothing. I was, in fact, so concerned about this aspect of the job that, shortly after gaining the position, I asked the chair of the Religious Studies Department, James Dittes, to see the written reports on my dissertation.[1] I wanted to see if my scholarship was appreciated and I was not being hired simply as a talented teacher who was, in the eyes of the faculty, equivalent to cannon fodder. Dittes, a psychologist, tried to persuade me not to seek access to the reports, and his reason was intriguing. I was, he told me, well known as a hothead (he had been present at my dissertation walkout), and he was concerned not that the reports would make me think less of myself but that they would lead me to despise the sloppiness of my new colleagues. I persisted, and Dittes's words proved true: I was dismayed at the lack of serious engagement shown by (my now) senior colleagues in their responses to my dissertation. I entered the position chastened. It wasn't so much that they rejected or scorned my scholarship; it was more that they didn't seem really interested.

Viewed from another perspective, a (possible) eight-year stint at Yale Divinity School, with colleagues like Dahl, Meeks, Malherbe, and Greer, could be viewed as a splendid postdoctoral program positioning a young scholar for a future in another university. Almost inevitably, though, as they moved through the years and received glad appreciation from the students, holders of this position tended to think deep in their hearts, "I will surely be the exception. They will change the rules for me. I will get tenure." Malherbe was particularly good at quashing such fantasies, telling me, after my first three-year period, "Start looking for another position; it may take a few years."

As I joined the faculty with whom I had worked in my own doctoral program, I met another junior faculty member, who had been appointed the previous year. Carl Holladay was from Tennessee, had been a student of Malherbe's at Abilene Christian Seminary, had received a ThM degree from Princeton, and had received his PhD from Cambridge University, working particularly with C. F. D. Moule and Ernst Bammel. On the basis especially of Hellenistic Jewish materials, Carl's dissertation challenged the then popular premise that a *theios anēr* ("divine man") Christology was behind some of the controversies in Paul's letters and the Gospels.[2] Carl and I were assigned to team-teach the all-important class in New Testament introduction, and we set to it with a will.

Carl and I bonded quickly, recognizing in each other (despite our widely divergent backgrounds) a partner in the pursuit of excellence. Joy and I became friends with Carl and his wife, Donna, and Carl and I spent many hours on Saturday mornings—having told our wives we were going down to work—sitting in our offices, trading tales, and finding the deep elements of similarity that lay beneath the wildly different surfaces of Roman Catholicism and the Church of Christ. This bond with Carl grew until (having beat me out for the job) he departed for Emory University in 1980, and it was renewed in a powerful and fruitful collaboration years later when I joined him on the faculty of Emory in 1992.

THE STRUGGLE TO SURVIVE

Every junior professor faces any number of new challenges. The most basic is adapting to the role of the teacher, after so many years as a student. But this transition must take place in the context of real-life (as distinct from professional life) difficulties. What Joy and I had to deal with, then, was not unique to us. Perhaps the transition was more severe for us because of the way we had each severed a long-standing commitment. Joy had been married to a multimillionaire businessman and had her name inscribed in the New Orleans social register. I had enjoyed the security of the religious life, which ensured, no matter if I was a good monk or a bad one, that I would get warm clothing and three meals a day. In any case, the kinds of difficulties we faced can be enumerated simply as a reminder that scholarly work is always carried out in the context of real life, and the pressures of real life are, well, real.

Financial. It might be supposed that professors, especially in elite schools like Yale, enjoy substantial if not munificent salaries. The truth is that most academics, even in elite schools, live (unless they have other sources of wealth) closer to the world of poverty than to the world of wealth. Academic families were most often, out of necessity, two-career families. Donna Holladay, for example, worked as a school counselor all during Carl's career as an academic. In our case, Joy's frequent and persistent illnesses prevented her from working.

After forty years spent at such top-ranked institutions as Yale, Indiana University Bloomington, and Emory—with the last twenty-four of those years holding a distinguished chair—my final salary was roughly equivalent to that of a first-year associate in a top law firm. The beginning salary at YDS ($12,000) was not competitive even in 1976, and far from a living wage. That salary, moreover, covered only nine months of the year—for twenty years, I had to scramble to fill the three-month salary gap. Worse, Yale offered no benefits to junior professors (no pension payments at all), apart from participation in the Yale Health Plan (YHP). Yale, indeed, specialized in obtuseness concerning the human issues of faculty and students alike. It failed utterly to reckon with the fact that in those years the oil embargo had led to heating oil prices in New Haven of $400 a month, or that real estate in New Haven was out of reach for most, or that the USA in those years suffered a yearly inflation rate of almost 4 percent.

In Louisiana divorce law, Joy could have walked away with a fortune. She chose instead to leave the money for the children, receiving from her divorce only the payout from the sale of the house. A woman who had formerly done her Christmas shopping at FAO Schwarz in New York City now had to do it at Bradlees and Big Lots in New Haven. And Joy, who never complained about circumstances, did so with a willing spirit. The money she did receive provided enough of a buffer to see us into a house and through the first five years of my career. Her ex-husband also paid for the children's education and provided a small monthly support payment for each child. Even with this help, however, we were stretched to the breaking point. By the time we left New Haven, I was a month away from bankruptcy. To compensate, I accepted every invitation to do series of Bible studies in suburbs all along Long Island Sound, driving on Sunday mornings to the Connecticut towns of Madison, New Canaan, Wilton, Darien, and Norwalk, to teach Protestant congregations at twenty-five to fifty dollars a pop, and riding the train into Manhattan for multiweek courses at Saint Peter's

Lutheran Church and Saint Bartholomew's Episcopal Church. When invited, I also spoke to Protestant clergy conferences. Along the way, my Christianity grew ever more broadly ecumenical, even as I added a few dollars to the family purse.

Medical. A great part of our financial distress was due to medical issues. Joy was at once a vibrant and active person and a seriously ill person. In addition to her long-standing chronic-periodic inflammatory condition, she experienced during our New Haven years her seventh pregnancy, fibroid tumors, severe dental issues, runaway migraines, and the clinical depression I mentioned in the previous chapter. The Yale Health Plan was ill equipped to deal with such long-term problems. The YHP's construal of the Hippocratic oath was to keep students alive until Christmas or summer, when they could see real doctors. The doctors in the plan were certainly not attuned to long-term and puzzling syndromes.[3] Some of Joy's condition, in fact, was iatrogenic: she had a hysterectomy after Tiffany's birth and then entered menopause; she was provided no hormone treatment for menopause and was administered massive doses of steroids for the inflammatory condition, which led in turn to a tremendous weight gain and the erosion of her teeth. The psychotherapy and the pain management that Joy required (each, by the way, excellent) were not covered by the health plan, nor were medicines. Although my own health was basically sound, I had a series of attacks during my first year of teaching that leveled me. The deeply Freudian doctors at the health plan attributed my spells to stress and anxiety, and misdiagnosed an obvious case of cholecystitis. It required an emergency visit to the hospital and, eventually, gall bladder surgery in the spring of 1977; in those days, gall bladder surgery was still a major surgery, as the scar on my belly attests. But I was back in the classroom within a week.

Children. It is common for young professors to be married and have children, so that their scholarly work must compete for attention with the needs of spouse and children. Carl and Donna Holladay, for example, had two small boys when we began at YDS and soon had a third. Our family's domestic arrangements were not therefore different in kind but rather in complexity. We had to contend with a nine-and-a-half-year difference in age between Joy and me, the continuing influence of a powerful ex-husband, and the wide range in the ages of the children—my oldest stepson was only ten years younger than I! Trying to establish a coherent family was difficult.

Joy's children also had a variety of issues with which they had to deal, not least among them that they were caught in a classic divorce-remarriage scenario. Add to this a variety of problems with school, drugs, alcohol, and gender identity. To top it off, we had not only the three youngest of Joy's children in our new family full time (the older ones came and went) but also our own daughter, Tiffany, who struggled to grasp how the strange dynamics of her world worked.

Faith. This was the hardest adjustment of all. Joy and I had cut ourselves off from the most important support in our previous lives. We dared not openly attend the churches where I had formerly worked as a priest or join the charismatic community at Yale that I had formerly attended. To raise Tiffany in the faith, though, we needed to participate in the sacraments; we consulted with each new pastor we encountered and explained our status and our desire—they were uniformly gracious and welcoming—and proceeded to take the risk of attending Mass and receiving communion. With my theological education, I was better able to distinguish obedience to God and obedience to the church than Joy was, but I still experienced a sense of bereavement, especially in the early years. I did not, for example, receive an invitation to speak to a Catholic audience until 1996, so I spent twenty years in the ecclesiastical desert. Joy never lost the simple and direct trust in God that she had from her childhood, but as the years went by, she grew increasingly angry at the institutional church, especially when the cover-up of clergy pedophilia was exposed, and she contrasted the leniency shown toward the abusers of children to the harshness she had experienced from the church during her divorce and remarriage.

I note all these situations and experiences because scholarship is never completely severed from the context of human embodiment. Considering these, it becomes clear how necessary it is to have "the mind in another place" to do real scholarship at all—otherwise, one can be drowned by quotidian concerns. It is also clear how having the mind in another place offers a healthful counterweight to the pressures of worldly existence. Certainly, I became increasingly aware of how my work gained in sharpness and urgency when I had less time to give to it than when I was a monk. And I grew more and more committed to develop a mode of scholarship that grew out of and responded to the experiences of ordinary people.

TEACHING

Carl Holladay and I were tasked with co-teaching the large introduction to the New Testament class. It enrolled 180 students, and we had at our disposal five or six teaching assistants (TAs), drawn from the Yale PhD program. We thus had the pleasure of working with such outstanding future scholars as John Fitzgerald, Michael White, David Worley, Jerome Neyrey, Alan Mitchell, Anne McGuire, Jackie Williams, Ben Fiore, and Larry Yarbrough. The class extended over two semesters, with two lectures and one discussion session led by teaching fellows a week. Carl and I hammered out the basic process: we would require two exams and two exegesis papers each semester. We would grade the exams together, and the TAs would give a first evaluation of the papers and submit to us their discursive assessments. All these (exams, papers, assessments) were to be placed in a student's folder, and at the end of the semester Carl and I would reread all of the students' work, write a separate assessment, and assign the final grade.

That was the easy part. Much harder was coming to an agreement on the way the New Testament was to be approached. I managed to convince Carl that we needed to start with the philosophical/historical questions of causality: Why was there a Christian movement in the first place; why did it produce writings; why do they look the way they do; why were they collected so quickly into a canon? He agreed that we would start with the movement and treat the writings as arising from that movement. I took on the critical opening lectures: the analysis of the first Christians' claims; their experience of power; the source of that power in the resurrection experience.

On this basis, we could move to the symbolic world of Hellenism and Judaism within which the Christian movement asserted its claims, and then deal with the respective New Testament writings as the ways in which experience forced the reinterpretation of the symbolic world. The influence of Peter Berger and Thomas Luckman on this model is patent. After the opening lectures, Carl and I alternated lectures on the respective compositions. I co-taught this class with Carl for three years, and when he left for Emory, I taught it alone for another three years.

I did not in the least regret the time and effort demanded by this large and unwieldy class. I was convinced then, and have remained convinced, that such an introduction, which gets at the causes as well as the shape of writings, is imperative for a true grasp of the canonical literature. With slight modifications, I continued to teach introduction in just this way for the rest of my career, both at Indiana and Emory.

Teaching such large numbers of students across my time at Yale, I inevitably became a fairly visible figure on the campus. And since I had not yet clearly worked out for myself the distinction between being a priest and being a professor, I spent many hours (up to twenty a week) counseling YDS students. In the process, I discovered how valuable our experiential starting point for teaching New Testament was. Students at YDS in the late '70s were decidedly smart—among the best students I have ever had—but many of them came without solid educations or any serious formation in the faith. What many of them did have were experiences in their lives that drove them, not to the church, but in our increasingly academicized world, to the seminary, as they sought to understand the implications of their turning from drunk to sober, or from drugged to straight, or from straight to gay, or from abused to liberated.

The classic historical-critical approach, which assumed a well-formed Christian identity and a churchly grasp of Scripture, was intended to provide a critical reflection on the received tradition. It turned out to be, for these students, a dismemberment of a body that they had never experienced as alive. They were expected to learn and love Scripture through the process of an autopsy, while never having experienced it in dance. Hearing the stories of hundreds of students at YDS was an important element in the development both of my teaching and of my subsequent writing. The same sense of immersion in the real lives of students came to me through six years of teaching "Pastoral Care and Counseling in the Parish" with the psychologist–social worker Lucia Ewing. Such field-based reflection on Scripture and on theological texts such as this course demanded gave a sharp existential edge to the learning and teaching of the New Testament.

I was also able to teach courses in elementary and intermediate Greek, as well as Greek exegesis courses in Romans, the Pastorals, and 1 Peter. The immersion in Greek was especially valuable to me, because my preparation for these classes was minute and exacting. I forced myself to parse every verb, break down all grammar and syntax, and do elaborate lexical research. I filled notebooks with such systematic observations. These habits were ones I carried over into my later writing of commentaries on the Greek New Testament. Also proleptic of later research was an English exegesis course in the Letter of James. Ever since my early days in the monastery, this sapiential/prophetic writing had intrigued me, and the process of working through it with talented students only spurred the desire to work in it more extensively. I was convinced by working through the letter in this class that the atomistic approach to the composition found in the leading commentary by Martin Dibelius was entirely wrong, and that James had far more literary unity than had usually been acknowledged.

Two further classes I taught at YDS anticipated later research and writing. The first was a limited-enrollment seminar called "Methods and Madness in New Testament Studies." Beginning with Walter Wink's *The New Testament in Human Transformation* (1971), the decade of the '70s saw the emergence of various "methods" that challenged the hegemony of the historical-critical paradigm. At the time I taught the class, such ideologically based approaches as feminist, womanist, liberationist, deconstructive, or postcolonial had not yet surfaced. But I was able to lead students through readings in the sociological, psychological, structuralist, and literary "methods" that had recently been proposed, testing them both for what they enabled and for what they necessarily precluded as interpretive perspectives. At the same time, students were able to recognize the relative rather than the absolute value of the historical-critical approach. This course set me on the path of a decades-long engagement with contemporary scholarship, and it set the frame for my later work in 1996 on the historical Jesus controversy.

The second class focused more precisely on the way concrete human experience can be analyzed theologically. I constructed a reading class ("Christian Existence as Life in the Spirit") for three very bright students (two women and a man), who met once a week at our home. Over coffee, I led them through basic theological concepts—power, idolatry, sin, grace, faith—and had them examine in journals their own life story through the lens, respectively, of each concept. We then extended the analysis to their experience of sexuality, possessions, anger, and freedom. This turned out to be such a powerful, even transforming, course that I then proposed it for a larger enrollment.

To my surprise, sixty students signed up. Now I had the problem of teaching a boutique experience of intimacy and reflection in a wholesale setting. Not daunted, I organized the large class into three-person discussion groups. Each week, I would lecture on the respective theological topics, the students would meet in their groups and discuss them, and then each individually would develop his or her own reflections in a theological journal. At the end of the semester, I was presented with a stack of sixty forty-page journals to assess, journals in which highly talented students dared to bare their souls to my eyes, revealing aspects of their lives they had not ever shown before. Many students used these journals as a means of coming to grips with their sexuality. I was stunned, honored, and deeply moved by reading these documents. These stories, plus the story of my stepdaughter's struggle to come out as a lesbian, turned me from a homophobic person to one who had to acknowledge the presence and power of God in the lives of all. I became more convinced than ever that the narrative of human experience had a deep theological valence and could indeed have the power to transform and convict, and that theology in the church ought to have an inductive character.

Faculty Service

I began my academic career at a point of institutional transition in higher education. The days of all-powerful presidents and deans who could recruit, promote, reward, and penalize faculty, as well as set administrative policies, were past. A lasting effect of the student and faculty unrest of the sixties was the bureaucratization of the academy. Faculty committees were intended to provide "advice and consent" in virtually every aspect of a school's life. Faculty committees were now tasked with searching for and recruiting new teachers, deciding on promotion and tenure, overseeing the curriculum, and deciding the fate of refractory students. Such committees did not, to be sure, make the governance of schools more efficient. Quite the opposite: administration and decision making grew ever more complex and cumbersome. To a very real extent, the latent social function of proliferating committees was to diffuse the discontent of faculty by providing the facsimile of a "participatory democracy."

While a junior faculty member of YDS, I was spared an excess of committee work—I obviously was not included in faculty recruitment or graduate admissions—but my work on the Professional Studies Committee, and especially on the Curriculum Committee (of which I eventually became chair), provided me with abundant insight into the power and weakness of such faculty service—the kind of citizenship that functioned silently as one of the genuine measures of whether a faculty member would gain tenure. The most critical question a faculty must ask itself concerning any potential new member is whether the person will carry her or his weight in the shared labor of faculty governance. More than either research or teaching, the question of "citizenship" matters most, because it is the hidden but essential glue of faculty cohesion.

Faculty committees became, and have remained, an essential feature of academic life. They are also, in many cases, the occasion of deep frustration. As chair of the Curriculum Committee at YDS, for example, I observed that the MDiv—supposedly a degree certifying a professional competence in ministry—was being awarded to students with the most diverse path through the school, many of whom, for example, bypassed New Testament introduction and other basic classes. So, I secured from the registrar 150 transcripts of students who had graduated with an MDiv in the past three years, fifty a year, and analyzed them in detail. My research proved what I had suspected, namely, that a professional degree was being awarded in many cases not on the basis of a coherent professional competence but on the basis of earning credits in highly personalized individual "curricula." My concern for the integrity—indeed, the plain honesty—of the degree was met with complete indifference by the full faculty when I presented it the data. Facts, I learned, never trump inertia.

Research and Publishing

I have talked about teaching and service first, because for academic scholars, these two activities always take precedence. They represent, in Carl Holladay's locution, "the tyranny of the immediate." Research and writing are done when possible, but especially for scholars of a more introspective temperament, who need time to get cranked up, time is rarely available in the hurly-burly of the school year. While work on a monograph might be put off, teaching a class or attending a committee meeting never can be. Summers and sabbaticals are craved for precisely this reason: they offer the time and space to work on what scholars think of as their most significant projects.

I certainly have elements of the introspective in my makeup, but in terms of work, I am the complete extrovert. The capacity to compartmentalize, to concentrate on each task as required, to summon the memory specific to that task, has always been one of my strengths. Indeed, I relish multitasking and have always found the interplay between teaching, service, and research to be enlivening rather than deadening. Teaching, in particular, has always been for me a stimulus to research. The dirty little secret, seldom shared with the public, is that academics stay intellectually alive (when they do) because of the bright minds they encounter in the classroom and in student papers; if teaching is genuinely an intellectual engagement with fundamental and difficult problems, it invariably gives rise to research.

Many junior professors who are in a position to seek tenure calculate what publications might best lead to that desired end. A premium is placed on books, especially monographs, and peer-reviewed articles. Since I was in a position that could not lead to tenure, and because I was convinced in any case that tenure and promotion were goals that should be met by an excess of accomplishment, I began at YDS my persistent pattern of writing and publishing in every direction, and at every level. There was method in this madness, but it was not always apparent to the casual observer.

I quickly came to think of my writing as falling into two categories. The first I called "jobs of work": these were things I wrote because I needed money, or because I was asked by an editor or fellow scholar. The second I called "works of love": these were the projects that I began and completed (sometimes over the course of many years) because I was passionately interested in a topic or question. The two categories certainly overlapped. Often, "jobs of work" became "works of love" because, once into the project, I was into it completely. A good example is provided by the commentaries I wrote over the years. All of them were in response to invitations. All of them were demanding in execution. And all of them provided me with some of the purest pleasure I experienced as a scholar.

As soon as my dissertation was approved, I submitted it to the Society of Biblical Literature Dissertation Series, which published dissertations as is, without revision. It was accepted and was published in 1977.[4] As is typical for young scholars (thirty-three is young in the humanities, especially in New Testament), I then set out to pursue aspects of my study of Luke-Acts that I had not examined in the dissertation. Scholarly conferences are the natural setting for such explorations. At three successive meetings of the Catholic Biblical Association, I presented papers investigating the intriguing narrative development in Acts 10–15. I suspected that the literary approach that had served well in the dissertation would yield results also in this passage. I was especially eager to pursue this because, despite the "conciliar" era through which Catholics were passing, virtually no theological use had been made of the first account of ecclesial decision making, in the Jerusalem Council of Acts 15. Why this neglect? I was convinced it was connected to the fact that the dominant modes of interpretation were interested only in historical fact and not in theological meaning.

I also delivered a paper at the Society of Biblical Literature in 1979, arguing that the current historical fad of finding "communities" behind or addressed by New Testament compositions—such as Raymond Brown's depiction of the "Community of the Beloved Disciple"—was, in the case of Luke-Acts, a mistaken venture, precisely because it failed to come to grips with the rhetorical character of the writing and the narrative argument made throughout the entire work.[5] This was my first, but scarcely my last, exercise in scholarly disputation.

I also began to publish peer-reviewed articles. I found acceptance for my long essay on the function of the polemic against false teachers in 2 Timothy—this was the paper I had done for Malherbe in my first year in the doctoral program.[6] I examined another aspect of Luke's narrative argumentation in "The Lukan Kingship Parable,"[7] and I drew on my experience of reading James in an exegesis class to publish an article on the rhetorical use of the Hellenistic *topos* concerning envy in James 3:13–4:10, a frontal challenge to the atomistic reading of Martin Dibelius.[8] And I entered the complicated area of dispute concerning the meaning of *pistis Christou* in Paul's letters: Did it mean our faith in Christ, or Christ's faith in God? I argued the latter position in Romans 3:21–26 and hunkered down for several decades of dispute, since this understanding ran clearly counter to all contemporary English translations of the passage.[9]

An example of my scattershot approach to research and writing was my eagerness to accept such "jobs of work" as book reviews and encyclopedia articles. I liked doing book reviews first of all because I got to keep the book! Having left the monastery with only a Liddell-Scott and two volumes of Epictetus—I reimbursed the monastery as soon as I was able—I was desperate to acquire books. Haunting used bookstores was one method. The other was reviewing any book offered. But reviews were also a wonderful way of exercising careful and precise critical judgment, and of staying abreast of scholarly literature.

I also wrote a long series of short entries for the *Encyclopedia Americana*. They paid by the word, which was welcome. But the word limitations forced me to cut my prose more finely, to combine, when possible, comprehensiveness with concision. Try writing an entry on "the kingdom of God" in five hundred words, or on "Hans Küng" in four hundred words! Such "jobs of work" repaid the effort put into them by improving my scholarly acumen, and in the process, my very tough reviews began to make my scholarly voice more widely known.

Two small books I wrote at YDS certainly count as "jobs of work." One was a small commentary on Colossians, Ephesians, and the Pastoral Letters;[10] the other was a book on the beatitudes in Matthew's Gospel called *Some Hard Blessings*—the small volume consisted of retreat conferences I had given as a monk.[11] Another book that began as a "job of work" became a work of love: John Hollar, the great editor at Fortress Press who died far too young, had read my dissertation on possessions in Luke-Acts and asked me to contribute a volume to a series called Overtures to Biblical Theology. In *Sharing Possessions: Mandate and Symbol of Faith* (1981), I made full use of the insights into body and spirit, being and having, that I had learned from Gabriel Marcel—nothing is ever wasted—in an examination of the language concerning possessions throughout Scripture. In this book, I felt that I was making a genuine contribution to a fundamental theological mystery, and in fact, this book has been—despite mixed reviews especially from those who thought I was too hard on social engineering—among the most useful for readers seeking a way to think about their own attitudes and practices. Thirty years later, another publisher would produce an enlarged version of *Sharing Possessions*, in which I had the chance to answer some of those critics.[12]

Over the course of my time at YDS, I pulled together several strands of experience and reflection into a new project, which was in every respect a "work of love." I had developed, the reader will remember, considerable remorse about my participation in the internecine battles within monasteries during and after Vatican II; I thought there must be some important difference between being "right" and deciding "righteously." At the same time, I was working on the theological implications of my work on Acts 10–15: surely Scripture was showing us how the early church made the most fundamental decision about the inclusion of gentiles without hindrance on the basis, not of precedent, but of the experience of God's Holy Spirit, and the narratives communicating that experience to the larger church.

And then, I had learned so much from the revelatory force of the student journals that I had read in the course "Christian Existence as Life in the Spirit." In my last year at YDS, I published with Fortress a book that became the centerpiece of my personal theological project concerning discernment and decision making in the church. *Decision Making in the Church: A Biblical Model* (1982) was a modest enough essay. It began on the ground, with an analysis of the factors involved in group decisions of every sort, arguing that every communal decision was a form of self-interpretation on the basis of fundamental principles ingredient to the group's identity, and that for the church, decision making ought to involve the hermeneutics of God's action in the world, that is, be an act of obedient faith in the living God. This was followed by an exegesis of Acts 10–15 that suggested that this narrative presented the church with a model for how it ought to make identity decisions. Finally, I applied this analysis to three kinds of decisions facing the contemporary church. The book received a handful of reviews and went out of print so fast that it left skid marks. But its afterlife would be interesting.

Toward the end of my time at YDS, I launched what would be up to then my most ambitious project, the writing of a New Testament introduction—very much a work of love. I was convinced that the standard versions of this genre were inadequate to the goal of engaging students—especially theology students—with the literature of the early Christian movement. Many seminarians throughout the country used the standard college texts that started with Jesus, then went through Paul, and then wandered off to "the later writings" in a simplistic narrative that did nothing to show the fascination and power of the writings. The alternative was to use some version of the German *Einleitung*, which amounted to little more than a technical description of the canonical writings.

I wanted to write a text that was a genuine "interpretation" of the New Testament writings, and that introduced readers to them precisely through such an interpretation. I wanted, in a word, to write a large book that would communicate something of the excitement and power of the highly successful class that Carl Holladay and I had developed, and that I had continued after Carl's departure. I was convinced that a book that didn't look like a textbook (no illustrations, real prose) but could be used as a textbook would have a wide and positive effect on students of theology, who longed for a reading of the New Testament that was critically respectable yet spoke to the experience of believers. An introduction that began with the experience of transformation among the first believers could open the way, I was convinced, to readers connecting the writings of the New Testament to their own experience. Not only would this be relevant to their lives, it would also be a more genuine and adequate historical apprehension of the Christian movement and the production of its earliest writings.

I wrote up a proposal for Fortress Press, and when they expressed a mild interest, I took the train to Philadelphia for a lengthy meeting with the editors. They were intrigued by the proposal but had reservations: Was I not too young and immature for such a venture? Would I not exhaust myself in the venture and fail to write anything further? Did I really think as an unknown teacher I could secure a place for such an innovative book within the market? They eventually allowed themselves to be persuaded, and they offered a contract. But before I could get to work on this project (which took a full two years of exclusive labor to complete), the need to secure a new position imposed itself.

The Job Search (Again)

Mindful of Malherbe's advice, I began the process of seeking a new position right after I completed the first three-year stint at YDS and had been promoted to associate professor (naturally, without tenure). I remain grateful for his firm but kindly direction, for it was easy to slip into the fantasy that Yale would after all bow to popular opinion—had I not been voted by the students the graduation preacher three out of my six years?—and consider me for tenure. With a sigh, I packed up those fantasies and started looking.

Now, those unacquainted with the process of hiring faculty in the academy may be astonished to learn how convoluted and drawn out it normally is, and how difficult the ordeal can be both for the institution seeking a new professor and for the candidate seeking such a position. In the military, as we all know, transfers are effective immediately at the behest of a commander. In business, positions are offered and taken up after a short interview with the boss.

In the American academy, however, the process is closer to that of a clumsy courtship. The school advertises a position in the fall of the year before it wants the candidate to join its faculty; the advertisement is often vague in the extreme, not only to court as many applicants as possible but also because departments often are not at all clear what they want or what they need. Candidates respond to the ad by sending letters of application, vitae, letters of recommendation, and writing samples. The search committee of the department reads through dozens and dozens of such portfolios and then invites a set of candidates to one national conference or another (depending on the discipline in question), where face-to-face interviews are held with the search committee. Weeks and perhaps months pass before the search committee is authorized by the faculty to invite two or three finalists to campus for (usually) a two-day intense courtship ritual with the entire faculty and administration: more face-to-face interviews with the search committee and with a select group of other faculty, lunch followed by questions and answers with the entire faculty, meetings with deans and presidents. And after all that, the candidate often must wait months before being offered the position—or not.

The process is time consuming and sometimes fractious for those doing the searching. Nothing reveals fissures (ideological and personal) within a faculty like a difficult search. After all, if tenure is in prospect, the faculty is choosing a lifetime partner. It truly is more akin to marriage than not. The process is also time consuming and psychologically wearing on the candidate, especially on one already holding a position, not only because of the pauses and delays, and the self-revulsion that arises from trying to sell oneself to people one is not sure one respects all that much, but above all because in order to want and really try for a new position, one must detach oneself from one's present placement. Such distancing is fine if one wins the new position. But if one does not, then there follows not only disappointment but also the task of falling back in love with one's present partner. From the wooer's side, the whole process is not unlike a seduction, and from the candidate's side, very much like an adulterous dalliance.

In the fall of 1979, the Candler School of Theology at Emory University advertised a position in New Testament. Carl Holladay and I both applied for the position and were, in the spring of 1980, both invited to interview. I gave the lecture "Romans 3:21–26 and the Faith of Jesus" that I later turned into an article. While on the Emory campus, I met and had lunch with Richard Hays, then a PhD student at Emory, who was writing his dissertation on the faith of Jesus in Galatians; it was the beginning of a long friendship. At the same time, I met a younger student in the PhD program, Steven Kraftchick, and we began a friendship that has endured from that day to this. When Carl and I returned to YDS, the next months were tense for both of us; we each jumped when a phone would ring in either's office. Carl deservedly won the position, and the thing that pleased me the most was that through the whole ordeal we maintained the bonds of friendship and mutual support. Nevertheless, I was disappointed, since it seemed to me then that a seminary was the natural setting for my teaching and writing.

Thus, when a position at Vanderbilt Divinity School opened the next fall, I put my name in again. I was asked to come to Nashville to interview. It was a weird experience, my first time of knowing from the moment I stepped off the plane that I did not have any chance to win the job, and that I was the "other guy" who had to be interviewed in order to fulfill all justice, while the job was already reserved for another. In this case it was Mary Ann Tolbert, who had spent the fall semester at Vanderbilt and had won plaudits for her teaching. At her public lecture, hundreds of students packed the auditorium; at my lecture (on James), some fifteen people fitted cozily into a classroom. The nadir of the interview process came when the divinity school feminist caucus—yes, things had come so far in so few years—sat me down and asked me why I considered myself a better feminist than Tolbert. Of course, they already knew, and I certainly knew, that there was no acceptable answer to that challenge-posing-as-a-question. Knowing that the deal was already done, I could not wait for the two days to finally end. When I returned home, I was thoroughly discouraged. Joy, who had in her first marriage experienced a great deal of corporate politics, told me that I should not take it personally, and that I should develop a thicker skin. Yes, yes, but.

So, I had struck out twice at highly desirable positions. Would I need to go the prep school route after all? Then, in the fall of 1981, I received a letter from David Smith, the chair of the department of religious studies at Indiana University (IU) in Bloomington. He had remembered my time there as an MA student, and he had heard about my teaching at YDS (from Meeks?), and he wondered whether I would be interested in applying for a position as associate professor at IU. I had never considered teaching in a state university, but at this point I was willing to try anything. I also had very fond memories of IU and its religious studies department, so I applied.

In the spring, I came to the beautiful campus in Bloomington for an interview. I lectured on the baptism of Jesus in Mark's Gospel. The interview seemed to go well, but my chances were uncertain. My competition was Dennis Ronald McDonald, a Harvard PhD who, at that stage of his career, was arguing that folklore was the key to understanding the New Testament. Later in his career he was convinced that much of the New Testament was directly dependent on a literary imitation of Homer. In any case, at least one voice within the department considered McDonald a much more "academic" type than me, more "scholarly" in the obvious sense, whereas I was much too theological, much too religious—could I ever fit within a religious studies department? And—a bitter twist—having started at Yale, would I be content to teach in a state university?

To my great good fortune, other voices—especially those of the student members of the search committee—were willing to take the risk, and I was offered the job. Better salary, better benefits, a fine university, a lovely town, affordable lifestyle, and in the Midwest. I did not need to ponder long. I would spend the next ten years at IU, teaching during the glory days of Bobby Knight and the Hoosier basketball team.

Chapter Six

INDIANA UNIVERSITY (1982–1992)

*W*HEN JOY, TIFFANY, AND I DROVE THROUGH THE southern Indiana cornfields on the way to Bloomington and my new position, we were aware that we were making a new start. This part of the country was familiar to me because of my four years at Saint Meinrad and my one semester on the Bloomington campus, but it was entirely new to Joy: the Midwest was truly *terra aliena* to this woman of the Deep South who had fallen in love with New England. But Joy was always ready to support me even when doing so meant walking into new and strange environments.

Joy was also glad to be able to live as a couple in a place where our names were not, among our fellow believers, scandalous. The events of her divorce and my departure from religious life were now nearly ten years in the past, and much easier to handle as backstory than they had been in the living of them. And although I had thought of the divinity school as my natural milieu, I was eager to see if I could meet the challenge of teaching in a religious studies department at a major research university.

Our family was now much smaller. The two older girls (Mary and Kimberly) had now gone off to college, and Joby chose to stay in New Haven, where he had joined a good friend in the construction (literally) of a magic act. Joby was powerfully drawn to artistic expression, and working in the magic act foreshadowed his years in a band. The magic act took him in the next couple of years to New Mexico and Los Angeles. His friend, with a new partner, eventually established himself and his show as a regular in Las Vegas. In 1985, though, Joby rejoined us and lived in Bloomington for the rest of the time we were there, marrying and, as a first-rate drummer, forming an alternative music band (Arson Garden) that performed through the USA and Europe for over a decade. To a real extent, though, our everyday family had shrunk to Joy, Tiffany (now eight), and me—the concerns of the older children intermittently intruded, but apart from those, the dynamics of daily life in Bloomington were less complex, if not much easier.

Although IU paid a better salary and offered pension benefits, our effective poverty was greater than it had been in New Haven, for Joy's divorce settlement had run out and we were now completely dependent on my salary and whatever moonlighting I could manage. Joy's health continued to be difficult, and IU's health plan was basically a system of reimbursement through Blue Cross Blue Shield. The system was cumbersome, requiring me to pay doctor and hospital expenses out of pocket, then fill out requests, and wait (it seemed interminably) for the plan to make me whole. During my IU years, I learned the fine art of managing credit card and department charge card credit—stretching to cover most of the minimum payments a month. I learned how to creatively kite checks, and frequently ran down Kirkwood Avenue to the bank on payday to cover the checks I had kited at Kroger. I just managed to pay Tiffany's modest tuition for parochial school—even while she would much rather have attended the public school! This was the decade when our school shopping took place at Marshalls in Indianapolis, and when Big Lots was our salvation for Christmas shopping.

For Joy and me, perhaps the best part of coming to Bloomington was that we could renew the practices of faith that still meant so much to us. We entered fully into the life of our local parish, Saint Charles. We attended Sunday Mass and received communion (with the tacit permission of the pastor); we took part in the sacrament of reconciliation; we formed a faith-sharing group that met for a number of years at our house; we felt positively normal, at last. Joy made friends in the parish and participated in a variety of volunteer activities. I began teaching Scripture and theology to adults in the parish who were interested—and many were. At IU, I finally was able to distinguish the roles of priest and professor. My life in the university was mostly all about the mind; my life in the church nurtured the commitment of my heart.

THE CITY

Bloomington was more of a large town than a city, in many ways the quintes-sential college town, with a population of perhaps seventy thousand wrapped around a university of some thirty thousand students. It maintained a small-town feel, with a typical Indiana courthouse square, no high-rise buildings, and few traffic lights—the locals grumbled about the "traffic jams" that occa-sionally developed at four-way stops. Bloomington was set in the rolling foot-hills of southern Indiana, and a short drive through those hills brought one to Nashville, Indiana, a former arts colony that had become a quaint tourist magnet, especially at the annual Bill Monroe Bluegrass Festival. The coun-tryside around Bloomington was dotted with played-out limestone quarries that had supplied stone to notable national monuments in Washington, DC, and to many of the grand buildings on the lovely IU campus.

The town did not entirely lack town-gown tensions—the cult classic movie *Breaking Away* was filmed just a few years before we arrived and accu-rately portrayed the resentments among the "cutters," whose contributions to the university had gone unnoticed and unappreciated. As the home of a liberal university set in a deeply conservative state, Bloomington could at times be a little precious in its efforts to distinguish itself from the reaction-ary types to the north in Martinsville and to the south in Bedford, a town nicely described as "Bloomington without the university." Still, it was a fine place to live. I could walk two miles to my office. Shopping was a half mile away. The streets were safe. Tiffany, who came to love Bloomington so much that she stayed on at IU even after Joy and I departed for Atlanta, could grow up as close to normal as our circumstances and characters allowed.

THE UNIVERSITY

Any thought that leaving Yale and going to IU would be a step down intellec-tually was quickly dispelled. Indiana is a Big Ten school almost exclusively devoted to the arts and sciences; its sister institution, Purdue University, specializes in agriculture, engineering, and the like. IU and Purdue com-bined in the Indiana University–Purdue University Indianapolis (IUPUI) campus, which specialized at that time in medicine and nursing. The em-phasis on arts and sciences at the Bloomington campus undoubtedly con-tributed to the decidedly liberal cast to the school and the town.

The faculty at IU, I found, was at least the equal of that at Yale, and perhaps even more intellectually stimulating because of a lack of posture or pretense. All that counted at IU was brains. Several of the schools and departments at IU were widely recognized for their excellence. The school of music was ranked nationally, and IU's opera company was renowned. Departments of language (especially German, Chinese, and Uralic-Altaic) were first-class. By the time I left IU, at a point when Emory was just moving from bookkeeping by hand, IU already had a computer science faculty of sixty, and the entire school was wired for Ethernet by 1985.

The undergraduate curriculum had been carefully planned and, in my view, provided the young men and women of Indiana the opportunity for a truly fine education. The student body included some drifters and slackers, to be sure, but among the thirty thousand students, I found that there was the equivalent of two or three Yale undergraduate populations. And unlike Yale students, those at IU were not in those years notably entitled. They were, for the most part, hungry and eager. They made for wonderful teaching.

As a Big Ten university, IU naturally also had a big-time athletics program. IU did not excel in football, but its swimming and diving teams were Olympic class. The athletic tail that wagged the academic dog at IU, however, was basketball. Hoosier Hysteria was real. The entire state was galvanized by basketball at every level (see the movie *Hoosiers*). The top tier was the programs at IU and Purdue, and during the time I was at IU, the legendary coach Bobby Knight was unrivaled king of all he surveyed. A consistent challenger for the NCAA championship, he had won the title twice at IU, and in 1987 won the championship for the third time. Fortunately, Knight was an avid reader, ran an absolutely clean program (all his players graduated), and was a significant patron of the new university library. Still, as I learned to my dismay, trying to conduct classes during a basketball team's run to a championship was a losing cause.

The Department

As associate professor of New Testament and Christian origins (an expanded description I have carried with me ever since), I was, rather than one of five or six teaching New Testament as at YDS, the only member of the religious studies department representing the life and literature of earliest Christianity. This arrangement seemed to me more beneficial than not, because I knew my colleagues would challenge and energize me from a greater variety of perspectives.

The IU faculty when I arrived in 1982 was a superb collection of teacher/ scholars in Sufism (Victor Danner), Jewish mysticism (Lawrence Fine), syncretic Chinese religion (Judith Berling), Indian religion (Patrick Olivelle), philosophical religion (James Hart), ethics (Barry Jay Seltser and David Smith), Catholicism (Mary Jo Weaver), Reformation and Enlightenment (Sam Preus), American religious history (Steve Stein), and Old Testament (James Ackerman). The department had a well-deserved reputation for teaching. Each year there were about one hundred undergraduate majors in religion, even though no student came to the university with that major in mind. The dynamic introductory courses that were the department specialty drew students to pursue this field of study—often despite the understandable objections of their parents, who wanted them to do something more practical. The faculty was also committed to serious publication, at a rate greater than that of the YDS faculty, and a number of the department's scholarly works were distinguished.[1]

The department had a lively inner life. We regularly peer-reviewed each other's classes and offered constructive criticism. We met monthly in one or another's house to read short papers or present ideas for the faculty's response. I not only have fond memories of the collegiality these sessions expressed, but I also am aware of how my intellectual horizons expanded through such exchanges. A key insight into the narrative of Acts, for example, came from a colleague who described the "turf battles" in China between local Taoist shrines and aggressive Buddhist proselytizing. The faculty was also willing to enter together into a sustained study that fell outside any of our areas of expertise. One year, for example, we committed ourselves to a course of readings in anthropology.[2] And if I was the only New Testament scholar in the mix, the study of the entire Bible was cultivated across the campus, and such study found an institutional home in the Center for Biblical and Literary Criticism, jointly administered by James Ackerman and Herbert Marks. The center sponsored lectures by faculty across the university as well as visiting luminaries like Meier Sternberg, Frank Kermode, and Emil Fackenheim.

Over the course of ten years, many faculty changes occurred, since the department typically attracted bright younger scholars who would then be recruited by other universities. Gregory Schopen, Robert Orsi, Hava Tirosh-Rothschild, Howard Eilberg-Schwartz, Rob Campany, and several others entered the ranks, sometimes as additions, sometimes as replacements. Such changes in personnel brought changes in outlook as well. I found myself, as time passed, increasingly out of step with the ethos of the department. When I first studied at IU and when I joined the department, religion was taught in a descriptive mode, avoiding both proselytism and disparagement—the model had been brilliantly displayed by William May and Wayne Meeks. I liked this approach. Slowly, however, and then more rapidly, the ideology of J. Z. Smith and Hans Penner—who regarded the teaching of religion as a matter of criticism and demystification[3]—began to shape the department's approach. I thought an approach that fundamentally reduced religion to little more than an academic category was a dead end. But as time went on, it was clear to me that I was not in the majority position.

High-Volume Teaching

In a large university, curricular offerings tend to be fairly stable, since predictability and word-of-mouth publicity are the keys to strong student enrollment. Thus, I inherited a group of classes that had been in place since the time of Wayne Meeks. "The Christian Church in New Testament Times" was basically the introduction I had taught at YDS, but now adapted to an undergraduate, nonministerial group of students (about two hundred a semester). The other large "service course" that I inherited was "Introduction to Religions in the West," covering Judaism, Christianity, and Islam. I had to scramble to get this together for my very first semester on campus, and I was happy to have had my Saint Ben's class in comparative religion to offer me some needed background. Judaism and Christianity? No problem. Islam? Crafting a set of responsible lectures in this tradition required a sprint of targeted reading. The payoff was the discovery of Islamic mysticism, which enabled me to think about the parallels between it and the Jewish mysticism I had studied (here at IU), and the Christian mysticism that had been such a large part of my former life. This class also drew approximately two hundred students a semester—the large enrollments were due not only to the faculty's reputation but also to the fact that religion classes could be used to fulfill a humanities requirement!

The large enrollment in these classes meant that, even more than at YDS, I spent huge amounts of time in reading and evaluating student exams and papers. I continued the practice I had established of assuming that students were doing B work—if they showed that they had learned what I had presented. If they fell away from that level in content or expression, they moved downward to C, D, or even F—a grade unthinkable in a seminary but common enough in a large undergraduate class, where some students, if not all, had the four *H*s: they were homesick, hungry, hungover, and horny. I customarily told students at the start of a semester that if they needed an A, they should take another course; I only gave As for truly exceptional work. I also told them that I would flunk my grandmother; the point is not love but performance. Amazingly enough, I never had complaints about grading . . . and some students did get As. But at the end of each semester, I would collapse for a time in exhaustion, such were the demands of time and energy in such a high-volume operation.

I developed a "correspondence" version of the "Christian Church in New Testament Times" course—a version of distance learning that predated the Internet—and won a national award. In fact, my time at IU was one of constant recognition of the effort I put into teaching, and the effect it was having. Perhaps the most gratifying of the five or six teaching awards I was given while at the university was the President's Award for Excellence in Teaching, which came not only with a certificate but also with a check.

Two upper-level classes drew more reasonable enrollments (about thirty-five each): "Jesus and the Gospels" and "Paul and His Letters." These classes enabled me to work more broadly in large parts of the canonical collection. Students in the department's thriving MA program could piggyback these classes—as I had Meeks's course on Paul when I was a student at IU. The master's students at IU tended to be very bright and highly motivated; many of them went on to doctoral programs in a variety of fields.

I developed two new courses for undergraduates. The first met a gap that I saw in the curriculum. Undergraduates had the opportunity to study a variety of religious traditions, but no class took up explicitly the question of the nature and shape of religion as such. In particular, there was no class that enabled them to read such classics in the field of religious phenomenology as those by Otto, van der Leeuw, or Eliade—the authors that Bill May had made available when I worked with him.[4] I offered this class as a capstone seminar for majors, and it helped them think more deeply about the subject matter to which they were devoting a considerable amount of academic credits. The second class was in service of the university honors program, with enrollment limited to students in that program. In "Ancient Moralists," I led a highly talented group through readings in Sirach, Philo, Paul, Epictetus, Marcus Aurelius, and Plutarch.

During my ten years at IU, there was a strong sense that the department should institute a PhD program. Like others in the department, I had already served as a reader on dissertations in other departments (such as English). I worked to help secure the PhD (see below), and when it was established, I offered doctoral seminars in Gnosticism, history of biblical interpretation, possessions and power, the letter of James and ancient wisdom literature, and the book of Acts and ancient novels. When Jason BeDuhn came to IU from Harvard to work for a doctorate with me, I read extensively in Manichaeism with him and served as chair of his dissertation committee. His doctorate was the first granted by the department; I returned from Emory to chair his defense of "The Metabolism of Salvation," a remarkably fine analysis of the religious practice of Manichaeism across multiple cultures and languages.[5]

Expanding Faculty Service

Service—the essential, though too often overlooked, dimension of scholarship in the academy—expanded for me during my ten years at Indiana University. Within the department, I naturally served on a large number of search committees and attended the de rigueur faculty meetings. My main service in the department was as undergraduate director and advisor. This job meant shepherding about a hundred young people a year through their course schedules, making sure they filled all the general requirements as well as those demanded of majors. An unforeseen aspect of this close contact with students (as well as of teaching classes with very large enrollments) was being asked to write letters of recommendation for seniors seeking a graduate position. From this point forward, writing such letters was a major part of my effort each fall—until my retirement in 2016, I wrote between fifty and a hundred letters of recommendation a year. As with the time and energy spent in the careful grading and commenting on student exams and papers, such labor largely goes unspoken among professors—it "goes without saying," as part of the social contract that once benefited us, and which we feel obligated to pay forward. It is a labor, however, that is unevenly distributed, so that the best teachers and advisors tend to carry a disproportionate amount of this important weight.

The Lilly Foundation in Indianapolis was generous in its support of universities and colleges throughout the state of Indiana. The foundation's charter, however, allowed it to donate only "soft" money rather than direct institutional support (such as faculty salaries). Over my IU years, Lilly money helped me offer seminars to business, clergy, and academic leaders in Indiana. The most fascinating experience was participating with David Smith in the series of seminars he offered on professional ethics that dealt, respectively, with moral issues in business, the military, health care, and media. To my surprise, by far the most coherent and sophisticated level of moral thinking came from business and military people. And by far the most puerile level of moral thinking was found among members of the media.[6]

Within the department, I formed (with Patrick Olivelle and Sam Preus) the committee that designed an innovative program in doctoral studies that made effective use of the department's strengths and could draw prospective PhD students. It was necessary to sell the program first within the department, since not all members were equally enthusiastic; they pointed out, quite justly, that we might replace a fine and flourishing MA program—one of the best terminal MAs in the country—for a weak PhD program.[7] It was necessary as well to sell the program to the College of Arts and Sciences, the university, and even state legislators. Fortunately, the seminars offered by Smith and others provided us with good contacts among state leaders, and we vigorously lobbied them. The PhD, as I indicated earlier, was successfully initiated, though during my remaining time at IU it remained a fledgling.

Citizenship in a large university means the willingness to participate in the faculty governance of the university as a whole. For a number of years, I served on the university curriculum committee, perhaps the most satisfying committee experience of my career because of the outstanding caliber of my colleagues from across disciplines. Our committee reviewed all curricular proposals, from the department of home economics to the physics department. We could reject proposals, send them back for further revision, or pass them. Not only did this work provide me an unparalleled vision of what actually happened academically across the university, it also gave me a sense of what truly bright and committed members of the academy could accomplish when they left their prejudices and pomposities at the door and worked together to secure excellence.

As one might expect, my stint on the university senate provided the counterpoint to my experience working on the curriculum. The senate was large, unwieldy, and the perfect expression of academic futility, taking public and lame stands on any number of issues, usually belatedly and always ignored. I worked on a subcommittee on "hate speech" (yes, we had reached that point), and we wrestled with the same ambiguities that still haunt that important but difficult subject. How could we navigate the ideal of free speech that ought to characterize the academy and also provide some guidance or control over antisocial expressions of that speech? And how does one determine what "hate speech" is? And who gave our committee, or the senate itself, the right to control anybody's speech? We solved nothing, but then, nobody else has subsequently, either. The university senate perfectly exemplified the combination of grandiosity and powerlessness—and the accompanying rage at powerlessness—that increasingly shadowed faculty governance in the wake of the sixties and seventies. It would, in my view, get worse with each passing decade.

In addition to the service given to students, the department, the university, and the public is the critical service that scholars give to maintaining the standards of scholarly discourse, through peer review. In addition to writing book reviews in an array of journals, including the *Religious Studies Review*, the *Journal of Religion*, the *Journal of the American Academy of Religion, Interpretation*, and *Theological Studies*, I accepted the invitation to become an associate editor of the two leading American journals devoted to biblical studies, the *Journal of Biblical Literature* (1982–1988) and the *Catholic Biblical Quarterly* (1985–1988). For a period of six years, then, I had to review one or two manuscripts a month for these journals. I also regularly reviewed book manuscripts submitted to publishers.

The process of peer review in the humanities is tricky. The standards of "replicability" or "nonverifiability" supposedly used in the sciences—though often fallaciously, as recent studies have shown—clearly do not apply in the humanities. But neither are judgments simply subjective or arbitrary. Peer review tests the plausibility of positions through analysis of the thesis, the evidence adduced in its support, and the logic of argumentation. A significant failure in persuading a fair-minded peer that one's thesis is reasonable, that one has provided sufficient evidence to support that thesis, or that one's argument is logical means that an article or book should not be published without amelioration of those defects. Honesty and clarity in carrying out such review are essential to the integrity of the scholarly process, and the failure to be honest or clear means a corruption of the process. As with the grading of student work, I regarded peer review as a matter of social justice, and I dedicated myself to its practice with diligence.

FRUITFUL RESEARCH

The first project I needed to complete was the introduction to the New Testament that I had proposed while still at Yale. Based on my Yale lectures (which had been typed single-spaced and read out loud to my classes), the book was composed on an IBM Selectric with moveable type-head and correcting tape—state of the art before the personal computer—with three carbons. The book took two full years to complete. It was, as I had planned, a genuine book—no maps, no pictures, no helpful breakout boxes, simply 618 pages of prose. I submitted the manuscript to Fortress in 1984, but because that publisher was committed to Brevard Childs's introduction to the Old and New Testament, and did not want to clutter its catalog, it postponed publication until 1986.[8] The delay was excruciating, not least because our finances were so underwater that I had hoped this book's royalties would at least get us to the surface. Eventually, they did, and although sales eventually diminished, *The Writings of the New Testament*, over thirty-plus years, served to introduce thousands of students to the New Testament in a way that made its writings transparent to the experience of the earliest Christians and transparent to their own experience of the Holy Spirit as well.[9]

My work on the Letter of James continued, as I wrote a series of thematic and exegetical articles and papers on aspects of the composition.[10]

These apparently caught the attention of David Noel Freedman, editor of the prestigious Anchor Bible commentary, and he asked me to undertake a new commentary on James that would replace the small and inadequate version by Bo Reicke that had appeared in the 1960s.[11] I was honored to join the ranks of scholars who had contributed to this series, and I began focusing my efforts on the eventual production of a fully realized scholarly interpretation of this precious and often neglected New Testament writing.

Among other things, I wanted the commentary to include a complete history of its interpretation, which had never before been done; under the influence of Luther, most commentaries and studies operated on the premise that James was a late writing (perhaps second century) that responded to a watered-down Paulinism. To set James properly within early Christianity, a comprehensive analysis of its reception and interpretation was required, as well as a full comparison between James and other ancient sapiential writings. I used some available Lilly money to pay a research assistant (Mark Pitts) to locate every mention of James in patristic and medieval literature; he compiled thousands of references from the pages of Migne's *Patrologia Graeca* and *Patrologia Latina*. At my first opportunity (a one-semester sabbatical), I then sat in the IU library and followed up these thousands of references, checking them for accuracy and analyzing modes of citation and of usage.[12] My work on James that had begun in a class at Yale, and was now being developed at IU, would not be completed until I was at Emory.

When I arrived at IU, I had the view that the commentary was an otiose form, and I thought I could never be persuaded to write one. My main complaint had to do with the inherently atomistic character of the commentary, which proceeds by breaking down a composition into intelligible segments and providing information about each such section. In series like Hermeneia and the Anchor Bible, this atomistic approach reached its apogee, as piles of information were stuffed into each segment, as though they were separate bags that needed to be filled to the top. Much of this information, furthermore, consisted of interactions with other scholars rather than interactions with the text in its ancient context.

With my conviction concerning the interpretation of the New Testament, namely, that the rhetoric or literary form of every composition should be the first key to understanding it, I regarded commentaries as an impossible instrument. As traditionally constructed, they offered information but very little interpretation. The challenge put to me by the invitation to write a commentary of James, then, was to find a way to offer needful information (such as commentaries from the time of Origen had done) while also providing a genuine interpretation of the writing's literary form and religious purpose.

Even as I was doing the preparatory work on the James commentary, however, another invitation came from the publisher Michael Glazier; he was launching a new commentary series on the New Testament under the editorship of Daniel Harrington, which he intended to fulfill the original ideal of the Anchor Bible, namely, to offer educated but nonprofessional readers a thoroughly critical yet thoroughly readable commentary. The title of the series, Sacra Pagina ("the Sacred Page"), echoed the patristic and medieval traditions so dear to me. To ensure the crispness he sought, Glazier wanted each volume to be done within a year! He asked me to write the commentary on the Gospel of Luke. But having argued for the position that Luke-Acts must be read as a literary unity, I did not want the volumes dedicated respectively to the Gospel and Acts to reflect entirely different perspectives. So I proposed that I do both volumes of Luke-Acts, and I pledged that I would complete the project in two years.

Not content with two (no, three) commentaries on my plate, I entered blithely into the controverted territory of Jewish-Christian relations. Using a lecture I had given at IU's Center for Biblical and Literary Criticism, I submitted "The New Testament's Anti-Jewish Polemic and the Conventions of Ancient Rhetoric" to the *Journal of Biblical Literature*, and it appeared in 1989.[13] This article, which sought to place the language of the New Testament in the context of the slander Greco-Roman philosophical schools used against each other, as well as the vitriol found in attacks between first-century Jewish sects, showed that, in historical terms, the NT's usage was unexceptional, indeed even mild, but that its power to harm later generations of Jews was connected to the changed circumstances of the two traditions and the (now anachronistic) normative force of the New Testament read as normative Scripture. The response to this article was both immediate and entirely positive, from the side of Jews as well as of Christians. My engagement with Judaism continued in a dialogue with the Jewish philosopher Emil Fackenheim, in which I responded to his important and provocative book *The Jewish Bible after the Holocaust*.[14]

During my IU years, I continued to accept invitations to preach and teach at Protestant churches, but all in the state of Indiana. My real traveling days were ahead of me. The opportunity presented itself, however, to stick my toe back into an explicitly Catholic conversation. The managing editor (later editor) of *Commonweal* magazine was my former YDS student Paul Baumann, who asked me in 1990 to review a book for that journal. *Commonweal* was (and is) a genuinely distinguished publication by lay Catholics that had published Dorothy Day, G. K. Chesterton, Michael Harrington, Daniel Berrigan, and Thomas Merton. It was a supremely desirable place for an obscure New Testament scholar to recover his Catholic voice. That first book review was the first of some sixty others over the years, and soon I contributed full articles as well, so that by the time I retired, I had appeared in the pages of *Commonweal* some ninety-six times, writing in response to books and movies as well as to issues in Catholic intellectual freedom, Jewish-Christian relations, sexuality, and theology. As it happened, the editor of the *Christian Century* during this same period was David Heim, also a former YDS student, who had me do a number of articles for that journal as well.

I regarded such popular publications in much the same way that I regarded teaching—indeed, I thought of them as a form of teaching that was not "downward" but "outward." Like teaching new courses, writing on new topics expanded my mind and imagination and provided new perspectives on my more technical work. Popular presentations and essays also reached ordinary people in a direct and powerful way. I grew accustomed to having essays newly submitted appearing in a matter of weeks (rather than months or even years as with books) and generating immediate responses. Such responses often appeared as letters to the editor, to which I was also invited to respond. Small whirlpools of controversy could unexpectedly occur, as when—a bit later—Cardinal Avery Dulles vigorously objected to an essay I had written on Christian supersessionism,[15] and I responded with equal vigor.

While spadework on James went forward slowly—there is no alternative to "slowly" when the research is both basic and vast—I turned my mind to the task of completing a commentary on Luke-Acts within a two-year period. If I succeeded, mine would be the first major commentary written on both New Testament books by the same author (Robert Tannehill had done his own narrative analysis of both volumes as a literary unity, but not in a commentary).[16] What I wanted to demonstrate was not simply that they had a single author but that they displayed a single literary and religious project.

The basic framework of my interpretation had been established by my dissertation: I read Luke-Acts as a single narrative argument defending God's fidelity to his promises to Israel, with the argument worked out through the pattern of God's sending prophets and of the people's acceptance or rejection of the salvation offered by Moses, by Jesus (the "prophet like Moses"), and by the men of the Spirit who, after Jesus's resurrection, proclaimed the good news of the salvation "in his name." After quickly dealing with the technical issues of authorship and date, then, my introductions to each volume laid out this argument and identified the subthemes that accompanied it. For each segment of text analyzed, furthermore, I tried mightily to show how the argument worked and how the narrative was both connected and coherent.

As anyone who has written a scholarly commentary can attest, the real labor as well as the real pleasure of the enterprise lies in the details. Here is where all the technical skills acquired through years of study come into play. First, one must determine the state of the Greek text, making decisions concerning textual variants. Then one must translate the Greek text. This task demands total commitment to the otherness, the strangeness, of the text; there can be no fudging or sloppiness. Decisions constantly need to be made concerning the rendering into English of a language that works in a manner quite unlike English; will one choose a wooden literalness at the cost of unintelligibility to contemporary readers, or will one choose to provide an "equivalence" translation at the cost of distorting the character of the text?

Precisely the commitment to absolute attentiveness—of having one's mind truly in this place and no other, in order to see the language clearly and without bias, and to hear the voice that speaks through the text from long ago and far away—is thrilling. The mind that engages with complete honesty the gnarly character of an ancient text experiences a sense of elevation, even of liberation—although the bondage to the text is total! The notes accompanying each segment of text thus translated seek to provide readers with an explanation of the translation choices made, of the debated aspects of grammar and syntax, and of the ways in which the text evokes the diction and rhetoric of other ancient compositions. It is in the notes that a scholar's depth of learning is revealed. In these and my other commentaries, I spent little time referring to secondary scholarship and used the space available to me for an examination of connections to other ancient texts.

Part of the joy as well as the challenge of writing commentaries is that they demand of the scholar a commitment of time and energy over an extended period of time. The task resembles ditch digging: each spade of dirt must be turned over, and there is no shortcut. Wake in the morning, go to the desk, work through this passage. Wake up tomorrow, go to the desk, work through the next passage. Do this until you reach the end. I completed the commentary on Luke in six months. The commentary on Acts I completed in eighteen months. In twenty-four months, slightly over a thousand pages. I had fulfilled my promise to deliver both volumes in two years.

Distractions and Advancements

Shortly after I settled in at IU, a position in New Testament opened at Emory University. This time the slot was in the department of religious studies rather than in the school of theology. My former YDS colleague and friend Carl Holladay had visions of us working together again and persuaded me to apply for the position, even though the religion department at Emory was decidedly inferior to that at IU. The attraction was the possibility of working with Carl and the chance with him to turn an average doctoral program into a truly fine one. I was invited to interview, but, as at Vanderbilt, I knew at once that the stars were not aligned in my favor. My competition in this case was Vernon K. Robbins, a nine-year veteran of the religious studies department at the University of Illinois. Once more, the department was less excited about my candidacy than was the faculty in the divinity school. Robbins could talk about his vision for what he termed "socio-rhetorical criticism" of the New Testament—an easily identifiable academic category; I chose to talk about the teaching of New Testament introduction (I was working on that book). I could see the needle tilting in his direction. The race was nonetheless a close one and was finally decided in Robbins's favor by the dean of the College of Arts and Sciences. I was now a two-time loser at Emory and figured that particular door was closed forever.

On the positive side, I was in a better teaching position at IU, even though in 1983 the doctoral program was yet but a dream. And as so often happens when a faculty member is recruited by another school, IU sped up my process of tenure, which was awarded that year. In my closing conversation with the chair, David Smith, however, I heard him state explicitly a bias that had been intimated, just below the surface, at Yale. Smith said, "No one will ever accuse Johnson of writing too little. But is there a genuine program of research?" In plainer language, I wrote too much and without a clear academic label by which I could be defined. Smith gave utterance to the peculiar academic bias that turns prolific production, even when of high quality, into a vice. By a strange inversion, academics with the narrowest possible focus, and who produce only one book, or better yet, none at all, enjoy a greater reputation among other academics than those who write widely and often.

Among literary chatterers, the same sort of perspective regards John Cheever as a greater writer than Joyce Carol Oates, because . . . well, she has written so many books! The profligate William Shakespeare should especially be embarrassed, along with Charles Dickens! How could what they write be great when they have written so much? Thus do smaller minds measure according to the measure of smallness. I was instinctively repelled by this "count-by-the-numbers" approach to scholarship. How little I cared about having a specific label is illustrated by what followed.

For the second great distraction that entered my life in 1987, I received a letter from Leander Keck, dean at YDS, asking if I would be interested in applying for a position in Pastoral Theology. Now, in addition to the seductive thought of teaching again at Yale, this invitation stirred in me the last vestiges of my priestly identity. I had, in my book on decision making in the church, proposed a model of pastoral care and counseling that was fundamentally hermeneutical rather than therapeutic. In this position, I thought, I could train a generation of pastors in the art of theological listening.

I was aware that such a move would have a severe impact on my identity as a "New Testament scholar," but I thought I could continue to work in the New Testament from a theological and pastoral perspective, or perhaps more accurately, work in pastoral theology from a scriptural perspective. Invited to campus for an interview, I gave a lecture called "Pastoral Theology as the Discernment of God's Word," which developed this vision. Yale eventually offered me the position, which demanded of me a truly serious discernment of my own. Not only would I be adopting a new professional guise, but I would be bringing my family back to New Haven, where Joy's health and our financial status had not been good. For once in my life, I drew up a cost/benefit analysis, which made me realize that even with the salary Yale offered, the cost-of-living differential between Bloomington and New Haven (where prices had continued to spike) made moving potentially catastrophic. So, I rejected the offer and stayed at IU.

Knowing that I had decided to stay within the field of New Testament studies, I took the opportunity to write a highly personal book called *Faith's Freedom: A Classic Spirituality for Contemporary Christians* (1990), which attempted the sort of "reading" of human experience that I had wanted to make the basis of a hermeneutical approach to pastoral theology. Although this small book has never sold many copies, it has miraculously stayed in print to this day, and has, of everything I have written, been shared most widely by friends and family, teachers and students. This interlude of dalliance with Yale also stimulated IU to promote me to full rank as a professor.

In the spring of 1992, I received a totally unexpected letter from Kevin LaGree, the new dean of the Candler School of Theology at Emory University. He invited me to visit Emory to consider the possibility of being named a Robert W. Woodruff Distinguished Professor of New Testament and Christian Origins. The Woodruff chair was the most distinguished university chair at Emory, created to attract outstanding talent to a university that wanted to reach the stature of Duke and Stanford. The chair was funded by the huge donation made to Emory by the chairman of Coca-Cola in 1979, the donation that enabled the school to leap from regional to eventual national prominence. There were usually only five or six Woodruff professors at one time, distributed in diverse disciplines.

This was quite an invitation, especially coming from a school where I had been a two-time loser in competition for much lesser positions. I correctly suspected the hand of my friend Carl Holladay, who had not given up the dream of the two of us forming a team that could make Emory excellent in our field. Carl had become associate dean of faculty affairs at Candler and had great influence over the newly appointed dean. Carl later assured me that it was Hendrikus Boers as well as himself who agitated for the appointment. A few years earlier, the chair had been offered to Raymond Brown when he was leaving Union Seminary in New York, but after some dalliance, he decided to relocate to Menlo Park in California. Failing to secure Brown, Candler entertained a number of visiting scholars (mostly European) in a variety of theological disciplines. If they could hire me, however, they would have secured a more permanent presence.

I agreed to the interview, which consisted largely in the Candler faculty seeking to persuade rather than to challenge me. I was, of course, well known to them from the searches in 1980 and 1983, and many of them had read my work. Because this was a university appointment—I would work at Candler but was funded by the university—I also had to interview with the provost, Billy Frye, and the president of Emory, James Laney. On this last exchange depended the offer of a Woodruff. The conversation went exceptionally well, and by the time I returned to Dean LaGree's office, he had been authorized to offer me the Woodruff position. At the age of forty-eight, I would be the youngest to hold that chair.

There were both negative and positive reasons for accepting the offer. Negatively, I felt that I had accomplished everything I could at IU; realistically, the only way I could improve my family's life—that is, earn a greater salary—was to turn to academic administration. But although there were aspects of administration that attracted me (I had discovered in myself a habit of thinking in terms of social systems), I by no means wanted to step away from serious and sustained scholarship. And, as I stated earlier, I had increasingly felt ideologically out of step with many in the department.

Positively, the Woodruff chair doubled my salary and added a research fund that was replenished annually; Emory had a long-established doctoral program that Carl and I could make even better; Candler enabled me to work once more with ministry students; Atlanta was a large and growing metropolis; and, it was in the South, so Joy would be closer to her family. Not insignificantly, Atlanta offered a climate that would be more healthful for Joy, who sank, as so many did, under the gray clouds of depression that covered Indiana from November to May. The first thing I did when I got LaGree's letter of invitation was to run to Hook's Drugstore, grab an almanac, and find that Atlanta had twenty-eight more days of sunshine a year than Bloomington! This fact alone was almost enough to push me toward the position. I accepted the position, and Joy and I began the process of house hunting in Atlanta, and of preparing our Bloomington house for sale. We were returning to the South, and we agreed that this was a very good thing.

Chapter Seven

EMORY UNIVERSITY (1992–2001)

*I*BECAME A WOODRUFF PROFESSOR AT EMORY UNIVERSITY IN 1992. I was forty-eight years old and still had twenty-four more years of hard work ahead of me before I retired in 2016. These twenty-four years were so filled with incident that I treat them in this and the next chapter. Since this book is not really an autobiography but the memoir of a scholar seeking to communicate something of what the scholarly life entails, I continue in these chapters to expatiate on aspects of academic life that, while not necessarily of overwhelming importance in cosmic (or even in personal) perspective, nevertheless reveal some of the context within which my scholarship was carried out.

In some obvious ways, the move to Emory was a blessing for Joy and me, but in less obvious ways, this latest migration proved to be both arduous and contentious in ways I had not anticipated. My mature scholarly years would be spent, not in a state of quiet contemplation devoted exclusively to research and writing, but rather in a state of fairly constant struggle and conflict.

I can start with the blessing. Most significant, Joy and I were now, for the first time in our eighteen-year marriage, truly alone. Our daughter Tiffany had elected to stay on in Bloomington and attend Indiana University. After a rough first year there, she prospered, and in four years she earned a degree in psychology. Joby also had married and had made Bloomington home base for his band. Joy and I now had the chance to discover—apart from the constant stress of parenting—who we really were as a couple. The good news is that we were both immensely pleased and grew closer with each passing year.

We found ourselves no longer in a middle-sized college town but in a large and growing city. Metropolitan Atlanta's population grew from 3 million to 6 million during these years, and especially after hosting the Olympics in 1996, the city became a vibrant and exciting place to live. We found a lovely townhouse surrounded by parks in the Druid Hills neighborhood, walking or biking distance from Emory, and only a few miles from the heart of downtown. The proximity to Emory was especially important to me. Both in Bloomington and now in Atlanta, I wanted to work no more than two miles from home. One obvious reason is that Joy's health could become critical within minutes, and I wanted to be close, just in case. The other reason is that walking was a precious part of my life. It was the only consistent form of exercise available to my once athletic but now aging body. For some thirty years, I walked at least four miles a day, not only to stretch out the body but also to liberate the mind. As both Kierkegaard and Nietzsche demonstrated, nothing so stimulates the imagination as purposeful walking. Like them (but without their genius), I have always found the silence available in an hour's walk a haven within which imagination and logic alike could flourish. Most of my creative impulses have arisen while walking. The silence of these walks also provided me with the prayerful contemplation that has always been dear to me and that the rest of my life precluded.

The common perception of Atlanta as a traffic-choked, soulless sprawl is based primarily on the experience of people who have known only the freeways or the airport. For its inhabitants, Atlanta is a loose conglomeration of charming neighborhoods, linked by roads that sinuously follow ancient footpaths to mills, shaded by urban forests with explosions of flowering bushes. Atlanta is situated in the piedmont of the Appalachians, and the distinctive topography of ridges and gullies has dictated its unusual pattern of growth. Once one has mastered the surface roads it is possible to get anywhere within the beltway in about thirty minutes. Having spent the last eighteen years in comparative wastelands, Joy delighted in Atlanta's abundance of good restaurants, music, drama, and not least, shopping centers like Lenox Mall and Phipps Plaza.

We both found a worship home in the historic Sacred Heart of Jesus church—now Basilica—in the heart of downtown, which combined a strong liturgical sensibility with a powerful commitment to social action. Before long, I was once more teaching classes regularly in the parish's adult education program. The seeds of my book *The Creed: What Christians Believe and Why It Matters* were planted in these courses, as were those of *The Revelatory Body: Theology as Inductive Art*.[1] For a number of years, Joy and I met in our house with a faith-sharing group from the parish. Finally, we were able to enjoy the company once more of Carl and Donna Holladay.

Best of all, Emory's benefits package was far superior to those of either Yale or IU, so that in addition to a good salary and research fund, the school contributed generously to my pension and, most significantly, offered medical insurance that was ample and flexible. The crushing weight of medical expenses was finally lifted from our shoulders. And since we could pick our physician, Joy found a fine female internist who finally combined the sort of medical acuity and human sensitivity that Joy needed; she remained her primary physician until Joy's death. Coincidentally or not, Joy began in 1992 the longest stretch of relatively good health she had enjoyed since childhood. This would eventually change, but the respite was a relief to us both. It enabled Joy in her sixties and me in my fifties to at last have something of a honeymoon.

Under the sponsorship of Provost Billy Frye, one of the unalloyed pleasures of the Woodruff appointment was the monthly luncheon he provided for all the holders of this chair—plus the superprofessor James Gustafson—at which matters great and trivial might be discussed. The chance to converse with distinguished scholars in ethics, anthropology, neurosurgery, psychology, philosophy, and genetics was appreciated by all of us, and we had stimulating and wide-ranging discussions. Occasionally ex-president Jimmy Carter would join the group, though his presence tended to flatten rather than elevate discourse.

Together with all these good things, however, my appointment as a Woodruff professor brought with it a weight of expectation that was not easy to meet. I was not joining the faculty as a junior member or filling an already established slot. Nor was I arriving as a scholar of age and dignity who had won a reputation at Harvard or Berkeley and who came to Emory as a sort of ornament with no obligation except to contribute my name to the roster, with nothing expected of me except more of my own research. It was made clear to me from the start that I was appointed at an early age and with only a slight reputation, precisely to be an agent of change both within

Candler and at the university. I was not appointed as an ornament but as a catalyst whose mandate was to be so excellent that I would raise the level of excellence across the board. Once more, it was my energy and idealism that appeared as my most valuable assets, and the president, provost, and dean all signaled that they wanted me to break the mold of Woodruff professors and be something of a supercitizen of the school.

Now, I should note at once that, while all social systems are inherently resistant to change—especially change initiated by newcomers!—the academy is particularly dedicated to inertia. As Bill Chace (the president under whom I served the longest) once observed, "What faculties excel in most is saying no." One reason for such resistance, to be sure, is simply the human craving for the regular and the predictable: "I have always taught this course in this fashion, and I see no reason not to continue teaching it in this fashion." Another reason is the built-in solipsism cultivated by many, whose eyes rarely rise above the level of their own courses and research. It has always amazed me to learn—over and over again—how few academics habitually think in terms of systems, even one so pertinent as the ecology of students' actual learning. Coming to Emory with the explicit charge to change things meant that I would inevitably meet resistance and sometimes resentment.

There was much at Emory, in fact, that needed improvement. The university displayed areas of true excellence (notably in biomedical research) along with patches of mediocrity. Billy Frye had recently come from the University of Michigan as provost precisely to create an atmosphere conducive to systemic excellence, but he faced uphill sledding. The Candler School of Theology, likewise, had some superb scholars and teachers,[2] but it also had other faculty who did not contribute much. Most of all, Candler lacked a coherent sense of program. Candler's main degree program, as at YDS, was the professional MDiv degree. The school's fundamental commitment was to prepare ministers for the United Methodist Church. But while the commitment was clear, the means by which the faculty sought to shape professional competence were not.

The quest of excellence at Candler also had to face the fact that the student body when I arrived was not impressively talented. There were, to be sure, a handful of brilliant students at the top, but there was also a truly deep and wide bottom, and little in the middle. Candler's faculty, correspondingly, was perfectly competent to recognize excellence and reward it, as well as to recognize stupidity and reject it. What many in the faculty lacked were the vision and energy necessary to help the talented but underskilled student seek and strive for competence. In a word, to teach. The Candler faculty had a communal commitment to "equality" (meaning everyone did every task, whether fitted for it or not) and "niceness" (meaning conflict avoidance at all costs). While admirable qualities, the combination did not make for excellence.

The Graduate Division of Religion at Emory, which, like Yale, drew its faculty from both the school of theology and the department of religion in the college, also lacked coherence. Some "tracks," such as Hebrew Bible and New Testament, were relatively strong, while others, such as Eastern religions, were not. PhD students at Emory, moreover, had little notion of what constituted "religious studies" as such, outside their own discipline. Within the New Testament area itself, much work was needed. The area was well staffed: in addition to Carl Holladay, the faculty included Hendrikus Boers, Vernon Robbins, and Arthur Wainwright. Fred Craddock taught preaching and New Testament, while Gail O'Day worked within the same double position. Carl's energies, however, had been siphoned by his administrative duties at Candler—he would, in the end, spend ten of his most productive years in the difficult and unappreciated role of academic dean. There were also personal tensions among Holladay, Boers, and Robbins, which made pulling together difficult.

The dysfunctional state of the New Testament PhD program is perhaps best illustrated by its weakness in two essential elements of a first-rate doctoral program. The first is recruitment: Emory was far from competitive with the top national programs, despite its enviably generous financial package. And without the best students, a program cannot turn out the best scholars. The second weakness was the production and publication of dissertations; although the program had produced some notable scholars over the thirty-four years of its existence,[3] the department had not produced many published dissertations (only nine of forty-seven) or placed many of its graduates in good academic positions.

Much more than in my first two academic placements, then, my position at Emory demanded of me a kind of scholarly leadership, which, while assuming that I would meet expectations concerning my own teaching and research, meant that, at least in the beginning, my citizenship and service would require a great deal of my best attention. As I recount my first decade at Emory, therefore, I will deal with teaching and service together—much of the service, after all, entailed pedagogy—and only then touch on some aspects of my research.

SERVICE AND TEACHING

As noted, Candler's main degree program was the MDiv, a professional degree. When I arrived, however, students could receive the degree by working through a set of distribution requirements willy-nilly, with a "professional assessment" tacked on at the end. With regard to the Bible, they could fulfill requirements by choosing any two courses in the Old and New Testaments. A graduate of Candler could have taken exegesis courses on Numbers, 1 Samuel, Romans, and Revelation and have been sent out to preach on Scripture every Sunday. Courses in introduction, which covered all the canonical literature, were completely optional. This was equivalent to a medical school granting a degree to students who had never taken anatomy. When I became chair of the biblical area, then, I pushed through—and "push" is the correct term—a complete overhaul of requirements. Now, students would be required to take two semesters of Old Testament introduction and two semesters of New Testament introduction; whatever else in Scripture they might take, Candler graduates would have some grasp of the anatomy of Scripture on which to build their future work in the ministry. I undertook to teach the New Testament introduction class, and I did so for most of my time at Candler, alternating with Carl when he was finally freed from the associate deanship.

Teaching New Testament introduction involved a huge commitment, not so much in the preparation of lectures (by this point I had them under control, although I wrote my outlines fresh every year) as in the management of teaching assistants. Five or six PhD students served as TAs each year. They led discussion sessions and graded exams and papers. I regarded the mentoring of these young scholars as a critical part of my teaching vocation.[4] Before each discussion session, I would meet with them for forty-five minutes to map our goals and propose strategies. After the sessions, we would meet again for a forty-minute debriefing and discussion of what we had learned about teaching from the process (I always took a discussion group myself). After the TAs read exams and papers, making comments and suggesting a grade, I would read the student's work over again and then assign the final grade—at the same time, I would discuss with the TA what the TA saw in the paper and why my grade agreed or disagreed with the TA's. Given an enrollment of over one hundred students, such mentoring was labor intensive but also deeply satisfying.

To my surprise, given the generally student-friendly and congenial nature of the school, the Candler faculty was not accustomed to making themselves available to students on a regular basis. Once more, a symptom of the view that the faculty taught but had little to learn. But how can effective teaching take place in ignorance of those being taught? I managed to get the faculty to agree (as we had at Indiana) that every faculty person would be available to students in the office at least three hours a week, with the times posted on a sign-up sheet on the office door. Three hours was a bare minimum, but even this was difficult to establish.

My next target was the signature ministerial course offered by Candler. When I arrived, it was called "Supervised Ministry": students were placed in church settings, and they met weekly with a minister-supervisor and a faculty member to discuss and integrate their nascent experiences of ministry. In theory, every member of Candler's faculty participated. The idea was certainly sound. But the structure of the course was based on "clinical pastoral education," which had originated in the training of hospital chaplains and placed considerable emphasis on the psychological assessment and reformation of students. Not only was Candler's faculty ill equipped to engage in this kind of psychological gamesmanship, but the process lacked any true theological character. Students resented the program as much as they learned from it.

The capstone of this process was the "professional assessment" (PA) that came in the student's final year. For the PA, the student wrote a short paper and presented a sermon before two faculty members and another student. By the time I arrived, the PA had become mostly an empty shell, redundant (ministerial boards did the same kind of thing) and even corrupt (students chose favorite faculty and best mates for the assessment). Working with several others on the faculty, I eventually persuaded the faculty to eliminate the PA[5] and to construct an alternative way to give integrity to the MDiv degree.

Consequently, as chair of what came to be called the Contextual Education Committee, I worked over a four-year period with other faculty to reimagine this central element in Candler's ministerial degree. We retained the basic notion of internships in ministerial settings, and weekly meetings with supervisors and faculty. What changed was our adoption of an umbrella concept that would subsequently pervade the entire curriculum, namely, that theology must always be "contextual," that is, emerge from and respond to actual human experience in the world. We chose to front-load the formation process, beginning with a more elaborate orientation for first-year students—immersing them in the city of Atlanta—and having them placed in contexts of immediate human need, such as homeless shelters, soup kitchens, orphanages, and hospitals. Only in their second year would students work in local churches.

The stuff of the weekly discussions with faculty and on-site supervisors, moreover, was theological rather than psychological—the emphasis was not on the psyche of the student but on the student's ability to think theologically about engagement with raw human experience among people in desperate circumstances. The faculty welcomed the new conceptualization and structure, and Candler's program soon became a model for other seminaries. My experience of developing and then teaching this course over many years confirmed my conviction that authentic theology is best practiced as an inductive art rather than as a deductive science.

Immediately upon joining the faculty at Emory, I sat on a committee that was tasked with creating some distinctive shape to the PhD program in religious studies. We agreed that students tended to focus on their disparate disciplines without a general awareness of the complexity of religious studies as a whole. Connected to such disciplinary isolation was little awareness of the work of their peers in the doctoral program or how to situate themselves in a department of religious studies when once they had attained their degrees. As a way of broadening students' vision and simultaneously socializing them into a coherent community of scholars, I developed and then taught for three years a proseminar required of all those entering the Graduate Division of Religion, called "Mapping the Landscape of Religious Studies."

I recruited faculty from every specialized track to take part. Each week, students would read and write a response to an article written by the faculty and considered representative by its author. In the seminar session, I would spend an hour interviewing the professors concerning their path to scholarship, the nature of their specialty and how it fit within the larger field of religious studies, and their own contributions to scholarship within this field. The interviews were rich and revealing; the scholars and students alike relished the individual face given to disparate and sometimes strange areas of inquiry. The second half of each session consisted of the students questioning the visiting professor on the basis of the interview and the article they had read. The course was remarkably successful in providing students with a sense of the wide field of religious studies and of the perspectives each of them brought to study. They discovered, for example, that scholars working, say, in ethics or New Testament not only had different methods, but they thought differently; they were possessed of quite distinct kinds of minds.

Change within one's own specialized guild is the hardest to accomplish. Everyone is an expert who resists challenge in an area over which he or she is an expert. Status, seniority, protocol, and precedent are all jealously guarded. Within the tight circle of Emory's New Testament scholars, consequently, change had to happen more slowly, by means of persuasion and example. The difficulty of positive change was greater because of the personal and professional dislikes and suspicions that existed within this faculty. The fact that Carl Holladay and I saw eye to eye on the goals we hoped to achieve, and that each of us brought serious energy and dedication to making the New Testament PhD program one of the best in the country, made all the difference. As Chesterton once observed, the greatest numerical leap is from one to two:[6] having a comrade in difficult struggles is a great advantage, especially a colleague as smart and decisive as Carl.

I subsequently chaired the search committee that brought Steven Kraftchick to the New Testament faculty. Steve had taught at Oberlin and Princeton Theological Seminary, and brought a well-honed literary and theological sensibility. With his addition, we had a solid core of faculty committed to excellence. Bit by bit, we managed to put in place the pieces of a program that could increasingly recruit the best students and produce the best scholarly dissertations. Within ten years, Emory's program in New Testament ranked among the top in the nation and was internationally recognized.

Together, Carl and I shaped a set of required seminars and examinations that made Emory's program as fully demanding as those at Harvard, Yale, and Chicago. In addition to in-course examinations in Greek, Hebrew, French, and German, candidates wrote lengthy examinations on exegesis, Jewish background, Greco-Roman background, and theology, and then underwent a rigorous oral examination conducted by the entire faculty. This process prepared students more coherently for the writing of a dissertation.

The possibility of directing PhD students in the writing of dissertations was one of the reasons I came to Emory, and it remained the most satisfying (if also the most demanding) form of teaching/mentoring I have ever done. Here one has the chance to work with the brightest minds, who are also the most intellectually ambitious and focused, and who have been trained to exercise scholarship at the highest level. The process of helping students discover their topic and craft their argument, align their sources, and structure their composition is time consuming but infinitely worthwhile. When the process is successful, as when three-fourths of the dissertations directed by Carl and myself were published by distinguished presses, and when newly minted PhDs find a place in the academy or church, then one knows that one has not only drawn from the tradition of scholarship at its highest level but also contributed to it in a fundamental way. Having Emory PhDs teach at Boston College and Boston University, at Duke and at Gonzaga, at Wake Forest and at Loyola of New Orleans, at Saint Andrews in Scotland and in the Protestant Faculty of Paris means that a certain vision of scholarship and a certain set of pedagogical values are being disseminated far beyond Emory itself.

Keeping to my commitment to serve the entire university, I taught courses on the Gospels and on Paul in Emory College as well as in the School of Theology. For three years I served as a member, and then president, of the University Senate and as chair of the University Faculty Council. Probably because of his contacts with me in these settings, President Chace (who began at Emory in 1994) asked me to sit on his newly formed President's Advisory Council, which not only offered him advice on knotty issues but also met regularly as the de facto tenure and promotion committee for the entire university. This meant that we dealt with especially difficult and disputed cases. We read portfolio after portfolio, debated, and then decided. It was important and difficult work.

During this same period, President Chace asked me to sit on the university's Strategic Planning Committee. Still later, Chace asked me to consider serving as provost of the university. Thinking that he was inquiring out of his rich sense of humor, I assured him that I was not good provost material, struggling as I did with my own checkbook. Similarly, a later invitation from Yale Divinity School to meet with its search committee for a new dean I took to be a kind gesture more than a serious inquiry. What I knew about myself was that, although I had the ability to think systematically, I did not possess the patience to be an administrator. More than that; because of Joy's health, I knew that I could juggle academic work, but that the full-bore dedication required of public administration would have been too much.

In service to the larger academic world, I agreed to be part of a team of three evaluators for the Lilly Foundation–funded Wabash Center for Teaching Religion. Each evaluator worked as a participant-observer for three of the summer workshops held at Wabash College in Crawfordsville, Indiana, and wrote a subsequent report. This meant flying to Indianapolis, driving to Crawfordsville, and spending two nights and days mingling with teachers from across many subdisciplines within religious studies. After four years, the team met with Lilly Foundation representatives in Indianapolis to make a final assessment of the program. The work was interesting if also exhausting. Positively, I became acquainted with a still larger circle of scholars in religion. Negatively, the experience confirmed me in my view that such programs that drew people from their home institutions for discussions with others in their discipline actually functioned—in this regard, like the conferences held by the Society of Biblical Literature and the Catholic Biblical Association—to energize individuals but did very little to improve teaching or collegial conversation within their home institutions.

This brief recital indicates, I hope, how my first decade at Emory was defined by the task of being, as a Woodruff Chair, an agent of change. I hope it also shows how much, especially at Candler and in the PhD program, pedagogy was at the heart of my endeavors. The PhD proseminar and structure of seminars and exams; the Candler Bible curriculum and contextual education courses—all this strenuous and time-consuming work had as its goal making the School of Theology and Emory more consistently excellent. My goal as a teaching scholar has always been student centered, in the sense that I have consistently tried to imagine a student's real needs and to find a way of meeting them through a coherent curriculum and through attentive teaching and mentoring.

I hope that my sketch enables those who know little of academic scholarship to appreciate how much effort and energy—and sheer time—a conscientious scholar spends in activities other than research and writing. If one adds in a scholar's commitment to faith, family, and friends, one understands why some scholars with great ability but limited energy and drive have a difficult time imagining and completing substantial scholarly projects.

RESEARCH AND WRITING

The habits I had acquired in earlier appointments—compartmentalizing, focusing, making every moment count—stood me in good stead as a Woodruff professor who, in addition to exceptional service and teaching, was expected to produce scholarship worthy of the appointment. The first thing I needed to complete was the Anchor Bible commentary on the Letter of James. The splendid Pitts theological library at Candler (one of the very best in the country) was of great assistance in completing the research for this project, which consumed approximately ten years of my labor at IU and Emory. It was published in 1995,[7] and its positive reception indicated that I had met my goal of changing the conversation concerning this important early Christian witness. This commentary stands with three or four others of my books as the basis for my claim to be a scholar who has carried out original and field-altering work.

To my surprise, I was approached by the editors of Abingdon Press in Nashville to produce a second and expanded edition of my short 1982 book on decision making in the church that had gone out of print so quickly. It seems that some of the ideas in the book had appealed to pastors concerned with actual decision making, and to some theologians (like Stephen Fowl and Gregory Jones) who were interested in narrative theology. So I added chapters that addressed some of the complaints by readers of the first edition (for example, the criteria for discernment), and the book appeared in 1996 with a new title: *Scripture and Discernment: Decision Making in the Church*. I was delighted to have this new version appear, for it contained the basic framework that had governed, and would continue to direct, my theological thought.

Almost simultaneously, I also published commentaries on Paul's letters to his delegates Timothy and Titus and on his Letter to the Romans.[8] These appeared in series that were more popular, but they nevertheless enabled me to develop further my perspectives on Paul. In the Romans commentary, for example, I extrapolated from my early work on the "faith of Jesus" in Romans to read the letter as having a fundamentally narrative character—an approach that has been usefully appropriated and extended by later works.[9] My popular commentary on the Pastorals coincided with a scholarly debate with Margaret Mitchell initiated by a paper on 1 Timothy that I had given at the SBL convention.[10] Mitchell is a first-rate scholar—in fact, Carl and I had seriously tried to convince her to leave the University of Chicago Divinity School and come teach at Emory—but I was convinced that her objections to my position were erroneous. The debate, however inconclusive for the moment, sharpened my appetite for further work on these letters, an appetite that found some satisfaction in a major commentary on First and Second Timothy in the next decade.

In these early Emory years, I also began to work with John Witte, a professor in the law school who combined true scholarly energy and acumen with a remarkably entrepreneurial spirit. He headed the Emory Center for Law and Religion; I became one of its members, and over the course of the next two decades presented major lectures and participated in faculty colloquies under its auspices. Witte specialized in large academic conferences dedicated to topics at the intersection of law and religion. The earliest papers I did for such conferences were entitled "Human Rights and Religious Texts" and "Proselytism and Witness in Early Christianity."[11] These papers enabled me to range well beyond the boundaries of the New Testament, to dialogue with scholars in disparate fields, and to grow into the role of a more public intellectual.[12] Such efforts were abetted by the remarkable research assistance given me by Mary Foskett, the first and probably the best of the assistants I was able to hire because of the Woodruff research fund. After Mary completed and published her highly original dissertation,[13] she began a long academic career at Wake Forest.

All these activities, however, were overshadowed by the publication in 1996 of *The Real Jesus: The Misguided Quest for the Historical Jesus and the Truth of the Traditional Gospels.* This publication had totally unanticipated consequences, and it illustrates the way in which a scholarly career can be as much a matter of accident and circumstance as of rational planning. The book was not at all in my personal plans. It came about this way: I had written a number of highly dismissive reviews of books that purported to deliver "the real Jesus" through historical methods. My reviews focused especially on the naïve conceptions of history employed by these books, on their erratic use of evidence, and on their inflated claims.[14]

Done and done, as far as I was concerned. But then an editor at HarperSanFrancisco named John Louden phoned and asked whether I would be willing to write a full book on the subject. Because of my other commitments, I told him yes, if I could deliver a manuscript in three months and could place the "historical Jesus debate" within an analysis of the confused cultural roles of the church, academy, and media. He agreed. I set Mary Foskett to scour all media reports on the infamous "Jesus Seminar" that had begun a decade earlier and had garnered to itself the greatest amount of publicity. Within weeks, Mary brought me a fat folder filled with newspaper and magazine clippings (note the predigital, pre-Internet character of all this). In the meantime, I organized my thoughts on the critique I would direct at the seminar and its founder, Robert Funk, and then on a series of historical Jesus books that had varying levels of plausibility (ranging from the ridiculous Barbara Thiering to the formidable John Dominic Crossan), but that shared certain fatal historiographical errors.

Although the historical Jesus commotion in general, and the antics of the Jesus Seminar in particular, with its deliberate cultivation of the media and its explosive pronouncements, was negatively regarded by most first-line scholars, very few in the academic establishment had deigned to confront or rebut it. Notable exceptions included Richard Hays, Howard Clark Kee, James Dunn, and N. T. Wright. Their criticisms had been public but had tended to focus mainly on the Jesus Seminar (rather than the whole movement) and often lacked a substantive critique of historiographic methodology. Although lightly written, my book was a genuine scholarly challenge to the entire enterprise, carried out with the sort of crispness that had characterized my book reviews. I named names, analyzed specific claims and arguments, and spoke plainly.

The part of the slender book devoted to the Jesus questers interested me far less than the cultural analysis I carried out in chapter 3. There, I showed how the two cultural institutions within which reasoned discourse and debate could be carried out—namely, the academy and the church—were both being bypassed through the manipulation of the media, which in matters of religion is truly ignorant and easily seduced by anything that smacks of scandal. The announcement that Jesus did not really say the Lord's Prayer, or that most of the other words ascribed to him in the Gospels were inventions of the church, was intended to titillate, and in the hands of the media succeeded.

I demonstrated how much of the historical Jesus commotion, which traded on the claim to represent the best in scholarship, did not follow proper scholarly methods and was, in fact, an effort to draw attention to its fomenters and to further erode the fragile grasp of contemporary Christians on their convictions. So-called educated believers (above all Presbyterians and Episcopalians) were the easiest prey to this seduction. Themselves decently well educated and quick to distinguish themselves from Bible Belt sorts, they no longer regarded their clergy as reliable tradents of truth; conversely, they displayed an almost superstitious reverence for the authority of academicians. The watered-down good news of Crossan and Borg—Jesus was not a divine savior but the purveyor of political correctness and the subversion of conventional piety—seemed the best news available to those Christians who took what was being peddled to be sound scholarship.

Fully aware of the irony of the procedure, I determined that my tract should not be buried in library stacks but should if possible effect a change in the national conversation concerning the historical Jesus. With Elaine Justice, the Emory University director of communications (who won a national award for her effort), I plotted a media campaign—yes, I know!—to ensure that this contrary voice would be heard, if not heeded. Coincident with the publication of the book, we held a small scholarly conference at Emory at which Richard Hays and I delivered papers, and to which other Candler faculty responded. The media were invited, and some came. At the national Society of Biblical Literature meeting in November, the book sold out within hours, and the buzz began.

Through the spring of 1997, I was interviewed by close to a hundred radio talk shows; gave interviews to CNN, CBS, and ABC; had the book discussed in *Time*, *Newsweek*, and *US News and World Report*; and was profiled by the *New York Times* and *Atlanta* magazine. I took part with John Dominic Crossan and Marcus Borg (two of the scholars whose work I had vigorously criticized) in a pioneering Internet debate, called *Jesus at 2000*, that extended over the entire period of Lent. And I participated with those two, plus N. T. Wright and Deirdre Good, in a national podcast from Trinity Church in New York, responding to questions put by viewers from across the country. The climax of this year of living dangerously came at the Society of Biblical Literature's 1997 meeting. The final session of the conference was devoted to my book. In a hall filled with hundreds of scholars and with television cameras running, Adela Yarbro Collins and Walter Wink presented their rebuttals to my little book, and I had the chance to respond, which I did, *con brio*. *The Real Jesus* turned out to be a best seller, not by the metrics applied to Harry Potter books, to be sure, but by those applied to books in religious studies, where the sale of over twenty thousand copies qualifies.

When I spoke above of "unintended consequences," I did not mean the publicity given the book; that, as I have stated, I had intended. I meant, rather, the changed perceptions of me consequent to this national exposure. One such perception was caused by John Louden's insistence, over my objections, that the subtitle of the book would be *The Misguided Quest for the Historical Jesus and the Truth of the Traditional Gospels*. I had wanted the main title *The Real Jesus* to be ironic: my whole point was that the claim to deliver "the *real* Jesus" through historical methods was bogus. I had as my original subtitle *Cultural Collusion and Confusion* (the present title of chapter 3), because that was the real thesis of the book: I challenged not only historical methods but also the breaking of cultural protocols in the marketing of ideas through the media rather than through contexts in which they could be debated in a face-to-face fashion.

As the editor, naturally, Louden prevailed. But the result was that I was perceived by many not as a critical scholar but as a defender of the historicity of the "traditional gospels," which was not at all what I was. On one side, then, I obtained admirers among the many Christians who considered all critical thought concerning the faith destructive. Most of such admirers saw only "truth of the traditional gospels" and not my far more critical argument. And on the other side, I was attacked by many academics precisely for being a spokesperson for fundamentalism and know-nothingness. Amusingly, I was also reproached by many academics as having been sarcastic and dismissive in my treatment of other scholars, so that I was in their view not only a conservative throwback but also guilty of political incorrectness, academic-style. To my regret, no matter what scholarly work I did subsequently, such perceptions lingered, and I had to strive mightily to recover the scholarly equanimity I had enjoyed before 1996. It caused me no small amount of chagrin to realize that a book that took three months to write threatened to eclipse books that had taken me years and even decades to write.

Seeking to provide a less polemical and more constructive treatment of the subject, then, in 1998 I published with HarperSanFrancisco *Living Jesus: Learning the Heart of the Gospel*. In this book I did not take up the historical quest but offered my understanding of the standpoint from which Christians ought to view Jesus, and the entailments of that standpoint. Thus, "living Jesus" refers to the belief that the "real Jesus" is not simply a historical figure of the past but a living presence in the present: the standpoint of believers is that the resurrection of Jesus defines his reality, with the resurrection understood not as an event of the past but as an existential condition of the present. The first part of the book teases out the implications for "learning Jesus" not as an academic pursuit but within the context of a community of believers who consider him the Lord who presses upon them urgently and seeks a response.

The second part of the book provides a reading of all the New Testament compositions based on this conviction: not only the Gospels but also the letters and book of Revelation are read within the community of believers, not as more or less adequate historical sources but as indispensable witnesses to the transformative life made available through the exaltation of the crucified Messiah, Jesus. The message of my book to the church, in short, was that the proper apprehension of Jesus came not through the epistemology of history but through the epistemology of faith. Predictably, this more positive treatment did not sell nearly as well as the polemical one!

My experience of riding the media carousel for a year was sobering. I saw, first, that the attention of the media is addictive. One can actually feel larger and more important because one speaks before a camera. Realizing that this was not an addiction suitable for a sober scholar (and ex-monk!), I determined to get off the media merry-go-round as fast as I could. I have avoided subsequent invitations to get back on. Life in the limelight is inimical to serious scholarship. I discovered, second, that such media exposure adversely affected my relationship with my students. They were thrilled that I was now "important," but they also began to view me as a more remote figure because of that "importance." Some students, I learned, feared coming to my office because I was such an "exalted" media figure. It was in this period that students began calling me "LTJ" and passing on urban legends concerning this "LTJ," which had little connection with who I was. All of this nonsense disgusted me, and it confirmed my determination to withdraw once and for all from the celebrity circus.

But it was impossible to avoid the fact that I was now a public figure (of a very minor sort) in a way that I had not been before. Invitations to lecture at churches and universities and seminaries multiplied, and I had to decide which to accept and which to refuse, committing myself to perhaps one in every three invitations. Before the publication of *The Real Jesus* in 1996, for example, I gave some nine public lectures through the first half of the decade, whereas between 1997 and 2000, I gave fifty-two. Some of these, naturally, were presentations on the question of Jesus. I was willing to engage real people on this issue, as opposed to pontificating in a TV studio, so, although I quickly grew tired of repeatedly dealing with the same question, I saw doing so as a legitimate entailment of having entered the fray in the first place.

Invitations also came to speak on a variety of other topics, and these I accepted more gladly. Perhaps the most energizing invitation was to be a Phi Beta Kappa "visiting scholar" in 1997–1998. This program funded public lectures for colleges that could not otherwise easily support them. The fact that I had never myself been Phi Beta Kappa was generally overlooked! I developed three formal lectures that I thought would display some of the intricacies of my own specialty while appealing to broader humanistic interests: "*Koinōnia*, or Unity and Diversity in Earliest Christianity," "*Paideia*, or Greco-Roman Culture and Earliest Christianity," and "*Thrēskeia*, or Greco-Roman Religion and Earliest Christianity." On each visit, I presented one or the other of these lectures, did classroom presentations, and met in discussion with faculty and students. I lectured at such fine schools as Mount Holyoke, Stetson, Furman, Claremont McKenna, Centre, and Wake Forest. Although exhausting, the experience was invaluable in providing me a firsthand look at higher education in schools where teaching rather than research was of paramount importance. Two of the lectures, moreover, began the process of thinking about Greco-Roman culture (especially religion) and Christianity that culminated in my book *Among the Gentiles* that I completed ten years later.

Another set of lectures that provided the impetus to new research was the Stone Lectures that I delivered at Princeton Theological Seminary in 1997. The five formal lectures had as their overall title "Religious Experience in Earliest Christianity." The first two lectures addressed the theoretical issues concerning the analysis of religious experience, entering into a detailed criticism of the reductionistic approach of such historians of religion as Jonathan Z. Smith at the University of Chicago and arguing instead for a more phenomenological approach to early Christianity. The final three lectures took up specific examples: "Ritual Initiation and the Politics of Perfection," "Glossolalia and the Embarrassments of Experience," and "Meals Are Where the Magic Is." After giving the lectures, I submitted them, complete with extensive footnotes, to Fortress Press, which immediately published the collection in 1998 under the title *Religious Experience in Earliest Christianity: A Missing Dimension in New Testament Studies*.

Another lecture that anticipated later work was called "What's Catholic about Catholic Biblical Scholarship." I delivered it in 1997 as an invited plenary presentation at the annual Catholic Biblical Association meeting in Seattle. The lecture asked the assembled scholars to consider whether the highly successful incursion of Catholic scholars into the historical-critical methods that had originated among Protestant scholars with quite different theological presuppositions might not have had as an unintended consequence the abandonment of some specific and important scholarly values ingredient to the Catholic tradition.

The lecture immediately divided the crowd, stimulating some angry comments from the audience, some of whose members (like John Meier) thought that I was attacking historical approaches as such—the right to employ which had been won by Catholic scholars with great difficulty and against sustained opposition. The eminent New Testament scholar Joseph Fitzmyer, in fact, was so outraged that the next morning he abandoned his planned seminar in order to spend the entire time rebutting my heretical proposal. Oddly enough, many of the Protestant scholars in the audience responded with enthusiasm. I subsequently expanded one section of the lecture into an article for the journal *Modern Theology* called "Imagining the World the Bible Imagines."[15] I was excited at the contemplation of a possible epistemological paradigm shift that would occupy my mind over the next decade.

My more public presence during this first decade at Emory was also abetted by my continuing to write book reviews on a wide variety of topics, and by contributing articles (by invitation) to *Commonweal*, the *Christian Century*, and the British journal *Priests and People*, whose editor, David Sanders, had the knack of enticing me to write three-thousand-word essays on everything from suffering and sacrifice to the pedophile crisis.[16]

DEATH AND DISTRACTION

The end of the decade brought heartache and grief. Our daughter Tiffany had married Gordon Hunter, a graduate of the Air Force Academy, and had begun life as a military wife in Minot, North Dakota. Joy and I celebrated their union with them in Bismarck, and we were ecstatic when we heard the news that Tiffany was expecting a baby. But in mid-December, just as final exams for the New Testament introduction course were handed in, we received a call from Gordon that Tiffany was in intensive care; she had suffered a fetal abruption, and it was uncertain whether either she or their little girl, McKenzie, would survive.

Joy and I flew that afternoon to Minot and found Tiffany alive after emergency surgery but still in danger because of blood loss. Her daughter, McKenzie, had suffered severe cranial bleeding in the process of trying to save mother and child and would not, the doctors told us, ever recover. All we could do was support Tiffany as she slowly recovered, and then keep watch with her by the infant's incubator as McKenzie slowly moved toward death.

In the middle of this crisis, I had to fly back to Atlanta, work three days and nights to correct one hundred plus exams, hand in the semester grades, and then fly back to Minot. I arrived the night McKenzie died and immediately set to work getting Father Paul DeRosier, Joy's friend and mine, and the priest who had baptized Tiffany, to Minot for the baby's funeral in the middle of a terrible winter season. The whole episode was profoundly traumatic for us all. Joy's inability to comfort Tiffany appropriately at the critical moment caused a rift between them that was never fully healed.

And I moved about for a considerable time in an emotional fog of which I was only partially cognizant. One consequence quickly became evident.

I had begun a yearlong sabbatical immediately after the shock of McKenzie's death. While at a conference for Congregationalist pastors at Louisville Presbyterian Seminary, Richard Hays and I spent a day and a half working with them on how to think about "boundaries that are not barriers" in the church. At the Brown Hotel the night after our first session, Richard asked me whether I would consider a position as Duke's equivalent to the Woodruff Chair. There was much that attracted me at Duke: the chance to work with people like Richard, Lewis Ayres, and Stanley Hauerwas (whose work I had always admired); the attractiveness of working with the dean of Duke Divinity School, Gregory Jones (with whom I had conversed when he was on the faculty at Loyola of Baltimore); and the opportunity to escape from the place where I had spent a decade exhausting myself in teaching and service, and which now appeared to me as without savor.

Joy and I therefore visited Duke. I gave lectures and sat through interviews. Joy was royally received. All good, but slowly, I became aware that my attraction to the more theologically conservative Duke was wrongheaded: it was much better, I realized, being a conservative in a more liberal school like Candler than being a conservative in a conservative school like Duke Divinity School. The kind of conservatism I observed at Duke, furthermore, was not like my own. I was uncomfortable with their particular way of being evangelical. It turned out that I was a lot more theologically liberal, in the long run, than I usually acknowledged—at least by comparison to the faculty at Duke. Moreover, Joy and I did not find the scenery or the housing in the Durham area in the least attractive—we had each had more than enough of piney woods, thank you.

Finally, and most important, I realized that the desire to "escape" had much to do with exhaustion, yes, but even more to do with the condition of grief through which I was passing. And Duke could not heal that. The offer from Duke, however, nudged Emory toward greatly enhancing my salary, and, even better, reaffirming my right to teach across the curriculum in both the school of theology and the university. The Duke distraction was the last I was to undergo. My final sixteen years as an academic scholar would be spent at Emory.

Chapter Eight

EMORY UNIVERSITY (2001–2016)

AT EACH STAGE OF THIS STORY, I HAVE TRIED TO PRO-
vide a sense of time, place, and circumstance, in the hope that the human
context of scholarship can be better grasped by those who live far from the
strange world inhabited by people whose minds are chronically in another
place. In my last (long) years at Emory, my own mind was constantly in
at least two places. One place was my life as a scholar, which became ever
more varied, complex, and challenging—recognition and rewards carry
with them their own imperatives. The other place was taking care of my
dear Joy, whose health declined steadily after 2003, and who required ever-
increasing amounts of physical and emotional attention.

By 2006, I needed to provide Joy with daytime care so that I could carry
out my service and teaching responsibilities. When I was away on speaking engagements, she needed twenty-four-hour caregivers. In the last years
before my retirement in 2016, Joy needed outside care for six hours a day,
five days a week (the time I spent at the office); the remaining hours of
the week, I was her caregiver. Because her attacks could come on without
warning literally within minutes, and became increasingly life threatening,
such care involved almost continual anxiety. Atlanta EMTs and firefighters
well knew the route to our house, and from our house to the emergency
room at Piedmont Hospital.

In earlier chapters, I mentioned the complexity of Joy's physical condition and the fact that she (and we) enjoyed a period of relatively good health
between 1992 and 2003. Beginning in 2004, however, Joy's health became

worse. She was now in her seventies, and a lifetime of chronic illness began to wear her body down. She had a stroke in 2005, and although she substantially recovered her basic faculties, she lost the ability to do the kind of serious reading that had always given her pleasure, and that had made her the compelling conversation partner who read and critiqued everything I wrote.

Her arthritic knees increasingly robbed her of independent mobility; in her last years, she got about in a wheelchair pushed by me or a caregiver. From 2016, her COPD had advanced to the point that she was dependent on oxygen concentrators to breathe; frequent bouts of pneumonia led to many hospitalizations, and in December of 2017, Joy's body finally relinquished her indomitable spirit. My beloved partner and friend of forty-seven years finally found peace and freedom from pain.

The dynamic of presence and absence that chronically characterizes the life of the active scholar became more acute for me in these years. With regard to Joy, I was physically absent far more than I wished to be, on quick lecture trips undertaken primarily to earn enough money to support her increasing need for care. But my mind never wandered far from her, and in the last years, mind and body alike were constantly at her side.

The dynamic of presence and absence, however, applied to Candler and Emory as well. On one side, I was obviously and visibly present in the life of the school. I chaired significant committees, taught large classes, held frequent office hours, preached in chapel, spoke at orientations and leave-takings, taped videos on behalf of the school. But this presence was one of public performance. I seldom attended chapel when not preaching; I did not meet with colleagues socially; I attended no student social functions; I did not meet with graduate students and other faculty for the monthly colloquy. In short, my public life as a scholar that seemed on the surface to signal success and good fortune brought with it real costs—separations from Joy even for a night were painful for both of us; being a resident alien in my own academic home was equally a source of stress and regret.

One moment in November of 2008 perfectly captures the tension within which I lived. I was preaching a sermon in Cannon Chapel on 1 Thessalonians 4. In this passage, Paul addresses the grief his readers were experiencing at the death of members. I was speaking about the inevitability and absolute character of death when, three minutes into the sermon, my cell phone rang. At that time, only Joy had my number. Although I was in midsermon, I had to answer, knowing that a crisis could come upon her in minutes. She said, "Honey, I need you now." I said, "I will be there in fifteen minutes." I closed the phone, told the congregation, "That was my wife. I must go home to help her." I stepped away from the pulpit, left the chapel, ran to my car, and drove home. Many students thought I had manufactured the moment to illustrate the suddenness of the crisis of death—to make a sermonic point. That was far from the truth. The moment illustrated rather the extent to which having the mind in another place can stretch bodies, minds, and hearts.

Another illustration of how Joy's fragile health affected my scholarly life was my relative lack of international travel. In my field particularly, scholars are accustomed to visit Europe and Asia (even Australia) for scholarly conferences. My colleague Carl, for example, has participated in and given talks at such conferences in England, Germany, Italy, Israel, Russia, Greece, Turkey, and South Korea. Although I traveled extensively in the USA, in contrast, Joy could neither accompany me on such long excursions nor could I leave her for the extended periods such excursions required.

Apart from a couple of lectures in Canada, then, as well as two in Dublin and one at Oxford (all one trip) and a series of presentations in Bangkok (on another trip), I was not able to attend such international meetings. I remember sending papers to be read at conferences to which I was invited and planned to attend but a crisis in Joy's health made impossible, such as ones in Boston, Rome, Canada, and Germany.

As I recount my properly scholarly activity during this period, then, it is important to remember that, with few exceptions, my research and writing were carried out, not in a library, but at home next to Joy, or in hotel rooms, or in airport terminals—I have written many chapters in those locations. Student papers were not read and graded in my study but in the kitchen, where my wife watched television while I worked, and where I could help her with meals, medicines, bathroom runs, and getting oxygen. These were years when the capacity for compartmentalization, focus, persistence, and patience was especially important if I were to have any scholarly life at all.

New Directions of Service

As a result of the negotiations with Emory at the time of the Duke dalliance, my service to Candler and the university became more varied and interesting. I was free to move in new directions precisely because of all the heavy lifting Carl and I had done in the previous decade. The changes that were most required had been made. The basic framework at Emory was solid. Within the graduate program, I shared with my colleagues the work of graduate student recruitment—a much more elaborate process now that we were competing for the best students in the country. In one case, the threat of losing a student we wanted led me to forfeit most of my yearly research fund to "top off" a financial offer. I joined my colleagues in teaching required seminars, in administering and evaluating qualifying exams, in participating in dissertation colloquia and defenses, and finally, in directing dissertations.

In Emory's doctoral program, dissertation directors were not assigned by faculty but were chosen by students. I was honored to have the opportunity to direct sixteen dissertations in this sixteen-year period, and to see twelve of them published. Apart from credit being given for teaching a seminar each year, it should be noted, graduate faculty receive no recognition or remuneration for any of their "supernumerary" labors. If ever there was a place in the educational system where the word "selfless" would be appropriate, it would be in the dedication of those who work to secure the future of the professoriate through the training of younger scholars. The amount of effort, the number of hours, spent in helping students complete the work that will introduce them to the world of scholarship is impossible fully to compute.

For the university, my main service was a year spent on the committee to select a new president to succeed Bill Chace. I was one of two faculty members of Emory on the search committee that chose James Wagner, who went on to serve in that position from 2003 to 2016. I subsequently also sat on the committee to select a new dean of the Laney Graduate School.

The most fascinating yet also expensive activity (in terms of time and energy) was my role in securing and shepherding a distinguished visiting professorship for Emory. I received a call one day from Bill Fox, the head of university development. He asked me to talk with Alonzo McDonald, a wealthy (and eccentric) entrepreneur who was also an evangelical Christian, and a man of fixed and fervent ideas about how to spend his money. McDonald wanted to support a chair on "the person and teaching of Jesus" but did not want to locate it in any department (such as religious studies) out of the fear that in such a context, his vision would be swallowed in the flow of institutional inertia. According to Fox, McDonald was ready to pull out of his conversations with Emory, since no options appealing to him had to that point been offered.

So, I met with McDonald for two hours in the administration building. I proposed a visiting distinguished professorship on "Jesus and culture," dedicated to the study of Jesus's cultural influence, as well as the effect of cultural shaping on the figure of Jesus. The visiting chair would give a series of public lectures but also offer a class to selected students. McDonald bought the idea on the condition that I would organize and run the lectureship, which I agreed to do. For five years, before the chair was finally brought within the management of the dean of Candler, I did the recruitment, secured the funding, provided the hospitality, and generated enthusiasm for the lectures and classes offered by the McDonald Distinguished Professor in Jesus and Culture. The chair continues and has been extremely successful in bringing to campus such splendid scholars as Jaroslav Pelikan, Wayne Meeks, John Noonan, and Garry Wills. But was it a lot of work!

Under Dean Russell Richey, I was asked to chair Candler's new strategic planning committee, which I did for three years until the planning process for the entire university was centralized. Strategic planning is not a habit instinctive to academics, whose antipathy to change and systemic thinking I have earlier noted. The process was therefore arduous (Are all faculty voices represented? How much homework can I ask of them? When can we find time for meetings in an already loaded schedule?), and the pace was glacial. In the first year, we managed a self-study of Candler by way of comparison and contrast to other leading divinity schools across the country, establishing a profile of Candler that corresponded to facts rather than to wishful thinking. In the second year, we hammered out (with much resistance) six fundamental values that should guide Candler's future. Well and good.

In the third year, however, when we took up the task of imagining and implementing a future for the school, resistance, not least from the dean himself, grew stronger. The dean, at least in my view, was the one most resistant to real change and was fearful of my proposal that we claim rather than camouflage Candler's liberal heritage—in the name of, rather than opposed to, the good news of Jesus Christ—and enter into serious competition with Yale, Harvard, and Chicago for national theological leadership.

Richey, it seemed, felt constrained by his (rapidly diminishing) southern United Methodist base, which was allergic to anything that sounded like liberalism. It was a relief to shift the burden to the university.

Finally, under Dean Jan Love, Russell's successor, and the most joyfully energetic of the leaders under whom I served, I was asked to coordinate Candler's centennial celebration. I chaired a committee of effective faculty and (most important) staff, and we set about planning a range of special events for the school year of 2014–2015. The culmination of the celebration was a theological conference in the spring of 2015, entitled "The Theological Challenges of the Next Century." The committee decided on four critical theological concepts that in our view would press upon the next generation: "Logos: Theological Imagination and Secularization," "Person: The image of God in the Contemporary World," "Cosmos: God's Creation and the Care of the Earth," and "Polity: The Kingdom of God and Global Pluralism."

For each topic, a major presentation was made by a Candler faculty member and responses were given by distinguished visiting scholars. I gave the keynote address, "Meeting the Theological Challenges of the New Century." Candler students attended each session and participated in group discussions of each topic. Like strategic planning, the work devoted to this centennial conference was time consuming; unlike strategic planning, the conference turned out to be signally worthwhile. Not only was it exhilarating to have all faculty and all students participating in the same event over a two-day period, but many of the presentations were of such excellence that they were published in diverse religious journals, and all of them were eventually collected in a book.[1]

More Freedom in Teaching

After having taught New Testament introduction for some forty years, I was glad around 2010 to relinquish this most demanding course to my junior colleagues. I continued to offer each year one of the required doctoral seminars (history of interpretation, Greco-Roman background, New Testament Theology) and occasionally had the chance to spend a semester working through one of Paul's letters in Greek with doctoral students. My desire to do close readings of letters such as Romans, 1 Corinthians, and

2 Corinthians in this fashion was part of my gradual turn from a focus on Luke-Acts and James to Paul, the most complex and most controverted of early Christian writers.

Within Candler, I was therefore free to offer a number of thematic courses on the New Testament. "Prophetic Jesus, Prophetic Church" was a course built on a series of conferences I had given to ecclesial groups and was my climactic interpretation of the composition, Luke-Acts, that I had worked on since my dissertation. The course, in turn, became the basis for a book by the same title.[2] My investment in Paul was amplified by a course I taught at least three times, called "Paul's Jesus." Students read all of Paul's letters with a single question in mind: How did Paul view and speak of the human Jesus?

The permission I had won to teach across the theological curriculum led to the development of two classes that were cross-listed with ethics and fulfilled students' requirement in that area. The first was called "The New Testament and Christian Ethics," which—uncharacteristically for me—focused entirely on secondary literature dealing with the moral dimension of the New Testament. A benefit of this course was that students learned how to engage well-known authors, whom they might earlier have held in awe, and critically examine their arguments on the basis of logic and their use of textual evidence.

Finally, I taught a course called "Sexuality and the Bible." The pertinence of this topic to ministerial students in the contemporary world was obvious, and enrollment in the class had to be limited. In contrast to the ethics class, this course dealt only with the primary texts of Scripture. I led the students through a reading of the entire Bible, "surfing for sex," attempting to get a handle on the wide variety of statements on sexuality and gender in Scripture and gaining a chastened stance with regard to the mystery of human sexuality that eschewed the easy and simplistic postures that proliferate around this difficult topic. Because of this course, the essays I had written mainly for *Commonweal*,[3] and the many discussions I held with LGBQT students on campus, I was considered "LGBQT-friendly" and was invited to address a spectrum of issues dealing with sexuality in a number of settings, which I gladly did.[4]

My enthusiasm for teaching undergraduates had never waned, so when Bill Chace, the former president of Emory who had returned to the classroom as a professor of English literature, asked me if I would like to team-teach a course with him, I immediately accepted. But how could a specialist in James Joyce and a specialist in the New Testament construct a course that would attract and challenge undergraduates? The first class we offered was "Suffering and Creativity: The Expression of Human Pain in Literature." With approximately sixteen upper-class undergraduates, we read great works of literature from Job to *Waiting for Godot*, from *Philoctetes* to *The Diary of Anne Frank*, probing the specific question of how pain gave rise to literature and how literature expressed pain. To an impressive degree, students showed themselves able in this class to probe deeply into their own suffering and that of others.

The course was such a success that we decided to offer another. But we disagreed on which direction to take. I wanted to offer a class on "the academic novel," since there was such a rich tradition of fiction set squarely in a university context (think of Snow, Amis, Smiley, Lodge, Russo, Hynes, and others). Perhaps because he had experienced enough of real-life academic silliness, Chace fought for a course called "Ancients and Moderns," and when I fully grasped the concept, I agreed. We read literature in pairs: The *Iliad* with *Red Badge of Courage*; *Oedipus Rex* with *Long Day's Journey into Night*—using the Ralph Richardson 1962 movie version—the *Inferno* with *The Wasteland*; *King Lear* with *A Thousand Acres*; the *Odyssey* with the movie *O Brother, Where Art Thou?* In each case, we asked what made something "ancient" or what made it "modern." Students were at first astonished and then delighted to see two senior scholars in actual argument concerning literary texts. It was, as you can imagine, a rare intellectual feast and pedagogical experience!

Beginning in 2000, my life as a teacher took on a new dimension. Apparently made aware of the teaching awards I had won at IU and at Emory, a new entrepreneurial venture then called "the Teaching Company" (now called "the Great Courses") sent a scout to record one of my lectures in New Testament interpretation, and on that basis invited me to Alexandria, Virginia, to audition for a slot as one of their teachers. I did a sample lecture for them, and then arranged to do a twelve-lecture course on the apostle Paul. The setup was simple in the extreme. Standing at a lectern before two cameras and a handful of volunteer auditors, I spoke *ad libitum* from notes, much as I had in my own classroom. I eventually did eight courses for the Teaching Company.[5] In all, I did over two hundred half-hour lectures. By the time I ended in 2012, the technology of production had advanced considerably: no lectern, script read from teleprompter, three cameras, no auditors. Although travel to the DC area meant extended absences from Joy (the two times I brought her, she ended up in hospital), the monetary rewards were significant, and I had the sense that it was worthwhile to make my teaching available to tens of thousands whom I would never meet in an actual classroom.

The same spirit animated my willingness to write popular essays (some fifty-one during these years) and book reviews (some sixty-seven in this period) in magazines and journals, as well as lecture at churches, seminaries, and colleges. Over these last sixteen years at Emory, I presented papers to twenty-two scholarly meetings. I also lectured and preached at some eighty-five churches and eighty-nine colleges and seminaries across the country. Visits to churches were most taxing, for they often demanded multiple formal presentations and discussion sessions, as well as preaching at worship. For someone who left the priesthood after only two years in ministry, I ended up doing a great deal of preaching, largely in Protestant churches and seminary chapels. I did not enjoy preaching as much as I enjoyed teaching. Indeed, I became quite neurotic about preaching.

In teaching, I felt free to point at the text from the side and interpret its meaning. In preaching, I felt under the judgment of the Word, which called me into account—not the meaning of the text so much as the meaning of my life was in question.[6] This awareness demanded of me a kind of integrity and transparency that teaching did not (at least not to the same degree). Because all my preaching was "celebrity preaching," moreover—that is, I was preaching to people I did not know, and who had elevated expectations of the visiting sage—my desire to be transparent to the text and simple conflicted with the need, driven by my public shyness, to prepare a written text, and once writing, to try to write beautifully. The tension between the desire to be simple and the desire to impress was a constant one. As I say, neurotic.

Lectures to colleges and seminaries were less fraught, but no less demanding in terms of time and effort. The romance of being a wandering minstrel quickly passes, after one has waited in hundreds of airports, white-knuckled difficult flights, endured jolting taxi rides, and survived dinners with faculty members (at which one is the entertainment), lectures followed by receptions, discussions with students, classroom presentations, and, worst of all, nights spent in lonely hotel rooms, far from home. I was willing to pound this soul-searing beat for two reasons. One was financial. The costs of travel and lodging were always covered by the host schools, who would add a small honorarium. Unless one is a Desmond Tutu, Colin Powell, or Hillary Clinton, however, the actual financial gain is minimal, if the stipend is prorated according to the hours spent in preparation, travel, and schmoozing, apart from the actual lecture.

The second reason for staying on the circuit was my appreciation that this kind of face-to-face teaching, like seeds strewn in a field, might possibly bear some fruit in the lives of those taught. As with the videos shot for the Teaching Company, such presentations extended my scholarship to thousands of people who would never attend the Candler School of Theology.[7]

Every public contact naturally created widening circles of further contact. I struggled to keep up with the volume of correspondence that my books, articles, and public presentations generated. In the field of New Testament and Christian origins, scholarship—especially when it is made accessible—stimulates the sort of intense response from the scholarly and nonscholarly public that is seldom roused by scholarship in other areas. Leave aside physics or microbiology, where an entire productive scholarly career can pass without stirring a ripple of general interest. Even in other areas of religious studies, scholarly work does not usually command attention outside the guild of historians, theologians, or ethicists. But the beginnings of Christianity are of intense interest to churchgoing Christians, to those who have rejected their Christian heritage, and to those who have lately converted to Christianity. In addition to the letters exchanged with other scholars and editors, and the perennial letters of recommendation, then, I responded to hundreds of letters each year written to me by ordinary people agitated by what I had written or said.

FOCUSED RESEARCH

Among the "jobs of work" expected of a senior scholar is writing entries for a variety of scholarly encyclopedias, anthologies, and collections. I wrote seventeen of these during this time, on topics ranging from sexuality and marriage in Christianity, through the role of law in early Christianity, to sacraments and sacramentality in the Letter to the Hebrews. Such essays, especially when they are lengthy, consume time and energy, but they also extend one's scholarship in unexpected ways. Best of all, the limitations of length force the sort of crisp treatment of which I am most fond.

During this extended period at Emory, I did substantial scholarly work in three main areas: the New Testament itself, Christian theology, and the historical study of ancient religions. I will briefly sketch what I tried to accomplish in each.

New Testament. The research I had begun already at Yale in the three letters of Paul to his delegates (the so-called Pastoral Epistles) was completed with my second entry in the Anchor Bible commentary series, *The First and Second Letter to Timothy.*[8] I did not treat the letter to Titus explicitly, because a volume on that short letter had appeared already in the Anchor Bible series, written by Jerome Quinn, whose untimely death prevented his working through all three letters. With the majority of scholars, Quinn regarded them as pseudonymous but made the innovative suggestion that Luke wrote them as the third volume of Luke-Acts.[9]

My approach was entirely different, arguing for the authenticity of all three letters, first, by challenging the conventional criteria for determining authenticity, second, by proposing a new model for understanding Pauline authorship—he "authorized but did not necessarily write" all thirteen letters ascribed to him during his ministry—and third, by showing that not the passage of time but the rhetorical purpose of each delegate letter best accounts for their distinctiveness within the Pauline corpus. As in my James volume, I provided a complete history of interpretation—more extensive even than that concerning James—from the patristic period to the present. Of particular importance was my demonstrating how the "consensus" view of scholarship was based not on the power of argument but on the weight of custom. My employment of the "sociology of knowledge" with respect to academic convention was never more pertinent.

Speaking of James, I was also able to complete the long years of research I had devoted to that letter when Eerdmans published in 2004 *Brother of Jesus, Friend of God: Studies in the Letter of James.* The essays collected in this volume served to amplify and supplement points made in my commentary on James. Thus, I included three essays on the history of interpretation of James in the patristic period that contained all the primary source evidence for which the commentary had no room. I added to the collection new essays on the place of James in earliest Christianity and the use of James in contemporary theology. Between the commentary and this collection of scholarly essays, I thought I had done what I could to make other scholars aware of the importance of this composition, and of the need to reconsider some of the conventional approaches to it.

More forward looking were my published studies of Paul. I wanted to complete my scholarly career with a major work on the New Testament author who had always been most dear to me. My extensive work on the Pastoral Letters was part of this agenda, as were the number of dissertations I directed on Paul's major letters. I noted above that my "Paul and Jesus" course fit this growing commitment. But I wanted most of all to lay the groundwork for a more substantial study with a series of scholarly articles. During this period, then, I published four new essays on Paul's letters to the Romans and Corinthians.[10] At the same time, I contributed an essay for a volume entitled *Four Views on the Apostle Paul*, edited by Michael Bird, with my "Catholic" essay appearing alongside one from an evangelical perspective, one from a Jewish perspective, and one from (I guess) a "post-new-perspective" perspective.[11] The exercise enabled me to sketch in brief the framework that I would use in the larger work that I had planned.

My study in the New Testament, then, was on one hand summative (James and 1 and 2 Timothy) and, on the other hand, proleptic (Paul). The apparent outlier to this neat schema was the major commentary I wrote for the New Testament Library series on the Letter to the Hebrews (2006). I say "apparent outlier" because, although I had not previously written extensively on Hebrews, this mysterious early Christian composition had intrigued me since I first read Ceslas Spicq's great two-volume commentary in French when I was a nineteen-year-old novice in the monastery.[12] My interest had been piqued even more by the course on Hebrews I took with Barnabas Ahern at Saint Meinrad School of Theology. And, like all monks of my generation, my sensibility was significantly shaped by this powerful composition that conceived of Christian existence as a pilgrimage to God, a journey whose "pioneer and perfecter" was the crucified and exalted Messiah, Jesus.[13] I took on the commentary as a "job of work" because the editor, Clift Black of Princeton Theological Seminary, asked me to, but as so often happens with me, it quickly became a "work of love." During a particularly rough patch in Joy's illness, the ability to sink myself—even if only for snatched moments—in the Greek text of Hebrews, with its astonishing vision of human existence as one transformed through suffering, provided me a kind of healing. In this case, "having the mind in another place" was therapeutic in a season of crisis.

Finally, my concern for proper methodology—going all the way back to my essay "The Lukan Community" and above all in the debate about the "real Jesus"—found expression in the book I cowrote with my Yale classmate William Kurz (we divided the book between us), called *The Future of Catholic Biblical Scholarship: A Constructive Conversation* (2002). Beginning with a version of the controversial lecture I had given at the Seattle Catholic Biblical Association meeting and ending with my essay "Imagining the World That Scripture Imagines," I argued that Catholic biblical scholarship, to be true to its nature, ought to embrace rather than reject so-called premodern biblical interpretation. In fact, I argued that for Catholic scholars, moving forward should mean an engagement of "postmodern" scholarship with "premodern," because those two modes have far more in common than either of them has with the historical-critical scholarship of "modernity." To illustrate, I wrote a chapter that contrasted the premises undergirding premodern and modern interpretation, and then a chapter each on the biblical interpretation of Origen and Augustine. As in my commentaries on James, the Pastorals, and Hebrews showed, such in-depth engagement with patristic and medieval interpretation was eminently worthwhile, providing support from the past for a positive view of the future.[14]

Scripture and Theology. A discernible theme running through my work, from *The Writings of the New Testament* on, has been the discernment of God's presence and power in creation. In that introduction to the New Testament, you may recall, I placed a strong emphasis on the experience of that presence and power among the first believers through the exaltation of Jesus as Lord. As I have mentioned before, my stress on the personal experience of God undoubtedly owes a great deal to my participation in the Catholic charismatic movement between 1970 and 1973, when I saw firsthand how the Holy Spirit could transform lives. Even more is owed, I am sure, to my own experience of "God's love poured into [my] heart" through the gift of Joy's love, which truly was a singular experience of grace that both upset all my previous false certainties and grounded me in what is truly certain, namely, God's presence.

I have also already recounted the way in which other experiences led me to write *Scripture and Discernment: Decision Making in the Church*. In that book, I laid out the framework for what I came to call an "ecclesial hermeneutics." Strikingly, virtually all theories of interpretation concerning Scripture, from Origen to Bultmann, have been based on the premise that Scripture is directed to the individual person. But in fact, Scripture is addressed to communities. The task, then, as I saw it, was to find a way that the church, reading *as* church, can interpret *for* the church. How can the church discern God's Word not only in the pages of Scripture but also in the living texts of human lives? The *Writings of the New Testament* sought to make the New Testament transparent not only to the experience of the first believers but also to the experience of readers today. Two other books, *Faith's Freedom* and *Sharing Possessions*, served to provide close phenomenological readings of actual human experience in the world. In a very nonsystematic way, then, I was clearly pursuing a systematic project.

The stimulus for a work to complete this project was an invitation to an interdisciplinary symposium on the phenomenology of the body at Duquesne University in March 2002. There, I engaged in dialogue with a psychoanalyst from England, a philosopher from Australia, and an MD/philosopher from the USA, Drew Leder, whose work had earlier impressed me.[15] My paper was called "The Revelatory Body: Notes toward a Somatic Theology," which was subsequently published in a book called *The Phenomenology of the Body*, edited by D. J. Martino (2003). In my paper, I argued that Scripture never refers to itself as revelatory but constantly points to the human body as the privileged medium of God's revelation in the world. In creation, covenant, prophecy, incarnation, and church, Scripture portrays the human body as the means of God's self-disclosure.

Building on this essay, I wrote *The Revelatory Body: Theology as Inductive Art* (2015). My thesis was that if spirit discloses itself in bodily activity, then the continuous self-revelation of God must be grasped inductively as a form of art, rather than deductively as a form of science. The suggestion, to be sure, completely reverses the manner in which theology has always been conceived. To illustrate how close attention to actual bodily conditions can be "revelatory," I then did a phenomenological analysis of the body in pain, the body at play, the body at work, the passionate body, the exceptional body, and the aging body. I am not sanguine about the possibility that my contribution will effect the Copernican revolution in theology I propose. We write, however, not in anticipation of success but in witness to the truth as we perceive it. Who knows whether some future theologian might stumble on this discarded book and find there the courage to forge his or her own vision?

Earlier in the decade (2003), Random House published *The Creed: What Christians Believe and Why It Matters*. As I mentioned earlier, this was a book that arose out of adult study classes in my Bloomington and Atlanta parishes. I began thinking and speaking about the creed—mainly the Nicene-Constantinopolitan version recited by all Catholic and many Protestant churches each Sunday—because I became increasingly aware, not least in the midst of the historical Jesus controversy, just how fragile was the hold many Christians had on their (supposedly) core convictions, as evident from their willingness to trade the Christ of the creed for the ersatz Jesus of historical questers. I sought to provide believers with a sense of identity-formative boundaries set by the creed, and then also, to see how the proposals of the creed entailed certain distinct ways of acting in the world. Thus the "why it matters" part of the title. Fully aware that creeds in general are the *bêtes noires* of modernity, I prepared for the composition of this book by finally, at the age of fifty-eight, reading great chunks of Nietzsche, the supreme voice of contempt for those adhering to traditional dogma.[16] I also kept in mind my atheist brother Pat, who similarly represented the scorn of evolutionary psychology toward conventional beliefs.

My goal in the book was to trace the origins and functions of the creed, and then provide an interpretation of each of its statements, using them as a point of entrance into Scripture. The conversation between creed and Scripture is intriguing particularly because of the inherent connection between them, and because of the way many Christians (especially in the free-church tradition) unthinkingly jettison the creed—which they tend to view as a form of tyranny—in favor of Scripture.

Readers of *The Creed* have praised its prose, and the book has found its way into a fair number of theology classrooms. I must confess, though, that the lucidity of style in this book is almost entirely due to an anonymous but brilliant copyeditor at Random House, who cut out huge globs of fatty prose and put my best sentences in a more convincing sequence. By this point in my scholarly life, I was only too aware of my own stylistic infelicities and was ready to welcome such kindly help.

Religion. My interest in religious studies, as distinct from theology, had remained consistent since my time at Indiana University. I saw no difficulty in taking off the hat of a theologian, bound by a certain set of premises and epistemological constraints, and putting on the hat of the student of religion, operating with other premises and epistemological constraints. Whereas theology is necessarily prescriptive, religious phenomenology seeks to be purely descriptive; whereas theology concerns itself with the integrity of Christian confession and practice, the study of religion concerns itself with how humans of the most widely varying beliefs and practices actually behave. In my Phi Beta Kappa lectures on *paideia* and *thrēskeia*, I had begun to apply the religious studies paradigm to ancient Greek and Roman religion and nascent Christianity. In the Stone Lectures of 1997 that became *Religious Experience in Earliest Christianity* (1998), I probed more deeply into the question of how Greco-Roman religious experience mapped onto the religious experience of the earliest Christians in initiations, ecstatic utterance, and ritual meals.

It was only upon completing the theological book on the creed, however, that the penny dropped, and I was able to perceive the categories that would enable me to forge a completely new way of analyzing the nexus between Greco-Roman religion and Christianity. I realized from working with the creed that my insistence that ideas shape practice for good or ill identified me as a certain kind of religious person. A "type," if you will, distinct from other "types" of believers. For all my attention to "experience," I realized, my own way of being religious was philosophical. I recognized the validity and importance of experience ("signs and wonders") in the empirical world, but my interest was much more in the transformation of the character and actions of persons. I began to grasp, with William James, that persons are different religiously—in what matters to them, in how they perceive reality—as much because of temperament as anything else.

Working with a neutral definition of religion, then, as "a way of life organized around certain experiences and convictions concerning ultimate power," I began to look at Greco-Roman religious behavior with new eyes.

I found that, as in every age and place, there were some people who were simply not religious, whether out of habit (simple profanity) or out of conviction (as with the Epicureans). Among those who were religious, however, there were distinct differences between "Religiousness A," those who regarded the divine power as immanently available through signs, portents, wonders, healings, and the external trappings of polytheism, and "Religiousness B," those who, while not in the least denying such realities, were not nearly so interested in them as they were in the power of the divine to transform lives from vice to virtue.

The supreme example of Religiousness A is the second-century rhetorician, Aelius Aristides, who spent his adulthood in pilgrimage from one healing shrine dedicated to Asclepius to another. He was far from being an uneducated simpleton; he was, indeed, among the most highly educated and sophisticated men of his time. But religious ideas mattered to him not at all; experience was the thing. The best example of Religiousness B is the first-century philosopher Epictetus, who fused his Stoicism with deep religious conviction, seeing the divine *dynamis* at work within the moral struggle of humans; he did not deny but rather affirmed all the external forms of Religiousness A, but that is not where his interest lay.

As I surveyed all the religious literature from the Greco-Roman world, however, I discovered two further ways of being religious. What I called "Religiousness C" was exemplified in those who saw the world as absent of any divine presence in the empirical realm and sought instead to free the soul from the body through asceticism; this is the Orphic strand in Greek religion, extending from Pythagoras to the *Poimandres*. Finally, I labeled "Religiousness D" the sort of "priestcraft as statecraft" found in people who supplied and ran the cults, and who thought of religion in terms of its stabilizing of the world/empire. Plutarch is the best example, as in his work *On Superstition*.

Having located four distinct ways of being religious in Greco-Roman culture—already an innovative approach—I applied the categories to first-century Judaism and found the same distinctions. The New Testament, which witnesses to nascent Christianity, shows the presence of only two types, Religiousness A (God is at work in human experience) and Religiousness B (God is at work in human moral transformation). But in the second and third century, the third way of being religious emerges in Gnosticism—flight from the empirical world—and eventually the fourth type emerges with the boundary marking and authority of bishops. By the time of Constantine, Christianity displayed all four ways of being religious that were present in Greco-Roman culture: many Christians sought relics and made pilgrimages; others became monks and sought moral transformation; others sought release through mysticism; and still others monitored the boundaries of orthodoxy and administered the ecclesiastical institution. Christianity in its mature form resembled paganism because it displayed the same range of religious temperaments as paganism, and continued to display it well through the fourth century CE.

The book *Among the Gentiles: Greco-Roman Religion and Christianity* was published by Yale University Press in 2009. It won the Grawemeyer Award in Religion in 2011. I was, naturally, pleased by the award with its stipend, but I was even more pleased at completing a task in which theory and evidence so perfectly coincided, and whose theory could be applied to other social phenomena.[17]

Retirement from Emory

The lack of a mandatory retirement age for professors has complicated life both for them and for the institutions they serve. For colleges, universities, and seminaries, planning for replacements depends on the whim of aging teachers. For the scholarly guild as a whole, delayed retirement means fewer available positions for new PhDs. For the professors themselves, multiple considerations come into play as they consider whether or when to depart from a school in which many of them have spent a not insignificant portion of their lives.

As I completed my work on Candler's centennial celebration, I knew that this would be my last hurrah, so I announced my retirement for the spring of 2016. I was seventy-two, and I had been at Emory for twenty-three years. Since I was a Woodruff professor, and not part of the basic faculty in New Testament, my staying or leaving would neither close nor open any slot for another. The decision to leave could be, and was, based entirely on personal factors. The first I have already mentioned, namely, that Joy's condition demanded ever greater amounts of my time and attention. The second is that I felt my physical strength diminishing. Until I was sixty-five,

I had been able to leap from a standstill onto the top of a table—much to the shock and delight of students. Now, I found it increasingly difficult to maintain the standards of grading that I had set for myself: my fingers would only with great reluctance do my bidding. Worse, I began to develop serious skeletal problems. In my last semester, while teaching a doctoral seminar, I had both a laminectomy and a hip replacement. At my retirement dinner, I hobbled to the podium with a walker. The third reason was the changing character of Candler. More and more of the faculty whom I had admired and with whom I had worked had either died or retired. The new faculty were, well, new, and some of their ideas and practices did not appeal. I found myself surrounded by strangers. I once coined the phrase "the world leaves us before we leave the world," and it certainly applies to aging academics.

Most of my office library I packed in boxes, and I delivered the books in a U-Haul to the library of Saint Joseph's Abbey, where I had spent my younger years, and for which I have never lost my affection—my leaving the religious life was not because of my fellow monks or the Rule of Benedict, it was because of my own choice of a more worldly life. The rest of that collection I merged with the books in my study at home. Once the books were removed, I was ready to move as well.

Chapter Nine

SCHOLARSHIP IN ACADEMIC RETIREMENT

I WAS NATURALLY CURIOUS TO SEE HOW RETIREMENT WOULD affect me as a scholar. Was all that work simply a matter of doing my job? Was it a role quickly to be shed so that I could go fishing or take up needle-point? Or did my scholarship stem from some deep reservoir of energy and ambition that would persist even though I was now an emeritus professor, and was now free, in theory, to do what I wanted?

As at every stage of my life—anyone's life, to be sure—the circum-stances of the life cycle make themselves quickly felt. The back troubles that surfaced in my last year of teaching grew worse, and I had a succession of skeletal surgeries (five in the next four years) to repair the mortal coil. The coronavirus pandemic hit in 2020, eliminating access to libraries, canceling invitations to lecture, and curtailing all normal human interactions. Most of all, Joy's death in December of 2017 forced me to face life without my dear companion of forty-seven years—grief over Joy's departure has not eased even after three years—and I am still struggling with how to live alone and how to cultivate the virtue of desire.

Despite these dramatically changed circumstances, I found that the hab-its of scholarship did not cease when my life as an academic ended. Strictly speaking, in fact, even my academic life did not completely end with retire-ment. I still was the director of five dissertations, so the pleasure of meeting with and helping these fine doctoral students only ended in 2019. Before the pandemic, moreover, I continued to give lectures at universities, confer-ences, and churches. Perhaps the most personally satisfying of these were the three lectures I was invited to give to the Benedictine Monks and Priors of North America in February of 2020, entitled "The Rule of Benedict and the Practices of Ancient Moralists: Monasticism in a Postmodern World," subsequently published in the *American Benedictine Review* (2020). In the end, it turns out, was my beginning: speaking to monks out of my long engagement with ancient philosophers and having the talks published by the same journal that published one of my first scholarly articles! Another example of coming full circle: in 2017, I presented "How a Monk Learns Mercy" at the International Thomas Merton Society conference.[1]

WRITING CONTINUES

In August of 2017, I also delivered a plenary address to the Catholic Biblical Association meeting in Washington, DC, entitled "Engaging Modernity: The Interpretation of Miracles, Then and Now," a paper that was subsequently published by *Commonweal* magazine.[2] The topic of miracles was much on my mind at that time, for a "job of work" that I carried with me into retirement was a volume on miracles for the series from Westminster John Knox Press called Interpretation: Resources for the Use of Scripture in the Church. Somehow, I had been inveigled into writing a book that I had never even remotely contemplating writing. "Miracles" were not part of my normal discourse about the life of faith; like many educated folks, in fact, I felt chronically uneasy when language about signs and wonders flourished around me. I had been caught in a weak moment.

As often happened during my life as a scholar, however, this job of work quickly became a "work of love," as I began to see not only the centrality of the issue of God's presence and power in creation but also the way in which the very idea of such presence and power challenged the epistemological premises of modernity.

The first part of *Miracles: The Presence and Power of God in Creation* (2017) dealt with the contrasting epistemologies of secularity and faith. I sought to show the severe limits of modernity in understanding reality even on its own terms, and I proposed the four dimensions of a faith perspective within which language about God's presence and power in the world makes sense. The first dimension is to imagine the world that Scripture imagines, taking "imagination" here not as a descriptor of fantasy but as a cognitive construal. Just as one must "imagine" education in order to perceive the role of lectures, study, exams, and degrees, or one must "imagine" democracy before elections, campaigning, voting, and the relinquishment of power make sense, so one must, with Scripture, "imagine" the world as one constantly open to the mystery of God in order to perceive God's presence in any aspect of empirical existence. The second dimension is a robust theology of creation, which understands God not as the unmoved mover standing behind the chain of worldly events but as the unseen power that sustains the entire chain in existence; creation concerns not the "how" of things coming into being but the "that" of human coming into being at every moment.

The third dimension is the privileging of human witness and narrative over universal laws and statistics: not every account by humans is true and not all of them are exceptional, but our age in particular has learned to recognize and honor the accounts of personal experience that escape the tyranny of the "objective" laid down by statistic and law. The final dimension is recovering and treasuring the language of myth, for if myth is the register of human language that enables people to speak of the mysteries that go beyond the quotidian and predictable, then miracles and myth go together—not as a reversal toward superstition and lack of reason but as an elevation to a higher plane.

Having made this argument, I took up the witness of Scripture in all its parts concerning God's presence and power in creation, showing that for Scripture, creation itself is a "miracle," as is the giving of the law, as is the incarnation and resurrection of Jesus Christ. The real issue with the subject of miracles is not whether Jesus walked on the water or multiplied loaves; it is whether God's presence and power in creation exist at all, for if not, then the entire Christian creed must, in the name of intellectual integrity, be jettisoned. In this regard, the "new atheists" like the late the late Christopher Hitchens must be acknowledged as having grasped the essential point better than some apologists.

Finishing *Miracles*, I was finally able to take on the project that I hoped to be the climax of my scholarly life devoted to the New Testament. I have already noted how, in the last decade at Emory, I had begun to increase my teaching and writing on the most controversial figure in earliest Christianity, the apostle Paul. I had during those years proposed a two-volume work on Paul to Eerdmans Publishers. They had waited patiently for it.

I normally hit the deadlines agreed to by publishers and myself, but in this case, circumstances of life and adventitious pop-ups like the miracles book delayed my progress. But finally, over the period of Joy's last illness and death, I was able to do the work.

I envisaged a two-volume work called *Canonical Paul*, the overall argument of which was that the entire correspondence ascribed to Paul by the New Testament ought to be the appropriate basis of scholarly inquiry and Christian instruction, rather than a diminished "Paul" based on dubious historical methods.[3] In a very real way, my defense of appropriate historiography over against distorted methods of historiography resembles the one I had made concerning the Gospels in *The Real Jesus*. The first volume provides a series of historical and literary studies concerning every topic necessary to reading the Pauline corpus: the sources for the knowledge of Paul; the shape of his ministry and correspondence—here the issue of "authentic" and "inauthentic" is thoroughly argued; what kind of Jew he was; Paul and the uses of Scripture; Paul and Greco-Roman culture; Paul and religious experience; Paul's convictions, symbols, metaphors, and myths; finally, I provide a reading of Paul's shortest letter, to Philemon, placing it in the canonical context of Ephesians and Colossians, in order to show how the composition makes more sense when read "canonically" than in isolation. Throughout these disparate studies, I tried to show that when evidence is drawn from all the canonical letters, a more satisfying portrait emerges of Paul's mission, correspondence, and convictions.

The second volume contains—in addition to an introduction and epilogue, which make the point that Paul's letters canonical should be read not to construct a singular "Pauline theology" but as a set of stimuli for thinking theologically—some twenty-six separate essays engaging one dimension or another of all the letters except Philemon (which was treated in volume 1). The essays range widely, from the topic of "the faith of Jesus" in Romans to "the pedagogy of grace" in Titus, with attention given not only to Paul's "thinking" but also to his pastoral practice. In several of the essays, the pertinence of Paul's rhetoric or argument to present-day circumstances is noted, as with the theme of truth and reconciliation in 2 Corinthians, or the movement from *eros* to *agapē* in Ephesians.

Concerning the eschewal of a Pauline theology, I make the comparison to the conventional understanding of the Greek philosopher Plato. Undergraduates in philosophy courses regularly are instructed in what is called "Platonism." This is a systematic arrangement of "Plato's thought" according to certain set topics: cosmology, ontology, epistemology, and the like. Yet if students are fortunate enough to read Plato's actual *Dialogues*, they have a difficult time finding the "Platonism" they had been taught. They come to realize that this abstraction had been drawn from a handful of passages in a handful of dialogues, but it never appears in the fashion proposed by philosophical textbooks.

In contrast, students reading the dialogues discover a wide-ranging and engrossing conversation on a world of subjects, and if they follow the actual line of these conversations, they discover themselves thinking in new ways about those subjects. This, I suggest, is analogous to the situation with Paul. The many "theologies" of Paul are but abstractions drawn from a handful of letters that fail to convey the richness of Paul's language, imagery, and thought. Far better is to engage Paul's letters in all their diversity and to learn how to think differently through such direct engagement.

It is not yet clear what large project might next catch my attention, or even whether my diminished physical capacities will make serious and sustained scholarship possible. As in so many matters, in old age, uncertainty is the new norm. As of this writing, I have a collection of my "public theology" lectures and essays in press with one publisher, while another publisher is interested in a collection of my sermons. But these are the leavings of earlier efforts. It remains to be seen whether my preparations for the McDonald Chair lectures—scheduled for fall 2021—will stimulate a new line of inquiry. The title of my lectures is "Imitation of Christ: Competing Visions of Discipleship." I hope to trace the ways in which Christians shifted from regarding their imitation of Christ as a matter of personal transformation to regarding it as a matter of social transformation. It is certainly a worthy and fascinating topic, but it is too early to know whether it will invite or excite my waning energies.

Reflections on My Life as a Scholar

Retirement and freedom from the "tyranny of the immediate" have meant more time to reflect at leisure on my life as a scholar. Before turning in the next part of this book to the qualities of good scholarship, then, I offer some summary observations abstracted from my incident-filled narrative.

I first consider myself singularly blessed by factors that had little or nothing to do with my own talents or efforts. My birth family, especially my mother, gave me a sense of the beauty, humor, and sanctity of life, encouraging and modeling a passion for wide reading and good conversation. My years in religious life provided a context in which depth of learning could be combined with piety. How gratuitous was the grace of being nurtured within a monastic tradition for which art, music, and literature were celebrated as expressions of, rather than opposed to, theological inquiry. How extraordinary were the gifts of time, silence, and prayer to the shaping of a young scholar's mind and heart. The significance of such early and totally unmerited gifts can hardly be exaggerated. I became more aware of their significance when I was able to compare the background with which I was blessed to that of many colleagues who had not been so gifted.

It was not by accident that I dedicated so many of my books to Joy. Her entry into my life was on the face of it cataclysmic but in hindsight can be seen as the most outstanding grace God gave me, for she broke through all the sterile obsessions and compulsions that had formerly bound me, and through her quiet insistence on truth, liberated me for a more difficult but also far richer life than the one that I had lived as a monk. Our life together was a true partnership. I cared for and supported her, true, but she was my lodestar, my muse, and—at a very practical level—my ideal reader. Until the very last years of her life, she heard me read everything I wrote and offered me both encouragement and caution. She insisted always that I be true to my own vision. She had a perfect ear for cant and nonsense. She made me want to be the best teacher and writer I could be.

Being able to study and to teach at schools such as Saint Meinrad, Yale, Indiana, and Emory also represents a kind of charmed journey not given to everyone aspiring to a life of scholarship. At Saint Meinrad, as I have noted, the stimulus of fine teaching was combined with rigorous demands, a splendid research library, and congenial and challenging colleagues— all this, again, within the context of Benedictine monastic life that made God's glory rather than human reputation the real goal of scholarship. At Yale, I studied and later taught with some of the most outstanding New Testament scholars of my generation: in the presence of a Wayne Meeks, a Nils Dahl, or an Abraham Malherbe, one did not dare be careless or sloppy; the standards were extremely high and were expected to be met.

Meeting and working with Carl Holladay similarly gave me a standard of intelligence and integrity that I constantly tried to match. My position at Emory, finally, while demanding much of me, also gave me much: financial security, professional status, scholarly resources, superb doctoral students, fine colleagues. Remembering these things, I call to mind the question Paul put to the Corinthians, "What do you have that you have not received?" (1 Cor. 4:7). With Paul, I prefer to see all that I have been given as the result not of random chance but of divine providence.

If a single term could be used to characterize my life as a scholar, I think it would be "energy." When I look back over my life, I am astounded at how I could do so many things with such a level of commitment. To be honest, I grow a bit weary even remembering the effort expended in service, teaching, and research—leave aside care for faith and family. To some extent, I am convinced that my energy was fueled by simple fear: for a great portion of my career, Joy's health and our finances (in combination) drove me to sometimes frenetic activity on every front. More positively, the energy I expended in teaching and research (in particular) was summoned by love for students and their learning, and by love for the subjects I was privileged to study. Imagine the excitement of being able to work, every day, in texts that are at once fundamentally formative of our shared history and, all during that history, contested! Scholarship in my area, I understood, mattered in a deeply existential way. Such love makes intelligible the final stimulus to my energy, which was anger. Healthy anger is a response to love threatened. Precisely because of my love for the tradition in which I was raised and which I still affirmed, my love for students and their proper formation, and my love for the proper apprehension of Christianity's founding compositions, anger drove me to defend the things I loved.

In a blurb for *Among the Gentiles*, Wayne Meeks referred to me as a "contrarian of the most constructive sort." Certainly, the contrarian element in my work is obvious even to the casual observer.[4] I never thought of my contrarian stance as a matter of temperament, still less as a hostile reflex toward any and all innovation, but as a matter of seeing error—error in my judgment, to be sure—and seeking to correct it. The number of such "correcting" projects is extensive.

In my New Testament Introduction, for example, I rejected the standard historical narrative in favor of a hermeneutical model, in which profound religious experience generated the reinterpretation of a symbolic world. With regard to the Gospels, I likewise challenged the adequacy of historical methods that, on one side, dismembered the narratives in the search for sources or for opponents and, on the other side, dissected the narratives in the search for a more usable Jesus. Instead, I argued for a reading of the Gospels as unitary compositions, taking equally seriously their rhetorical shape and their religious purposes. Putting these two corrections together, I consistently argued that the experience causing the writing of the New Testament and the experience creating believers in every age are the same: the experience of the risen and exalted Lord, Jesus Christ. The "real Jesus" is not one recoverable by scholarly methods but one accessible to the eyes of faith.

In my study of Paul, I fought against the conventional scholarly position (conventional for over 150 years) that Paul wrote only seven of the letters ascribed to him and argued for regarding the complete "canonical Paul" as having been written under his authorization during his ministry. Just as vigorously, I resisted efforts to construct a "theology of Paul" from this reduced selection of compositions, arguing that the diversity among all the letters, not only in diction and rhetorical argument but also in substance, makes such an effort at best misguided and at worst an exercise in scholarly *mauvaise foi*.

Similarly, I worked hard to turn around the lazy scholarly consensus regarding the Letter of James (exemplified by the commentary of Martin Dibelius) that located its composition late, its outlook anti-Pauline, and its literary structure absent. Against this construal—again, held by most scholars who had never actually worked in the letter—I showed the plausibility of its early dating (possibly our earliest extant Christian writing), its complete independence of any Pauline influence, and its coherent rhetoric.

More mildly "contrarian" was my argument in *Among the Gentiles* that the centuries of polemic and apologetics concerning the relationship between Christianity and Greco-Roman religion on the basis of "influence" or "causality" needed to be replaced by a more neutral sort of analysis made available by religious studies (rather than theology), which could show both the diversity of ways of being religious among Gentiles and Jews and the manner in which Christians shared progressively in all these same ways of being religious.

In my book on miracles, I directly and without equivocation combatted the epistemological framework of modernity that shapes secular culture and enables "new atheists" to dismiss belief in the presence and power of God in creation as superstitious claptrap that must be abandoned for humans ever to be liberated from the shackles of dogma. In agreement with Augustine, I concluded that the central factor in speaking about the miraculous is in fact epistemological, that is, the overall construal of reality that governs particular judgments concerning facts and events, and that the major problem facing Christians in today's world is that they are themselves double-minded, with one part of their minds in the symbolic world of Scripture and an even greater part of their minds in the world constructed on the basis of measurement and calculation.

My life as a contrarian in all these contested issues in the New Testament and the history of Christian origins, however, was matched by a "constructive" side to my work.[5] Much of this more constructive side appeared in the articles I wrote for magazines such as *Commonweal, Christian Century*, and *Priests and People*. These essays characteristically took up some aspect of Christian theology or discipleship in the light of Scripture and contemporary experience, in the hope of providing an interpretation that was faithful both to experience and Scripture. Two books that had a similar constructive character were *The Future of Catholic Biblical Scholarship: A Constructive Conversation* (cowritten with William Kurz) and *The Creed: What Christians Believe and Why It Matters*. In the first case, Bill and I tried to show how Scripture can be studied, not over against tradition, but in concert with tradition, without such study losing its critical edge. In the second case, I tried to demonstrate how Scripture and the Nicene Creed work together to form the symbolic world inhabited by believers.

The most obvious constructive project that occupied my mind throughout most of my scholarly life was to find a grounding in Scripture for, and then to theologically shape, a properly ecclesial hermeneutics that was based solidly in the actual practice of believing communities. As I noted in my narrative, the impetus to this project arose from the convergence of a number of questions: Why, in a conciliar age, did the Catholic Church make no use of the Jerusalem Council (in Acts 15) in its theological reflection? Did the neglect of the Acts narrative correspond to the neglect of the theological valence given to narratives of faith *within* Acts 10–15? How could

I and my young monastic colleagues be so right about the reforms after Vatican II and yet proceed to impose those reforms in such an unrighteous manner? How could my own experience of failure as a monk yet new life with Joy be understood in the light of Scripture? How could the revelatory force of student journals that disclosed disapproved sexual identity within lives of deep faithfulness be reconciled with the explicit condemnation by Scripture of the forms of sexual desire that were ingredient to their identity? The key work for teasing out these questions was *Scripture and Discernment: Decision Making in the Church,* but other books (*Writings of the New Testament; Faith's Freedom; Sharing Possessions; The Revelatory Body*) also filled in important pieces of this nonsystematic systematic project. If I have failed to have any effect on the understanding and practice of the church, I have the satisfaction of establishing markers that some future theologian might notice and employ to better effect. Witness, after all, is not measured by success, but by fidelity.

That is, in the end, probably a good way to sum up how I now view my many years of scholarship. All the effort that I put into changing academic institutions was not wasted—it was a necessary and useful aspect of academic citizenship—but no changes (even if they are improvements) have a significant shelf life. Many of the things for which I struggled are now forgotten. Institutions use our energy and enthusiasm heedlessly, and, when we are spent, they use the energy and enthusiasm of the next generation. Nothing tragic to this. I was glad to pay that price to do the work of teaching and research.

But neither did my passionate classes, public presentations, videos, sermons, and conference participations—with easily tens of thousands of auditors—have any real or lasting effect on the world, except perhaps in a glancing way on a few people. This does not dismay me. Sowing seeds by scattering them in every direction means much waste, and yes, the sower seldom actually sees whether any of the sown seed yields a crop. But I would not trade the hours I spent in preparing and presenting all this array of words for any other task I might have been assigned. As I gladly learned, so gladly did I teach.

As for properly scholarly writing and publication, I am acutely aware how few minds I have changed or improved. I know, in fact, that some of my views are regarded by many other scholars as wrongheaded or eccentric.

But I am also aware that I never stinted in the effort to make a difference in how important issues are understood. I know that I have employed the gifts God has given me—a modest intelligence, a wealth of energy, a passion for truth and beauty—as fully as time and circumstances have allowed. I have never wasted time, and I have never allowed circumstances to be an excuse for less than full effort. I have pursued truth as I have seen it. With that realization, I must be content.

PART THREE

A Scholar's Virtues

Chapter Ten

INTELLECTUAL VIRTUES

*T*HE TERM "VIRTUE" TRANSLATES THE GREEK NOUN *ARETĒ*, by way of the Latin *Virtus*. I am using it as much as possible in the way ancient Greeks used it, to refer to "excellence" in any arena of human activity, be it war, poetry, politics, athletics, philosophy, or morality. The greatest theorist of *aretē* in antiquity was Aristotle, above all in his *Nicomachean Ethics* (see especially books 1–4), who carefully analyzed both intellectual and moral forms of excellence. For Aristotle, *aretē* was a quality of character (or disposition) that was, on one hand, inherent in some people, and, on the other hand, capable of being developed. Such development came about through repeated practice, or habit, which, when steadily cultivated, became a *habitus* (or dominant trait) that helped form the character of a person: habit (*ethos*) led to character (*ēthos*).

When I speak here and in the next chapter of the scholar's virtues, then, I have in mind those dispositions and practices that express and lead to excellence in scholarship.[1] I ask the reader to remember that I am speaking of scholarship of a very special sort. I am thinking of scholarship in the humanities rather than in the sciences—although many of the qualities I name translate into that area of endeavor as well. I speak out of my experience as a scholar in the ancient Mediterranean world, with a specific interest in the interactions of Greco-Roman, Jewish, and nascent Christian cultures.

The reader should also be assured that I do not pretend to have displayed all these forms of excellence in my own teaching and writing. I have fallen short in many ways and on many occasions from the ideals I sketch here. But I can declare honestly that these are the standards by which I measured myself as a scholar. They are the qualities that, after a long career as a scholar, I can identify as ones that I wish I had consistently embodied.

As I speak of intellectual excellence in scholarship, I also assume a certain baseline of qualities that can be supposed of anyone who even thinks of pursuing this manner of life. A certain level of (especially verbal) intelligence is presupposed, as well as a memory that is both capacious and tenacious. So also are sufficient energy to perform quotidian obligations and still have some left over for intellectual labor, and a speed in reading that makes mastering secondary scholarly literature a minor rather than a major hurdle to be surmounted. I assume as well—for work in my area— proficiency in the pertinent ancient and modern languages, and at least a competency in the basic issues and disputes in philosophy, religion, and theology.

My catalog of virtues identifies some of the ways these baseline gifts and accomplishments can move toward genuine excellence. In every case, *aretē* comes about through steady application over the course of years. Such excellence cannot be expected of the young scholar, but the desire for such excellence can be expected.

Finally, my catalog of virtues focuses specifically on research and writing rather than on teaching, although it can be stated emphatically that all truly great scholarship is also a form of teaching at a high level, just as all truly great teaching is a form of scholarship distilled for communication to others.

CURIOSITY

When I began thinking about a list of qualities that made for great scholarship, curiosity was the one that first popped in my mind, and it has refused to be dislodged. By "curiosity," of course, I do not mean the sort of socially disruptive nosiness—poking one's nose into other people's business—that both ancients and moderns rightly perceive as a vice rather than a virtue. Nor do I mean the sort of random mental restlessness that is distracted by every new shiny thing. Curiosity of this kind makes people *Jeopardy!* champions, and queens of Wikipedia, but it does not lead to excellence in serious scholarship.

What I term "curiosity" could also be called the spirit of inquiry. At the most basic level, scholars are people who want to *know*, and to know as much as possible and at as great a depth as possible. Curiosity is the intellectual itch that research scratches. As with physical itches, however, the more one scratches, the greater the itch grows.[2] Curiosity, then, is the sense of unease, distress, or simple wonderment that propels the process of research in the first place, and keeps the process going as new questions emerge from the ones first raised. It is such intellectual curiosity, above all, that asks concerning any phenomenon the fundamental question *why*. Such a spirit of inquiry drives the best and most original scholarship.

It does not, alas, characterize everything that is called scholarship. Too often, academic works peddle received opinions without rigorous examination, build on premises that have not adequately been tested, content themselves with observations concerning events without probing the causes of those events, draw out minute sequelae of previously established positions, and offer rote answers to unexamined questions. The lack of real inquiry, much less a sense of intellectual urgency, in so much of published scholarship—together with often mind-numbingly bad prose—accounts for the atmosphere of boredom pervading it. In my field, biblical commentaries that fail to interrogate the original language of the text, or that simply pass on without examination the same views that can be found in virtually every other commentary, cannot be considered genuine scholarship. They are examples of repackaging.[3] Similarly, articles that take their start from a *status questionis*, without asking whether that *status* should have the standing ascribed to it, can be termed academic productions but not real scholarship.

Likewise, one can read dozens (or even hundreds) of books called introductions to the New Testament written by certified members of the academic guild that offer a historical "account" of an utterly predictable sort: the historical Jesus is followed by Paul, who is followed by "the other writings," strung out in a chronological sequence. The impression given by the sequence is of a "development" from the prophetic ministry of Jesus and the proclamation of freedom by Paul to a progressively sterile and institutionalized "early Catholicism." Pick up virtually any college or seminary text, and you will find the same pattern.

The procedure resembles histories of philosophy that move from Socrates to Plato to Aristotle to Plotinus (as the obvious figures to consider) without ever inquiring into the influence of the pre-Socratics on shaping the questions they pursued, or other thinkers (like Xenophon and Epicurus) who should be taken into account, or without ever asking the most important question, which is why this distinct mode of thinking arose in that time and place rather than in other times and places. The typical introduction to the New Testament, in sum, expatiates learnedly on the content of early Christian writings as a form of history without ever raising the most pertinent historical questions.

In my own examination of New Testament literature, in contrast, I pursued a set of what might be called existential (in the sense of philosophical) questions that led to a historical inquiry of a more fundamental sort than that found in typical introductions. My sense of curiosity led me to four *why* questions never asked by such treatments. First, why was there a religious movement based in a failed messiah that spread throughout the Mediterranean world with astonishing speed? It is not obvious that a crucified Jewish teacher should be the center of a cult *after* his crucifixion by Rome as a slave or rebel, or that any such cult should find adherents. Second, why did this movement prove to be so prolific in the production of literature within decades of Jesus's death: letters, visions, and multiple (and not entirely agreeing) narratives of Jesus's ministry? Other historical messianic and millenarian movements rose and fell without such literary productivity—a productivity, moreover, that did not cease but grew ever greater in the next centuries. Third, why did the earliest Christian writings look the way they did? Why these kinds of writings? Why their peculiar shape, looking so much like the Jewish Scriptures—indeed, employing the Jewish Scriptures—yet using them from the perspective of premises that were repugnant to other Jews? Fourth, why were the earliest Christian writings so quickly collected and made into a canon that in a remarkably short time (compared to other religious movements) was joined to the Jewish Scriptures to form a Christian Bible?

Such *why* questions demanded a new paradigm for explaining and interpreting the New Testament, a paradigm that could account for the rise of the movement as well as the production and shape of its writings. The paradigm of "symbolic world reinterpreted in light of experience" owed a great deal to my reading in the sociology of knowledge and in cultural anthropology, but its employment would never have occurred to me had my intellectual curiosity not led me to ask such basic questions—questions that other introductions apparently considered either not worth asking, or already answered and not needing consideration. But in fact, they are the questions most worth asking, and by no means did standard treatments either ask or answer them. Lack of curiosity leads to the endless repetition of the same "historical but not really historical" accounts.

Sometimes, curiosity can be piqued by a sense of shock or surprise. Shortly after starting work at Yale, I joined the Luke-Acts task force of the Catholic Biblical Association. Wanting to extend my inquiry beyond the bounds of my dissertation, I decided to write on a section of Acts that did not figure in that study of the literary function of possessions. I began to prepare a paper on the use of Acts 15—the narrative of the apostolic council in Jerusalem that opened admission to gentiles without circumcision—in contemporary Catholic theology. I figured this would be an easy five-finger exercise. For Catholics, this was, after all, a conciliar age—Vatican II dominated all theological discussion—so what would be more obvious than that the singular New Testament narrative concerning a council should serve as a theological *exemplum*? To my utter surprise, there was no such use. I scoured systematic theologies, ecclesiologies, biblical theologies. Nothing. Nowhere did such worthies as Congar, Daniélou, Lubac, Rahner, or Schillebeeckx make use of Acts 15. So here is where curiosity kicked in. Why this negative result?

Probing further, I discovered that contemporary theologians, unlike their predecessors in the patristic and medieval periods, interpreted Scripture according to the dictates of professional biblical scholars; what biblical scholarship made available to them, they would employ. In their own eyes, such subservience to another academic guild fit their self-understanding as proper academic theologians. Looking therefore at professional New Testament scholarship on Acts 15, I found that the historical-critical method employed by exegetes restricted interest in this passage to a set of strictly historical issues: Did the council really occur? Is the version in Acts more or less accurate than Paul's version in Galatians 2? Was the so-called apostolic decree in Acts 15:29 ever issued, and did it have any effect? All strictly historical questions.

New Testament scholars made no use of Luke's narration of the council, or of his story leading up to its deliberations, because at that time they literally did not see "narrative" as a significant aspect of interpretation. This realization pushed me to realize the severe limitations of the historical-critical method, not only with respect to its conversation with theology but also with respect to its adequacy to see and interpret much of the New Testament. Seeking to recover a mode of interpretation that took narrative seriously led, in turn, to seeking out the significance of personal narrative in contemporary theology—the way toward thinking of theology as "inductive art" started with these small steps stimulated by scholarly curiosity.

RESPECT FOR EVIDENCE

Scholarship in the humanities—in my case, ancient religious traditions—is at once similar to scholarship in the sciences and dissimilar. As in science, scholars seek to test a hypothesis (or theory) against the pertinent data, seeking to establish the truth or falsity of the hypothesis—or better, its adequacy/plausibility—on the basis of the available evidence. Unlike science, however, scholars in the humanities deal with products of human imagination, above all language, rather than material objects accessible to direct observation. Such products of human imagination in art, music, and literature are notoriously resistant to empirical "testing"; they are indeed available for as many "interpretations" as there are human imaginations at work on them. Even the most "objective" data from antiquity (material texts, archaeological finds, inscriptions) often turn out to be highly problematic with respect both to dating and to decipherment.

Here is the reason why scholarly positions with regard to, say, ancient Greco-Roman religion are so unstable and susceptible to constant revision—sometimes because of the discovery of new evidence but sometimes simply because, with the passage of time and with further experience, expert perceptions have shifted. This is also the reason why, unlike science, scholarship in the humanities must embrace the entire history of interpretation rather than only the most recent theories espoused in journals, for it is possible that much older readings continue to have value, and equally possible that what purports to be a new theoretical perspective turns out to be—sometimes because of the ignorance of the investigator—simply the rehash of a much earlier position.

There is, then, a necessary tension between the formation of hypotheses (or theories) and the use of evidence. On one side, data does not even become "evidence" unless some kind of hypothesis has been formed. Respect for evidence cannot mean a passive expectation that the data will explain itself. On the other side, the need to form and the desire to demonstrate hypotheses (or theories) can lead to distortion of the data. The virtuous sweet spot within this tension lies in the vigorous formation of reasonable hypotheses, already based in a first apprehension of the data, and then the honest and transparent testing of the hypothesis through the rigorous examination of all the pertinent data. It is curiosity that drives us to research; it is respect for the evidence that keeps our research honest.

Precisely here is why good scholars place such a high premium on the practice of *exegesis*. Exegesis is a close and disciplined examination of a text. It begins with the awareness of the text's linguistic and cultural "otherness" to the examiner and works to find the plausible range of meanings offered by the passage in question. Exegesis demands a sure grasp of the diction of the ancient language, the grammar and syntax of its sentences, the logic of its argumentation (or narration), and the conventions of its rhetoric. These determinations bring the scholar in the New Testament and other ancient literature closest to what scientists would term "data" or even "facts," as close as scholars in the humanities can come to "objectivity," for things like grammar, syntax, and diction resist a reader's tendency toward projection ("eisegesis") and can be debated apart from ideological premises. Exegesis reins in overenthusiastic imagination. It is the scholar's best defense against the tendency to manipulate evidence.

The failure to accept the *limitations* of evidence is common in the sort of New Testament scholarship that seeks to advance a highly specific theory. The best example is the proliferation of historical Jesuses offered by contemporary questers. Was Jesus a charismatic Jewish *chasid* (charismatic), or a revolutionary zealot, or a guru of oceanic bliss, or a cynic philosopher, or a subversive peasant, or a prophet of Israel's restoration?[4] Each of these portraits employs the same canons of the historical-critical method with respect to sources. Each uses some theoretical or comparative framework as a way of establishing and testing evidence. Fair enough. But in the execution of such studies, textual evidence tends to be dealt with selectively (only that supporting the theory is employed) and to be pushed beyond the limits of historiographical plausibility. Such widely diverse results—within a self-proclaimed "scientific" method—themselves suggest something wrong in the process. The same failure is found in contemporary efforts to read Paul's letters from a "postcolonial" perspective; in this case, the theory is used to expand beyond recognition the minimal evidence that Paul is, in any meaningful way, anti-imperial.

Sometimes simple ignorance accounts for the failure to respect evidence. Perhaps better stated, ignorance of evidence that ought to be considered. There are instances of New Testament scholars, for example, refusing even to investigate Greco-Roman literature or Hellenistic Jewish literature, out of the benighted conviction that these invaluable resources are not relevant to the interpretation of Scripture. Such cases of willful ignorance cannot be taken seriously. But even when a gesture is made toward using all the available evidence to interpret the New Testament and other early Christian literature, a full recognition of all the pertinent data is often missing.[5]

Some scholars seem to disregard data because of an ideological posture. Out of a politically correct desire to remove from the New Testament the basis for Christian anti-Semitism, for example, some scholars insist on translating the Greek term *ioudaios* as "Judean," as though it had only a geographical significance, with no ethnic or religious connotation.[6] The evidentiary basis for the claim is found in the Gospel of John, where such a geographical sense is pervasive. But knowledge of Jewish literature written in Greek (as in Philo and Josephus) shows that *ioudaios* did in fact frequently carry ethnic and religious connotations. The use of the term by the apostle Paul (above all in Galatians), furthermore, demands more than a geographical meaning. When Paul speaks of "judaizing" (*ioudaizein*) in Galatians 2:14, he certainly does not mean "act like someone from Judea"; he means "act like someone who is circumcised and obeys the law of Moses." John's usage simply cannot be extended to every use in the New Testament. The failure to take all the pertinent evidence into account negates the pious wish to remove the cause for scandal from the New Testament.

Another example at the basic level of diction: the verses in the letter of James 4:5–6 are notoriously difficult to translate—or even punctuate. Commentators expatiate at great length on the fact that, although James seems to be alluding to Scripture in 4:5, no passage in the Greek translation of the Old Testament corresponds to his words. Translators and commentators, nevertheless, convinced that 4:5 must have God as its subject, translate it as a declarative sentence along the lines we find in the New Revised Standard Version: "God yearns jealously for the spirit he made to dwell in us," with the phrase "yearns jealously" rendering the Greek *pros phthonon epipothei*. In sum, the translation treats *phthonos* (envy) as though it were synonymous with the Greek word *zēlos* (jealousy).

But this is impossible. In the entire world of Greco-Roman discourse—including Hellenistic Judaism—the term *phthonos* can refer only to the vice of envy, the evil disposition that seeks to take away what another has. A standard *topos* of Greek philosophy, indeed, is the *aphthonia* of God: God cannot be envious.[7] Cultural tone-deafness leads in this case to a disastrously erroneous translation. James 4:5 should be punctuated as a question rather than a statement, and its subject is the human spirit rather than God; *phthonos* is the vice that is the subject of the entire section between James 3:13 and 4:10. The translation should be, "Does the Spirit he made to dwell in us crave enviously?"[8] Respect for the evidence demands knowledge of the pertinent evidence, in this case the simple way in which terms are used in the world of the New Testament. This leads to the next topic.

MASTERY OF THE SUBJECT

Two points need to be made at once concerning this heading. The first is that the term "mastery" is deliberately chosen. Basic knowledge is to be assumed of the younger scholar, but the path to excellence (*aretē*) is the path to mastery, which denotes a knowledge that is wide, deep, flexible, and creative. Such an advanced form of knowledge in the humanities is the result of time sedulously employed. If there is no difference between the novice and the elder in their range and depth of knowledge or in the speed and agility with which they can deploy it, then the elder has failed to properly cultivate scholarly virtue.

The second point is that what "the subject" means needs sorting out, because not all those considering themselves scholars agree on what ought to be included as the range of their eventual mastery. It should be clear to the reader by now that I consider that the widest possible understanding of my field's "subject" should define the boundaries within which mastery is sought.

Let me begin with the ways in which the subject over which the scholar seeks mastery is deliberately narrowed. Some who call themselves biblical scholars, for example, restrict their study to the books of the Old and New Testament. They read them in the original languages; they use the tools of textual criticism; they employ the methods of historical criticism for questions of chronology and intertextual relations. In these ways, they seem able legitimately to claim the name of scholars. In truth, however, such efforts are better termed a more sophisticated form of the "Bible study" found in many churches. Even at the linguistic level, such scholars think in terms of "biblical Greek," as though scriptural language was a self-contained universe rather than a language best understood within the context of ancient *koine*. The restriction of attention to the biblical books alone, in fact, can be designated as a variety of a "higher fundamentalism." No genuinely critical questions are allowed; no contribution of knowledge from outside the "revealed truth" of Scripture can be entertained; indeed, nothing genuinely new is expected from these practitioners of biblical catechetics: the entire point of their work is to confirm what was already known, to secure the answers that have always been given.[9]

Another sort of delimitation derives from the sort of hyperspecialization that I have mentioned several times earlier, in which a scholar locates his or her work in a single part of the New Testament. There have existed "Johannine" scholars who have never, in their entire careers, written on even another of the Gospels. There have been "Pauline" scholars who have evinced no awareness of any other part of the canon; indeed, there are "Romans" scholars and "Galatians" scholars who show no knowledge of or interest in the rest of Paul's letters. There have certainly been "Revelation" scholars whose work has never moved from that fascinating composition.

I remember how shocked I was when, after finally reading Helmut Koester's *Introduction to the New Testament*, I found that, despite his innovative views concerning the gospel traditions (in which he had done significant work), his treatment of Paul (where he had done less work) was entirely conventional, and his treatment of the "catholic epistles" (James, 1 Peter, etc.) would lead one to conclude that he had never read these compositions, so out of touch was it with current scholarship in those books.[10] And he was professor of New Testament at Harvard! Koester's lack of mastery over even the compositions of the New Testament might be excused (although not really) because of his heavy investment in both the Dead Sea Scrolls and the Nag Hammadi Library. He was one of the key (and contentious) figures in the publication of these hugely significant discoveries of literature pertinent to the study of early Christianity.

Another sort of restriction of the subject matter occurs when a scholar takes his or her stand on some aspect of the New Testament's symbolic world (sometimes called "background") and interprets everything in the compositions of nascent Christianity exclusively from that standpoint. Such scholars illustrate the old maxim about hammers and nails: if one knows only one tool, everything is approached in terms of that tool. Remarkably, this form of restriction (or focus) is not scorned but rather praised within the academic guild. It would be possible to make a lengthy list of highly esteemed scholars in my field whose work can be adequately defined in terms of one or the other of these contexts: Dead Sea Scrolls; Jewish apocalyptic; Jewish mysticism; rabbinic Judaism; Hellenistic Judaism; Greco-Roman archaeology, rhetoric, fiction, philosophy, and religion; Gnosticism. By no means do I want to suggest that any of these contexts should be ignored. Just the opposite, I believe that true mastery in my field involves an ever-increasing knowledge of *all* the New Testament's symbolic world (or worlds). What I object to is precisely the elevation of *one* aspect over others, and the delimitation of a scholar's interest and effort to only that one.[11]

A similar sort of limitation is found in scholars who spend most or all of their careers cultivating a single theoretical perspective on Christianity's earliest writings. I have already suggested that knowledge of theory is important, and that the formation of hypotheses (or theories) is ingredient to the scholarly process in the humanities. What I have in mind here, though, are theoretical perspectives (and sometimes methods) borrowed from other fields and applied, usually woodenly, to these ancient compositions in the fashion of a Procrustean bed. Just as it is possible to list renowned scholars in terms of their exclusive approach from some aspect of the symbolic world, so can a register of scholars be constructed whose work can adequately be categorized in terms of one or another theoretical perspective: psychological (Freudian, Jungian, Adlerian), sociological, anthropological, narratological, structural, deconstruction, liberation, feminist, postcolonial.

Please note again: I am by no means denying the validity of using a theoretical perspective. My objection concerns the exclusive and amateurish use of such theories.

What should mastery of the subject look like, then, for a mature scholar in New Testament and Christian origins? It must include, I think, not only the comprehensive knowledge of the content and rhetorical character of each OT and NT writing but also a firsthand grasp of all the critical questions concerning those compositions. It should include significant research into more than one section of the New Testament. It should embrace appropriate interaction with all of Greco-Roman literature, Jewish literature, and early Christian literature at least to the time of Constantine. The mature scholar ought to be as comfortable with the *Sentences of Sextus* as with the *Sentences of Pseudo-Phocylides*, with the Pirqe Avot and the Avot of Rabbi Nathan as with the Sifre on Deuteronomy, with the varieties of Jewish mysticism as with the hermetic literature, with Epictetus as with Plutarch, with the Didache as with Dionysius the Areopagite. Such comfort can arise only from sustained firsthand reading in the primary sources. This takes time, energy, and steady application.

WIDE AND CRITICAL READING

Speed and accuracy in reading are essential skills for scholars in the humanities. No matter what the level of the scholar's curiosity or passion, if reading is a laborious chore, no real excellence in scholarship can be expected. High scores in the verbal graduate record examinations do not predict success for would-be scholars in my field—too many other factors come into play—but dramatically low scores accurately predict failure. The life of a scholar in the humanities is a life of reading. The mind is nourished and challenged through intercourse with other minds, and reading enables such interaction across a range of intelligent discourse that is, to this point in our evolution, unsurpassed. For the scholar in the humanities, Emily Dickinson's line "There is no frigate like a book" is simply and self-evidently true.

Because there is no end to the publishing of books (and articles), all of us are in a catch-up ball game with respect to wide reading. Those who have not cultivated the habit of voracious reading early in life are, however, particularly disadvantaged. Without the broad knowledge and critical sense that serious reading from the time of childhood provides, scholars are naturally prone to narrow their scope. Their vast ignorance in general can be camouflaged by an impressive expertise in a particular area. Thus, the hyperspecialization even within the small compass of New Testament studies, with research carried out in only one or two books of the canon; thus, the seizing of a single theoretical perspective. I have spoken to New Testament scholars, for example, who purported to apply "literary criticism" to the Synoptic Gospels while confessing that they simply "did not have time to waste on novels."

Excellence as a scholar demands more than a narrow expertise. It requires a broad knowledge that can be acquired only by constant reading both within one's field, in cognate scholarly fields, and in the humanities generally. Clearly, the path to excellence in this matter is long, indeed neverending. We do not expect the range of comprehension and sureness of touch in the young scholar that we do in the senior scholar.

For scholars in early Christianity, two practices in particular are useful for gaining a wider knowledge and greater critical acumen. The first is mastering the history of research on any project undertaken. In writing a scholarly New Testament commentary, for example, hundreds of books and articles must be read and assessed. Clearly, speed and incisiveness are keys to success in this endeavor. But so is the ability to remember the salient points made by previous researchers. The three elements go together: rapid reading seeks those salient points, incisiveness closes on them, and memory recalls them when needed in the composition of one's own work.

The second practice is the writing of book reviews in one's own and cognate fields. I have always been startled when reading the vitae of senior scholars who have written only a handful of reviews in their careers, because I have always regarded this practice as essential to gaining a wider knowledge and to cultivating a critical spirit. In reviewing, once more, the elements of speed and incisiveness are most important (memory less so); the good reviewer reads to find an author's thesis, mode of argumentation, use of evidence, consistency, and coherence. Setting high standards in such reviews serves as a reminder also to oneself of the standards to which one is committed. Conversely, failing to hold authors to these standards—approving of them even when they fail in one respect or another—represents a corruption of one's own judgment that has serious consequences. If we corrupt our judgment out of the desire to please or the fear of offending, we may end up with our capacity to judge severely compromised. I have always thought of writing reviews as analogous to playing baseball in the major leagues: if I play fast and hard, I must expect reviewers of my books to also play fast and hard. If I ask them to be smarter and more convincing, I must expect them to return the same kind of criticism. Fair play. The constant writing of reviews across my career has certainly widened my knowledge, and I think it has also kept me more honest in my own work.

My appreciation for the benefits of serious reading in cognate scholarly fields really took hold when I had the chance to study in the context of a religious studies department at Indiana University (1969–1970) and then teach for ten years in that same department (1982–1992). Within schools of theology such as Yale Divinity School and Candler, biblical scholars need to work extra hard to converse outside their specialization, precisely because there is a significant number of faculty within the same specialization. Even reaching out to faculty in other theological specialties does not extend one's range a great deal. But in a religious studies context, pluralism is real. Not only is a great range of religious traditions represented (often by adherents to those traditions), but the intellectual framework for analyzing and interpreting traditions involves a diversity of fields other than theology: anthropology, psychology, sociology, phenomenology, history.

In my first classes back at Saint Ben's in 1970–1971 after my sojourn at IU, I already employed the analysis of body language as well as anthropological analyses of play and ritual in my course on the history of the liturgy. And I used the categories of the phenomenology of religion as a way into diverse traditions in my class on comparative religions. My literary approach to Luke-Acts in my dissertation was clearly influenced by my wide reading in that field when, as a monk, I midwifed a dissertation in English literature. A reviewer of my dissertation asked why I did not include a "theoretical" section on literary criticism—a very academic question. The reason I did not is because my reading in literature and literary criticism had been so consistent and wide that it had formed a *habitus* that was connatural to me. Perhaps naïvely, I did not think what I was doing represented the application of a "method."[12]

The same could be said of the philosophical sensibility I brought to my analysis of possessions in Luke-Acts and the rest of Scripture. I readily acknowledge the clear influence of Gabriel Marcel, but his influence is so mixed with all the other existentialist philosophy I had read a decade ear-lier—where does Marcel leave off and Ortega y Gasset begin?—that the sensibility was, once more, shaped by a variety of thinkers (mixed with my own thinking) rather than an "application" of a theory to a subject. In my introduction to the New Testament, similarly, it is easy to see how my interpretive model owes much to the work by Berger and Luckmann in the sociology of knowledge, but equally important was my earlier reading in Durkheim, Mauss, Geertz, Gennep, and Turner.

The point I am trying to make about wide reading in other fields, even in those not connected in the least to religion, much less early Christi-anity, is that such reading supplies the scholar's mind with a rich mix of theories, examples, and analogies that may be pertinent to the study of early Christianity. A New Testament scholar wanting to engage the topic of "mythology," for instance, does well not to rest simply with the views of a Rudolf Bultmann but should be aware of the vast literature on the subject by linguists, anthropologists, sociologists, and philosophers, in order to understand that the topic is not monothetic but polythetic in character. The benefit of such reading is not that some field supplies a particular theory or method that becomes an open sesame to the New Testament, but rather that the scholar immersed in the reading of all these fields gains a variety of possible insights on the New Testament.

The applicability or usefulness of such insights can vary tremendously. In my study of glossolalia, for example, I was able to draw from many psy-chological, sociological, and linguistic experts in the study of the contem-porary phenomena, as well as anthropologists, comparative religionists, and classical scholars in the study of the ancient practice, in order to expand and clarify the scant evidence offered by the New Testament and suggest reasons why a practice so enthusiastically embraced by some should be-come an embarrassment to others.[13] In contrast, my literary study of Luke-Acts did not need to move much beyond Aristotle and Northrop Frye to have a theoretical grasp of narrative sufficient to work with Luke's story.

One of the most important forms of reading for the scholar in the hu-manities tends to be the most neglected, especially by those who work in theological disciplines. I mean a constant, daily, reading in literature, broadly construed, and above all, reading in fiction. Nothing so feeds the scholar's imagination as imaginative literature. Nothing gives so firm a grasp on the character of narrative, for example, as the reading of short stories and novels. Nothing gives a better sense of what genuine historiography is than the reading of great histories and biographies. Nothing provides a better ear for language than the reading of poetry. Scholars' regular failures in imagination can be traced to their failure to feed their imagination. Scholars' notorious infelicities in style have much to do with the fact that they do not have beautiful prose running in their veins.

If one wanted to be utterly pragmatic about it and ask "what use" is fiction to a New Testament scholar, one need only mention novels that have illuminated aspects of the Mediterranean world in fictional accounts that are also historically accurate. I have in mind novels like Gore Vidal's *Julian* and *Live from Nazareth*; Robert Harris's *Imperium, Conspirata*, and *Pompeii*; Anne Perry's *The Sheen on the Silk*; and Margarite Youncenour's superlative *Hadrian's Memoirs*. But it is important not to be utterly pragmatic, for the point is not gaining more specific knowledge about one's area of research but rather expanding and enriching one's capacity for an imaginative apprehension of the complexities and inexplicable strangeness of human behavior. And all great fiction, no matter what period in which it is set, no matter the circumstances of its characters, opens up a world that provides nourishment to the one who "puts the mind in [this] other place."

IMAGINATION

The form of excellence called imagination is as rarely found among contemporary New Testament scholars as is robust humor. The reasons are many: the highly technical character of advanced training in the field; the attraction of obsessive-compulsive types to this sort of technical education; the pedestrian and pedantic character of so much discourse in books, journals, and (Lord save us) academic conferences; and, above all, the lack of the sort of deep culture that accrues from long immersion in art, music, and great literature. But imagination is the surest mark of truly great scholarship in the humanities—as it is, for that matter, in the sciences as well.

By imagination I mean a combination of synthetic thinking and intuition that apprehends in a single vision both the whole of a subject and its parts. It is an apprehension of the whole that encompasses and makes intelligible all the data that previously had lacked such a comprehensive interpretive framework. If analysis properly is understood as the mind breaking a subject into constitutive parts and showing the internal connections among its parts, synthesis means the mind gathering all the parts into a coherent whole and then linking them to other wholes within a mental structure that is now seen to contain them all. Such synthetic thinking begins with and is guided by a sort of intuition, a guess, a glimpse of something larger lying just beyond reach.

Sometimes the vision given by imagination is thrilling, a *coup de foudre* that reorganizes the mind's categories. I have in mind, as an example, G. K. Chesterton's distinctive way of viewing the world in terms he called "topsy-turveydom," which challenged the epistemological strictures of the Enlightenment. In his biography of Saint Francis of Assisi, Chesterton described the young Francis as standing on his head and seeing his city for the first time as it truly was; not as a massive weight set solidly on the mountain, but rather as a delicate and fragile web hanging over the abyss of the sky.[14] In that simple image, Chesterton captured the essence of what is meant by "contingency" and by an "existential" view of life.

Imagination effectively deployed in the humanities often arises from a long and complete immersion in a mass of data that apparently suddenly—but not really suddenly—suggests a new synthesis. The scholar's mind now sees connections within the mass of data that had not previously been obvious or even evident. When that synthesis is competently communicated, the field of study can be reconfigured. In the last century, two impressive examples from the field of Jewish studies present themselves. The first is the pioneering work of Gershom Scholem in Jewish mysticism (*Major Trends in Jewish Mysticism*, 1941). Disparate manifestations of Jewish mystical practice had long been practiced and studied individually, to be sure. There were extant no end of detailed studies dealing with kabbalah, Lurianic mysticism, or Hasidism. But Scholem's deep immersion in the most ancient manifestations of mysticism within the rabbinic tradition, which he called, somewhat misleadingly, "Jewish Gnosticism," enabled him to trace lines of continuity through all the varieties and, for the first time, show similar impulses and expressions within what appear at first to be totally disparate phenomena.

The second example is Erwin Goodenough's imaginative construction of ancient Hellenistic Judaism as a "mystery religion." Taking his start from puzzling archaeological evidence, especially from the synagogue at Dura Europos, and connecting these archaeological finds to scattered textual evidence in Josephus, Philo, and fragmentary Hellenistic Jewish texts, Goodenough proposed that Judaism among Greek-speaking Jews, especially in the diaspora, was a syncretistic merging of Torah observance with pagan mystery cults (*By Light, Light: The Mystic Gospel of Hellenistic Judaism*, 1935). Goodenough's synthesis was impressive and turned out to be highly controversial; most scholars in the field did not accept its most extreme form. But his imaginative vision that pulled together evidence not previously seen together proved generative of further research and itself stands as a form of scholarship that displays imaginative excellence.

In much more modest fashion, my own contribution to the question of the authorship of Paul's letters depends on an imaginative reconfiguring of the debate. Since the early nineteenth century, New Testament scholars had argued back and forth: Did Paul himself write five, seven, ten, or thirteen letters? And if he did not write eight, six, or three of the letters ascribed to him, how do we account for their production? The debaters shared the same premise, that at least some of his letters were sufficiently consistent in style and theme as to represent the "undisputed" Paul, and that the remaining letters could be measured against this consistent core. Thus, the conventional solution almost universally accepted today: Paul himself wrote seven of his letters, and after his death, one or more "Pauline schools" produced six pseudepigraphical letters. No one was much worried by the lack of positive evidence for such schools apart from the letters themselves, or that the assumptions concerning "authorship" tended to be anachronistic.

My deconstruction of the conventional position (in *Constructing Paul*, 2020) began with a neutral examination of the correspondence, which shows that there is not a "core" in the correspondence against which outliers can be measured. Quite the opposite: the correspondence falls into discrete clusters that while internally similar are sharply dissimilar from other clusters. The Corinthian letters cannot be mapped stylistically or substantively on the Thessalonian letters, while Galatians/Romans does not match up with Colossians/Ephesians. With the disappearance of the core, what imaginative picture of Pauline authorship might be employed? I argue that the internal evidence across the entire correspondence suggests the production of Paul's letters as a social process undertaken by Paul and his associates. The Pauline "school" was at work during Paul's ministry in the composition of all his letters. Pauline authorship, then, is to be understood as entailing the "authorizing" of each of the letters ascribed to him, while not necessarily the "writing" of any of them. My solution is certainly imaginative enough; whether it will appeal to the imagination of other scholars is much less certain.

CLARITY AND COGENCY

The intellectual virtues I have discussed up to now have all concerned the pursuit of knowledge or insight, what the ancient would call the *via inventionis* ("the path of discovery"). My final category addresses the most important virtues in scholarly writing and speaking, the *via demonstrationis* ("path of demonstration/proof"). One might hope that written or spoken scholarship possesses touches of grace or even elegance, but if scholarly writing or speaking is to be considered excellent, it must at least be clear and convincing.

The two qualities go hand in hand: confusing prose usually indicates a confused argument. If syntax is confused, so is thought. Apart from the realms of poetry and mysticism, everything needing to be said can be said in plain prose. Obfuscation is not a sign of deep thinking but of the inability to see and state plainly what one's argument is. A bad argument usually involves bad writing, whereas good thinking leads naturally to clear writing. Although they go together, so that the absence of one also means the absence of the other, the virtues of clarity in writing and cogency in argument can be considered separately.

The sins of academic writing are notorious and easily parodied. Long and syntactically impenetrable sentences; the overuse of passive constructions; the avoidance of first-person statements ("this author holds"—"it is the position of this paper"); the heavy use of specialized jargon; the endless citation of secondary authorities—all these characteristics serve mainly to assert the academic qualifications of the writer and to repel readers who have not been initiated into the arcana of the academic mystery. But the use of such language does not indicate the presence of genuine scholarship; it may, in fact, suggest the opposite, namely, a pretentious posturing that seeks to camouflage the lack of evidence and logical argument.

I used the term "arcana" deliberately, for people do not grow up speaking and writing this way. They need to be initiated into the argot of the guild. Such initiation begins in college. Young adults who write perfectly lucid letters home or speak in a straightforward way to friends are coaxed or coerced by their professors into adopting a language that is truly foreign to them. They must learn academese as the first of their collegiate languages. Progress in the academy, moreover, demands the constant use of this artificial and esoteric way of speaking and writing. Sometimes, obscure prose is taken to be the mark of profound thought. Small wonder, then, that many scholars never recover any fluency in simple, everyday language when they write for publication. The periphrastic style of academics is indeed the contemporary equivalent of scholars' Latin following the medieval period. It is a mark of belonging to a specialized group. It is a necessary tool for communicating with others in that group. But it is not a living language. And it is never lovely.

Scholarly writing is excellent when it is simple and straightforward. The marks of good prose should be found in scholarly as well as nonscholarly writings: active sentences that move from subject to predicate to object; the sparing use of adjectives and adverbs; the preference for paratactic over hypotactic clauses; the avoidance of jargon and the use of vocabulary that can be found in the lexicon of any well-educated person; the making of short rather than long sentences; the appropriate deployment of the first person ("I think"; "I propose"); the establishment of clear syntax by means of strong connectives between sentences and paragraphs. Such clear writing is a form of honesty. Style is not used to hide thought but to make it clear. Simplicity in exposition forces the scholar to reveal his or her argument openly. This is a great gift to the reader.

The ability to write about serious things clearly can be learned through the wide reading that I recommended in the previous section, above all, in the reading of poetry. Immersion in the poetry of Emily Dickinson, Robert Frost, Philip Larkin, John Crowe Ransom, or Karl Shapiro cannot help but chasten one's own diction. Likewise, constant exposure to the prose of an Anne Tyler, Denise Mina, Elmore Leonard, Laurie Colwin, Alice Adams, Annie Proulx, or Richard Russo cannot help but improve one's own making of sentences. The scholar can also cultivate the virtue of clear writing by reaching outside the bounds of the academic guild through publications and presentations for nonacademic audiences. It is impossible to hide behind academic jargon when speaking to a crowd of highly intelligent but nonprofessional people, or when writing on a serious issue for a nonacademic journal. I found such writing for a general audience to correct my tendency toward pomposity. Indeed, for me, the best discipline of all was preaching. I could not get away with any academic dodge when standing in the pulpit. I had to learn how to say something significant directly and crisply and within severe time restraints.

Clear writing connects to cogency in argument. Scholarly writing in its truest form is not the display of a scholar's erudition but a contribution to the erudition of others. Even in scholarship that is primarily expositional—say, adding to the store of data in a specific field—a certain level of argument is required. I want to report an archaeological finding such as a manuscript fragment. My report should at least touch on questions like these: What is this new discovery? What is its importance? How does it add to what is already known, or correct previous perceptions? Why was it not previously known? What means were used to reach the discovery? What further paths of research does it open? The reader's interest in the research of others is piqued not by the mere assemblage of information but in the presentation of that information in a manner that demonstrates its significance.

Excellence in publications and presentations can be measured by the perspicuity of their argument. Ideally, the path of demonstration should reverse the path of discovery. In the *via inventionis*, curiosity has driven the scholar to an examination of a set of data. The careful analysis of the pieces leads eventually to a working hypothesis (this is synthesis rather than analysis) concerning the interpretation of the data. That working hypothesis is tested against the data, which is now weighed as evidence for and against the hypothesis. Satisfied that the testing supports the hypothesis, the scholar draws a conclusion. In the *via demonstrationis*, that conclusion becomes the thesis of the lecture, article, or book. In the argument seeking to demonstrate the thesis, however, the messiness of the analytic process is not repeated. Rather, in publication, the evidence that supports the hypothesis is laid out as the demonstration of a thesis, QED. In scholarly works that are more contentious in character—challenging a dominant paradigm, correcting an earlier assessment of data—the need for clarity and cogency in argument is even greater. Here, it is not a matter of adding a bit to the storehouse of knowledge; here it is a questioning of the state of the storehouse. The tools need to be sharp.

As a reviewer of hundreds of published books, as a previewer of many books seeking publication, as a responder to papers in dozens of scholarly conferences, I can assert with some confidence that the difference between mediocre and excellent scholarship lies precisely in this area of compositional clarity and argumentative cogency. Many academics abound in sheer knowledge of their field, or (let's be honest) a portion of their field. But far fewer show the ability effectively to marshal that knowledge. It is not uncommon for academic productions to fail in answering these basic questions that every good reviewer asks: Is the piece accurately entitled, written in plain speech, and intelligible to any other scholar in the larger field (i.e., not participant in a particular methodology or ideology)? Is there a thesis, and is it clearly stated? Is there an argument that demonstrates this thesis and not some other? Is the evidence adduced appropriately and logically? Is the conclusion a logical deduction from the exposition?

Such are the intellectual virtues as I have come to understand them at the end of a long scholarly career. Others may be equally important, but these are the ones that have impressed me as critical to what can be called excellent scholarship. But the mind is not all that is at work in the scholar's life. Emotional and volitional factors also have much to do with making scholarship excellent. In the next chapter, I turn to such "moral virtues" of the scholar.

Chapter Eleven

Moral Virtues

S THE NARRATIVE OF MY OWN LIFE MAKES CLEAR, chance—or providence—has a great deal to do with both becoming and being a scholar. In my case, the religious impulse that led to the seminary and monastery provided me with the ideal setting within which to cultivate mind and spirit. Between the ages of thirteen and twenty-five, I was immersed in a world so constructed and vivified by Scripture that "the love of learning and the desire for God" were mutually reinforcing goals. My context as much as my intellectual ability shaped the future direction of my life and work.

That said—and constantly acknowledged—it is also true that certain intellectual abilities are necessary to become a scholar. Difficulty in reading quickly and accurately, a porous memory, problems with concentration— all these are insurmountable obstacles. Abilities alone, however, are not enough. I have had many colleagues and students whose mental acuity greatly surpassed my own: they scored outrageously high on tests; they grasped difficult concepts quickly; they were at ease with every sort of theory; they learned languages with ease; they sparkled in academic conversations. Yet they never moved much beyond their impressive starting point. They never became productive, much less creative, scholars. Why? As I have tried to show, to become a genuine scholar, certain intellectual "virtues" (or forms of excellence) must be cultivated. In the previous chapter, I described a set of such intellectual dispositions that have seemed important to me.

But neither are intellectual virtues alone sufficient. Emotional and volitional dispositions are also critical to success. A state of chronic depression, for example, can effectively suppress or derail even the greatest of mental gifts, just as chronic anxiety can require so much psychic self-care that "having the mind in another place" than on one's own well-being is impossible. Addiction to alcohol, drugs, sex, or gambling has waylaid promising academic careers. More subtly, simmering or barely controlled anger can distort the efforts of even fine minds. Scholars are as subject to emotional liabilities as are other people. But the production of worthwhile scholarly work requires that they somehow convert depression into appropriate anger and anger into focused energy, that they transform anxiety into disciplined attentiveness, that they turn a tendency toward obsessiveness into a healthy respect for detail. In fact, for many productive scholars, channeling their neuroses into their work has proven therapeutic in their lives and profitable to their study.

Such emotional alchemy is highly individual as well as mysterious. We wonder at the way in which a deeply flawed and fragile person can produce scholarship of a high order. And we grieve at the way emotional dysfunction curtails the potentially great work of a gifted mind. It is very clear, however, that emotional factors play as significant a role in the formation of excellent scholarship as do qualities of mind.

Volitional health is also critical to the development of great scholarship. I consider some of its dimensions under the rubric of "moral virtues." I use the term "moral" not in the sense of behavior that is right or wrong but (once more) in the Aristotelian sense of "more excellent" as opposed to "less excellent." Although there are undoubtedly emotional as well as intellectual factors involved in each of the virtues I describe, there is also an element of choice, and my focus is on this element.

Fine scholarship in the humanities, I think, requires what I think of as a "passionate detachment." In the tension between the virtues that push scholars to strive and those that provide them some distance is found the Aristotelian balance between extremes. I first consider the virtues I connect to "passion" and then those I link to "detachment."

COURAGE

Aristotle himself held courage in high regard: "Courage is the mother of all virtues, for without it we cannot consistently perform the others."[1] He locates courage (*andreia*) between the extremes of brashness/arrogance on one side and cowardice on the other. For scholars in my field, I think, courage fails more often out of cowardice than rashness. I have come to regard courage as the singular disposition that distinguishes truly excellent from mediocre scholarship. For the scholar, courage is expressed in at least three ways.

The first, and most important, is the courage to trust one's own perception of a subject without being co-opted by the opinions of others. Scholarship in the New Testament is so vast and so ancient that it is easy to be swayed by a "consensus" view and turned from the evidence as it appears to one's own eyes. Such trust in one's own intelligence is demanded first in the simple act of exegesis. As I mentioned briefly in my narrative, an instance of the temptation to be co-opted by the majority occurred when I first experienced a cognitive dissonance between my reading of "the faith of Jesus" in Romans 3:21–26 and the overwhelming, almost universal interpretation given by other scholars (including all the standard translations), namely, that it was not "Jesus's faith" but "faith in Jesus" that should be read in this passage.[2]

Even though I was appropriately fearful in reaching and advancing my interpretation in light of such massive agreement against it, I could not disavow what my own intelligence showed me. If, out of cowardice, I abandoned my own perception, I would have been utterly lost as a scholar. What do we have, after all—what can we contribute to the world—apart from the witness we bear to reality? If we allow that witness to be weakened or watered down because of the pressure of human opinion, then we really have no business teaching or writing. We have given up the one thing that is distinctively ours and have thereby abandoned our vocation.

The second expression of scholarly courage is the clear and forceful presentation of one's perceptions through publication, even if these perceptions do not agree with those of other or even most scholars. I greatly admire the contrarian argument of William Farmer, for example, even though I strongly disagree with that argument. In *The Synoptic Problem* (1981), Farmer lays out with considerable vigor his conviction that, contrary to the view of the majority of scholars, Matthew rather than Mark wrote the first gospel, upon which the other synoptic writers depended. I disagree with him. After decades of firsthand exegesis and teaching by means of the Greek Synopsis,[3] I am convinced of Markan priority, not because it is the standard view but because study of the actual text has persuaded me. Nevertheless, I think Farmer is correct when he claims that many contemporary scholars accept Markan priority not because of their own research but simply because it is the majority position. And I admire his courage. I appreciate his minority position precisely because it reminds me and all other scholars in this field that the "Markan Hypothesis" is just that: not a fact but something to be demonstrated rather than assumed.

The writing of book reviews likewise provides scholars with the chance to state their views clearly and without equivocation. But this is a place where pulling punches is, alas, all too common.[4] Some scholars forget that the give-and-take of academic exchange is not in service of popularity but in service of truth. In the desire to appear "nice" to readers (that is, other scholars), reviewers too often give bad books and articles a pass. They seem to forget that the only contribution any of us can make to the common cause of scholarship is not collegial chumminess but the rigorous application of standards. There is certainly no guarantee that my criticism in any given case is correct. Other readers may not see the same flaws I do, or they may interpret them not as flaws but as strengths. Fair enough. But if I fail to state my judgment candidly out of a desire to please others, I have failed in scholarly courage.

A scholar's courage is tested most of all when his or her clearly stated positions are met with severe and sustained criticism, and even personal hostility. The longing to be part of a herd is deep within us. Few of us relish the sort of excoriation and even excommunication that occur when the academic tribe gathers itself to repel challenges that it regards as threats. Certainly, the scholar who is consistently labeled by the establishment as "out of bounds" has the obligation to look carefully at his or her methods and conclusions. It is always possible for the tribe to be right even when it is acting tribal. But the scholar is also called to the practice of courage in the face of general disapprobation when, after appropriate review, the scholar determines that his or her mind must stand in this specific place and no other. There is nothing quite so painful, as *Philoctetes* reminds us, as the isolation imposed by social ostracism. And nothing so demonstrates scholarly courage as holding as true what everyone around me declares as false.

AMBITION

I have struggled with naming this virtue. I have considered other terms, such as "desire," "fantasy," "drive," and "energy." But I think "ambition" is the best name for the "motor" that pushes the scholar to significant accomplishment. It is ambition—not in the competitive sense of seeking to outdo others but in the sense of desiring excellence—that moves us to accomplish great things. Athletes must have ambition if they are to "be the best they can be." Artists must have ambition if they are to overcome all the roadblocks to artistic achievement. Musicians must have ambition if they are to endure the toll of endless practice. All humans fall short of their goals. The violinist desiring to be another Heifetz or Hahn may end up in a local orchestra—or teaching band in high school! When personal goals are insignificant, accomplishments will fall even shorter. If an academic only seeks tenure, there is a distinct possibility that the academic will fail at tenure. If a full professorship is the goal, the probability is that the rank will not be reached. Similarly, if one's ambition is to change the shape of an entire discipline, one will fall short; but remarkable things can result from that "failure."

When I was recruiting students for Emory's PhD program in New Testament, the main quality I looked for (assuming the usual battery of intellectual abilities) was such ambition. No matter how marvelous a chassis, a vehicle will not move without a motor. It was important for me to determine what the candidate desired (I worked in the post-draft-dodging days): Was the PhD sought because it was the next step on the academic *cursus honorum*, or because, since the candidate had always liked studying, it offered the gate to a lifetime of staying a student? Such desires might get a student to the dissertation but not much beyond it. The best candidates were those who had, however inchoate and ill formed, a desire to become someone who contributed creatively to the field, and someone who wanted less to stay a student than to become the teacher of others. All else being equal, the more powerful the motor of ambition, the more successful these fledgling scholars would be.

Ambition can be distorted or even evil, it is true, when driven by the spirit of envy. Such envious ambition is revealed by the need to diminish others in the effort to assert oneself. Such personal savagery, it should be noted, is something quite different from scholarly argumentation or even polemics, which have as their target intellectual positions rather than persons. Envious ambition measures the self (positively and negatively) against those one regards in competition with oneself (for position, for status, for recognition, for funding!). The ambition that seeks excellence, in contrast, measures the self against figures who represent greatness in the endeavors one has chosen to engage.

In my own case, once I discovered that I could hold my own with other talented doctoral students, I began to measure myself by the standard of scholars of great accomplishment. My reach certainly exceeded my grasp, but the horizon marked by Dibelius, Bultmann, Cerfaux, and their like was the one on which I fixed my gaze. Tenure, promotion, a chair—these were never my goals; they were comforting in that they gave some academic security and freedom. Still less did becoming a dean, or heading a scholarly organization, motivate me.

But I did want to write a New Testament introduction that could be compared favorably to Kümmel and Wikenhauser. I aimed at a commentary on James that could stand with Dibelius's. I sought out and wrestled with J. Z. Smith—the most prominent contemporary theorist—on the nature of religion,[5] and I tried to write an account of Greco-Roman religion and Christianity that was better than those of Nock and Metzger. And so forth. I gladly admit that I fell far short. But having such large ambitions at least pushed me to what accomplishment I managed.

DISCIPLINE

The energy provided by drive and ambition needs to be focused if it is not to be dissipated. The ability to focus on a task, to stay steady in the analysis of complex data, to be constant in the meeting of obligations, to teach and write no matter what the circumstances depends on the virtue of discipline. The ancient philosopher Epictetus constantly stressed the importance of discipline (*askesis*) as he taught his students how to govern and control their mental impressions.

Discipline may begin in a sense of dedication or duty; the importance of an obligation demands attention and concentration: the farmer awakes before dawn to milk the cows because cows need milking; the soldier does not sleep while on watch because the enemy might attack; the mother stays by the bedside of a feverish child because the illness might grow worse; the athlete refuses to break training because the Olympic games are near. In like manner, the teacher prepares for every class and stirs the embers of enthusiasm for the sake of the students, because ignorance is an evil that must be fought. And the scholar returns again and again to a research project because the question the scholar is pursuing really needs answering.

As a virtue, however, discipline is a habit that is formed through the repetition of such commitments and engagements. Discipline is what enables continued commitment and engagement when motivation runs dry and inspiration is absent. The excellent scholar displays discipline across the spectrum of activities. It is an essential component of great teaching. No matter the weather, no matter the cataclysms in the news, in good health and in bad, the teacher's discipline makes her prepare meticulously, drags her to the classroom, draws from her inner resources a spark of excitement, props her up through fever and weakness, for the sake of instruction. No matter how pressing other obligations, the true teacher grades hundreds of exams and papers carefully and fairly, maintaining the same judiciousness in the last paper as in the first, commenting on work in a manner that encourages improvement, submitting the results on time, for the sake of student progress.

Discipline is equally needed in research. Simply to "put the mind in another place," when that place seems arid and the circle of family and friends seems an oasis of ease, demands discipline. The academic scholar constantly turns to research when already fatigued from the obligations of teaching, or university citizenship, or domestic chores. Getting back to a research project—or worse, getting started on one—when the rest of the household is asleep requires discipline. So does waking three hours before one's family to find a specific passage or parse a few lines or write a few sentences.

Discipline is the virtue summoned when the scholar sits to read. I listed "respect for evidence" as one of the scholar's intellectual virtues. It is the habit of discipline that activates and maintains that respect for the otherness of textual or material evidence. Exegesis is, indeed, nothing more than such a disciplined reading that refuses to project or impose meaning but seeks constantly to discover the meaning embedded in the specific diction, grammar, and syntax of the text being read, or the specific shape, size, style, and siting of the material object being "read." Similarly, discipline enables the scholar fairly to read arguments in disagreement with her own, to characterize the positions of others in an evenhanded and unprejudiced manner, and to bracket her own biases when assessing the work of others.

In scholarly writing, discipline is needed for the consistent elaboration of an argument (deciding correctly what counts as evidence and what does not), as well as for setting and maintaining the level of discourse—these are not easy tasks in compositions of considerable length and complexity. Discipline likewise comes into play in the loathsome details of publishing: meeting deadlines, reading and correcting proofs, compiling accurate indices.

In short, a scholar without discipline is a would-be scholar, and although discipline cannot replace curiosity, intelligence, or imagination, without discipline those qualities will remain simply the adornments of an intellectual and not the marks of accomplished scholarship.

Such constant exercise of discipline by the scholar has, it is true, a significant cost. The productive scholar is an expert in deferred gratification and in the suppression of desires, not least among them the animal warmth of human companionship and the simple pleasures of rest and relaxation. Serious scholarship demands constant effort, and with that effort come fatigue and eventually pain. Putting the mind in another place has a somatic price, and all true scholars know the truth of this.

PERSISTENCE

Persistence is the virtue of discipline extended through time. It is most clearly manifest in those encyclopedic works that require decades to complete—great accomplishment in scholarship is sometimes a function of longevity. Think, for example, of the seven volumes of the *History of Philosophy* published by Frederick Copleston between 1946 and 1959, or, even more impressive, the multivolume *Science and Civilization in China* by Joseph Needham. Beginning in 1948, Needham pursued just one question: Why had China, whose science and technology had preceded those of the West by centuries, apparently lost its capacity for invention? He began with seven volumes, then expanded his work to fifteen volumes, then reached twenty-seven volumes by his death in 1995. Discipline of a high order— even a kind of ruthlessness—is necessary for such impressive scholarly projects to be brought to fruition.[6]

Another way of thinking about persistence is as a scholar's ability to conceive and then pursue topics as new data comes to light or as new ideas and insights are gained. The pursuit of such topics ought not to be a matter of repetition, but of genuine development. Sometimes, the passage of many years is involved. In my narrative, for example, I noted how the insights into the Letter of James that I first had through teaching in 1978 were developed by a series of articles between 1982 and 1990, then brought to a focus in the Anchor Bible commentary in 1995, and concluded in a collection of studies on James in 2004—this is a span of twenty-six years, during which, in one way or another, my "mind was in another place" that was James.

The same picking at a specific topic over time characterizes much of my scholarship. My convictions concerning prophecy in Luke-Acts, for example, found first expression in my dissertation (1977), then were elaborated in great detail in the two-volume Sacra Pagina commentary (1990–1992), and were brought to completion in the monograph *Prophetic Jesus, Prophetic Church* (2011)—a span of thirty-four years. The importance of body symbolism in Luke-Acts is only suggested by the dissertation (1977) but becomes explicit in *Sharing Possessions* (1992), *Scripture and Discernment* (1982/1996), and *The Revelatory Body* (2014). Across these thirty-seven years, the basic insights into somatic experience and expression (that I owed in the first place to readings in existentialism and phenomenology) remained constant, but time was required for their implications and applications to unfold.

The conviction that experience precedes expression (including literary expression) has been a dominant theme in my scholarship, from the time I first taught New Testament introduction at Saint Ben's in 1970. In particular, the resurrection of Jesus, understood as the religious experience of his followers that generated the Christian movement and the composition of its first writings, has been for me not only the central theological conviction of Christian faith but also the critical historical datum for the explication of Christian literature. My emphasis on this point is obvious in *The Writings of the New Testament* (1986) and is pivotal for my extended debate with historical Jesus–questers in *The Real Jesus* (1996), *Living Jesus* (1998), and finally my more recent work, *Miracles: God's Presence and Power in Creation* (2018). I have persisted in engaging this all-important topic for a span of almost forty-eight years.

Two further examples. My book *Among the Gentiles: Greco-Roman Religion and Christianity* (2009) did not arise from nothing. The pertinence of Greco-Roman philosophy and religion to the nascent Christian movement had been teasing my mind for decades, finding written expression through five articles between 1978 and 1997 and in the book *Religious Experience in Early Christianity* in 1998. The ideas in *Among the Gentiles* could not have been developed without my having taught for ten years within the context of a religious department, or my having thematized them in my Phi Beta Kappa and Stone Lectures in 1997–1998. Finally, the two-volume work on Paul that I have published in 2020–2021 grew out of lectures and publications that began in 1980—my mind has been in Paul for over forty years.

The moral virtues I have identified and described to this point all express the passion side of "passionate detachment." Courage, ambition, discipline, and persistence all combine with the intellectual virtues of curiosity, respect for evidence, and imagination in connecting the scholar to his or her work so that it has focus and productivity. But it is important to recognize other dispositions that not only psychologically relieve the scholar of some of the intensity suggested by this list of virtues but also enhance the quality of scholarship itself.

Detachment

One aspect of detachment is the scholar's freedom from distractions that impede research and writing. I do not mean here the worthy "competing loyalties" of which I will speak below, but the less worthy preoccupations that can inhabit the scholar's mind and inhibit it from successfully being in another place. Worry about reputation is an obvious example. The scholar who frets over the possible responses of readers (especially reviewers and most especially tenure committees) is not free to fully engage a scholarly project on its own terms. Closely connected is the concern for the effect of one's research on one's scholarly career: Will my essay or book advance my standing in the eyes of the grandees of the field—or some small fiefdom within the field?

Less worthy by far is the distraction of writing for financial remuneration; often enough, getting paid for work is harmless. But sometimes when a scholar has been given a grant by an organization with a decided ideological bent, that scholar dances—even if not fully consciously—to the tune called by the benefactor/piper. Even less worthy a distraction is the scholar's desire to make one's work a weapon of destruction—not only trying to score legitimate debating points against opponents (for opponents are a feature of disputed territory), but seeking to silence or shame them. Detachment from such distractions and corruptions is necessary for the scholar to engage research and writing as honestly and cleanly as possible.

Another side of detachment is the volitional disposition corresponding to the intellectual virtue of "respect for evidence." Borrowing from ancient skepticism, phenomenologists speak of the importance of the *epochē*, the bracketing of presuppositions and prejudices when approaching any specific phenomenon. In phenomenology, the *epochē* represents a form of detachment that frees the subject matter to be apprehended as much as possible as it is. Rather than impose meanings that are important (for whatever reason) to the researcher, the scholar allows meanings intrinsic to the phenomenon to emerge.

Such detachment, to be sure, is never fully achievable. We cannot easily or once for all shed the desire to find what we want to find. This is a major reason why a community of scholars is critical, for others can spot my biases better than I can, just as I can detect theirs. By mutual correction among scholars, some progress toward the truth of a situation might be made. Working within a community of scholars, I can be relieved of the obligation to purge (by an infinite regression of self-reflection) my consciousness, because I know that others will gladly identify the ways in which my attempts at full *epochē* have fallen short.

The virtue of detachment is easier to cultivate when a scholar recognizes that scholarship itself—much less one's own contributions to scholarship—is not an ultimate but only a relative good. The destiny of humans seldom rests on a scholarly investigation. I am certain that nothing in my many projects is critical to the survival (or even the thriving) of the human race. Scholarship, indeed, is a form of play. It is serious, it is highly ruled, it dislikes cheating, it enhances the minds and hearts of participants. But it is best approached as a game. G. K. Chesterton drew a sharp distinction between seriousness and solemnity. To be serious about one's work is good; to be solemn about one's work is to be silly. The point of this is that scholarship is much improved when it is played as a game. It is much distorted when the scholar places his or her own identity and worth in scholarly accomplishments. The world (quite rightly) does not care whether you use italics or not; get over yourself.

Contentment

By the moral virtue of contentment, I certainly do not mean self-satisfaction or smugness. The term "contentment" is one of the several possible translations of the Greek *autarcheia*, which can also be translated as "self-sufficiency" or "self-control." In ancient moral discourse, it is opposed to the vice of *pleonexia* (avarice)—the "craving disease" that Paul identifies as a form of idolatry (Eph. 5:5). I use it here as a pointer to the volitional disposition that is, like detachment, a form of freedom from a scholarly possessiveness manifested by obsessiveness, compulsiveness, and perfectionism.

I speak of a form of possessiveness because, like more obvious varieties of avarice, it is a need to acquire and to cling that arises from anxiety. The logic of avarice builds on the premise that to be is to have, and to have more is to be more. The always ambiguous link between human being and having—"I both am and have a body"—is here made absolute.[7] I am only insofar as I possess. To the extent that I do not possess, to that extent, I do not exist. Such is the engine of anxiety that drives possessiveness. To share what I have represents a fearful self-dispossession: Who am I if I have not?

The logic of avarice applies to all forms of acquiring and owning, including scholarship. Is what I produce as a scholar the source of my identity and worth? Then my anxiety will drive me to obsess about its adequacy and compulsively to seek its perfection (it is "me," after all). It is extraordinarily difficult for me to release what I have made, not only because it is "mine" (or "me") but also because when I expose it to others, they may judge it negatively—a harsh review of my scholarship is the same as an attack on me.

But if my identity and worth are not to be identified with my scholarship, then what I research and write can freely and generously be shared with others. As in other areas of life, so in scholarship: liberality and even prodigality reveal a freedom that is the opposite of a cramped perfectionism driven by anxiety, that only with great reluctance shares with others what I have discovered or crafted.

Voltaire is credited with the aphorism "the perfect (or the best) is the enemy of the good"—although he attributes the axiom to an Italian proverb. Whoever first crafted it, the maxim's practical wisdom applies to scholarship. There is something terribly sad about scholars of exceptional ability failing to produce what they might have, because of perfectionism. Their obsession over details, their compulsive need to cross every *t*, their reluctance to publish until they have produced a small but wondrously shaped excretion—all these are painful to contemplate.

They resemble brain surgeons who refuse to operate on patients unless the result can be certified as ideal in every respect. Excellent surgeons want to operate as often as they possibly can; the proposition that they would operate only a handful of times in order to perform "perfect surgery" would strike them, quite rightly, as ludicrous: if there is anything like perfection in surgery, it lies in the repeated practice of the art.

I do not in the least mean to suggest that prolific scholarly production is necessarily excellent in quality, but I also do not consider paucity in publication to be the mark of superior scholarly standards. The quality of scholarly work does not correspond to size or number; a finely crafted essay may be as important in shaping a field as is a massive tome, just as the writing of many studies may or may not be as worthwhile as a single monograph. The length of a scholar's vita has little to do with the value of the scholar's contribution to scholarship. That said, the question remains: Why do so many highly trained men and women within the scholarly guild publish so little? Why do they resemble surgeons who space out three operations over thirty years, or, more dramatically, stop operating altogether after performing perhaps two?

Many reasons may be invoked to explain why a scholar's production does not match his or her intellectual gifts: perhaps energy is directed to teaching rather writing; perhaps health or domestic problems inhibit research and writing; perhaps the scholar simply does not have a great deal of energy available in the first place; perhaps curiosity has burned low; perhaps ideas seem ephemeral and not worth pursuing. But perfectionism is certainly one of the reasons.

If scholarly perfectionism arises (at least in part) from existential anxiety concerning identity and worth, and (in part) the false equation of being with having, and (in part) the idolatrous impulse that makes something nonultimate to be treated as ultimate—manifesting what William Lynch calls "the absolutizing instinct"—then scholarship is being taken too seriously by far.[8] When the writing of a book becomes the demonstration of my worth, the proof of my intelligence, the assertion of my place in the world, then it has acquired an over-the-top importance that can have the effect of crippling the very capacity to compose the book.

Authentic contentment (*autarcheia*) with regard to scholarship means severing the connection between scholarly activity and self-worth. Work is work. It is important, but it is not all-important. I have put a lot of myself into it, but it is not myself. I need, first, to remember the true basis of my identity and worth as one created in the image and likeness of God, as one gifted with intelligence and the ability to praise my creator through my work, but also as one who cannot add anything to my identity or worth by means of that work. God's measure is not that of the Society of Biblical Literature. Second, I need to cultivate a spirit of playfulness with regard to my scholarship. It is, after all, a game. A serious game, to be sure, to be taken seriously. But it is not ultimate. Like other serious human games, it is contingent. To play the game well, one must be relaxed and loose, fluid and flexible, willing to take losses as well as win victories, knowing that in the end, playing well and joyfully is the entire point.

MULTITASKING

Multitasking is certainly not one of Aristotle's virtues, and I suspect that many would regard it as a necessary skill imposed by the circumstances of modern life rather than an excellence in scholarship. And it is certainly true that scholars in the twenty-first century face a bewildering barrage of expectations that earlier generations did not. A quick example: In the first half of my academic career, professional secretaries typed manuscripts, copied them, and mailed them; they handled arrangements for speaking engagements; they kept a record of future obligations; they stood as guards before the office door. In the last half of my time as an academic, all these tasks were mine alone to do—the theory being that the computer, e-mail, and smartphones adequately replaced secretaries. They did not. The highly engaged academic scholar today must be his or her own travel agent, compositor, printer, and record-keeper. The time required to do these tasks is carved, naturally, from the time that formerly could be spent in reading, preparing classes, or doing research.

This minor irritant can be taken as a token of other alterations in an academic's world that tend to fill available time with anything but scholarship: the endless "assessments and evaluations" demanded by academic bureaucracies; the grinding and mind-numbing cycle of committee meetings and faculty meetings; the perpetual recruitment of new students and faculty; the stream of correspondence recommending and reviewing students and faculty; the hosting of learned dignitaries; the celebrations of faculty and staff birthdays, promotions, leave-taking—you get the idea. A less-than-virtuous form of the required multitasking in this new world is all too familiar: the "tyranny of the immediate" captures all of a scholar's attention, and life is dissipated in an endless round of ephemeral chores. The focus required for genuine scholarship is lost in a sea of "distractions." Among all the other tasks required of the academic, the conditions needed for fine scholarship to be done are treated as optional. To the degree that schools continue this trend toward consuming all their teachers' time and energy in institutional maintenance and upkeep, to that degree the academy has truly lost its way. That which was intended to serve has become that which is served. But given this reality—and this growing tendency—how can the scholar cope?

The virtue I am getting at combines efficiency—doing these and other tasks quickly and without hesitation—and an equanimity that derives from the perception that there is something good for scholarship in having many different tasks to perform. As my previous paragraphs suggest, to be sure, there are limits to that perception. Some tasks imposed on scholars in today's academy are deleterious and deplete the energy that ought to be given to worthier challenges.

The virtue, then, consists first in the cultivation of a "rapid response" form of focus: one moves from one task to another with appropriate attention and concentration but is able always to stay in touch with "the mind in another place" that is the world of learning. The time when scholars were granted time and leisure in order exclusively to cultivate their art is definitively over. The ability to focus quickly, turn one's focus to another subject or task, then refocus, is distinctively demanded of today's scholar. Certainly, quick mental apprehension, retentive memory, and the sort of detachment I have described above are all aspects of this form of excellence. But so is the calm receptivity that comes from a positive perception of multiple tasks and competing loyalties that challenge today's scholar. My premise here, shaped by my own experience and by observation of colleagues over the years, is that scholarship is not improved but diminished when the mind is unrelievedly and exclusively devoted to research and writing. I think of the mind, on analogy with diet, as healthiest when omnivorous.

Quite apart from the demands of academic citizenship, there has always existed a tension between teaching and research. Some scholars have regarded the tension as intolerable and have opted to concentrate entirely on one or the other. I have mentioned the way that scholarly monks at Saint Meinrad poured all their learning into their classes—certainly to the benefit of their students. The opposite option is frequently found in "research" universities, in which full-time faculty assign many of the pedagogic chores to assistants, so that they can spend their time in reading or writing. Still others, especially in doctoral programs, only offer seminars in the subjects they are presently researching, whether these subjects are particularly germane to student needs or not. In this case, teaching is a way for the scholar to pursue research in another form.

I have come to think that the tension between teaching and research is best left unresolved, and that scholarship gains in imagination and insight when each is maintained in its respective integrity. Thus, I have found that courses seeming to have little to do with what I am working on at the time have tended to accomplish two things: first, relieve my research mind—which tends to demand an exclusive focus—by providing momentarily still "another place" for its attention; second, frequently offer unexpected insight into the material I am researching. I choose the adjective "unexpected" deliberately, for such cognitive happenstance cannot be programmed. It results from the free play of the mind alternately engaging disparate topics. Looking back at my teaching over a span of some fifty years—and teaching the widest variety of subjects—I cannot think of a single class that actually affected my research and writing negatively; to the contrary, I frequently found my research and writing drawing on classes that I had taught in the past or was currently teaching.

The contemporary scholar also lives within the tension created by non-academic commitments and obligations. The leisure available to German academics of the mid-nineteenth century, who had few students to teach, and whose every material need was attended to by wives or servants, is unimaginable today. Family life, with all domestic chores shared between spouses, demands time and attention. The young scholar today who longs to add another footnote to his or her study of an ancient author finds that picking up the children at school or soccer practice takes priority. Commitments to church and society also require time and attention. Indeed, leaving apart scholarship, commitments to family, church, and civil society can themselves enter into fairly stiff competition. I argue, however, that for the dedicated scholar, such competing loyalties need not simply represent "distraction," or be regarded entirely as inimical to the life of the mind. In a manner different from teaching, the "empty time" spent in the parking lot waiting for school to let out, or at the sink washing dishes, or driving to a church benefit, or keeping watch over the sickbed of a loved one need not actually be "empty" at all but may be the contemporary moments of leisure within which creative thought can occur. The truly wonderful thing about the mind is that it actually can "be in another place."

I am sure that these intellectual and moral virtues are not the only ones that make for excellence in a scholar, but they are the ones that seem important to me in the light of my fifty years in scholarly pursuits. Nor, I emphasize once more, are they the virtues that I unfailingly displayed in my own work. They do represent, though, the measure by which I tried to measure myself. And as I look back over the list, I must agree with my placement of curiosity and courage at the head of each category of virtue.

Epilogue

Looking Back and Forward

B Y TELLING MY OWN STORY AS A "SCHOLAR'S LIFE," I HAVE aimed at more than a set of reminiscences that might be of interest to family and friends. My goal from the start has been to provide some sense of what this manner of life is. I have had in mind especially those who might be considering this vocation, as well as that large group that may or may not have some acquaintance with academic types but who have little sense of what scholars actually do. The life of each scholar is, to be sure, distinctive, but my hope has been that by digging into the particularities of my own life, some insight might be gained into elements common to scholars in the humanities, above all those whose careers are spent in colleges, universities, and schools of theology.

Looking Back

I am aware of the peculiar and nonduplicable aspects of my own progression toward becoming and then being a scholar of the New Testament and Christian origins. Not all, or even very many, other scholars of my generation have found in the religious life a refuge from the chaos of being orphaned and culturally transplanted, or have been exposed to the astonishingly rich traditions of monastic learning, or have ruptured the connection to the religious life through a scandalous marriage to a chronically ill woman with six children, or have worked in the same mix of secular and sacred academic contexts as I have.

My life as a scholar was both long in its development and marked by abrupt and sometimes dramatic alterations. The most consistent threads of continuity I can discern as I consider my story are my intellectual avidity, my self-confidence, and my abiding sense of living under the gaze of God. As I said in the introduction to this book, the desire to be a saint has never left me, even as I grow ever more aware of the ways I fall short of that goal.

The attention I have given to the specifics of my own experience has had the purpose of suggesting the way all scholarship is located within a complex and always changing set of circumstances. People become scholars for a variety of reasons, find themselves studying this topic rather than that as much by chance as by choice, are influenced in ways beyond their awareness or control by their teachers as well as by the academies within which they work and the students they teach. Scholarship does not exist in a privileged realm rising cloud-like over the complexities of everyday existence. Scholars work out of and respond to the circumstances of their diverse lives.

By going into such detail concerning my own service, teaching, and research within each of my settings, I have also tried to give a sense of the range of activities engaged by academic scholars. Everyone knows that they teach classes, but few outside the guild know what goes into preparing classes, advising students, administering and grading exams, evaluating and grading papers—or how many hours these activities require in a class with an enrollment of from eighty to one hundred! Likewise, everyone knows that scholars write books and articles. But few who do not write and publish understand that research and writing encompass the mastery of library protocols; the reading of hundreds of other scholars' books and articles; the composition of book reviews, conference presentations, and responses; as well as, for some, the writing of popular essays, lectures, and sermons.

Most of all, nonacademics have little idea of the enormous amounts of time and energy that are devoted to service activities that are little noted (often even by the institutions scholars serve). Committees of every sort are simply the surface, although it is worth noting that a search committee for new faculty may require hundreds of hours of each of its members. Add to them the processes of recruitment and direction of graduate students, peer review of colleagues, the writing of recommendations for colleagues and for students seeking academic positions, and on and on. All these activities, in turn, compete with those owed to faith and family and society. I have tried to show, in sum, that scholarship today is, for the most part, emphatically not an ivory-tower exercise. Just the opposite: contemporary scholars must struggle to "have the mind in another place" as they are overwhelmed by other commitments and obligations.

By placing so much stress on the arduous aspects of the scholarly life, however, I may, without intending it, omit the most important part of the answer to the question, "Why do people seek to become scholars?" What I refer to, of course, is the simple pleasure, fun, and even joy that scholars take in their activities. All teachers know what an exciting, even intoxicating, experience it is to have a student suddenly "get it," or to have a class laugh in response to a casual aside, or to see genuine progress in learning. But imagine the thrill of coaching a superbly talented doctoral student through a dissertation, and then seeing his or her work become part of the larger scholarly conversation. Teaching at every level is, for those fitted to it, a kind of addiction—but one with no bad side effects.

More mysterious, though no less real, is the excitement a research scholar feels when grappling with an ancient text or artifact, or the pleasure attendant on assembling all the pertinent evidence for the solution of a problem, or the satisfaction deriving from a well-made argument, or the sense of high purpose accompanying the approach to a truly significant issue. In the end, I think, genuine scholars spend their lives doing scholarship because they like it; they really like it.

Thinking back on the many moments in which my life was lit by such pleasure and enjoyment, I better understand the compelling attraction the activities of the teacher and writer held for me. From the time I first experienced the distinctive fun to be had in this playground, I knew I wanted more of this. And it is one of the sorrows of late-life diminishment to realize that those distinctive pleasures must fade ever more as my physical limitations inhibit my mind's still eager pursuit of "other places."

Looking Forward

Already in the introduction, I noted the ways in which scholarship in the humanities—and specifically in the New Testament—had changed over the fifty-odd years of my active life as a scholar. I noted how changes in technology, social arrangements, ideology, and institutions made the sort of scholarship that first attracted me and to which I devoted my best energies less and less possible and even plausible to a new generation of academics. Such changes will certainly accelerate as the inhabitants of so-called first-world culture find themselves in the midst of cognitive and cultural upheavals that can accurately be termed revolutionary.

Predictions of any sort are notoriously risky. The student of history most of all should know how events, discoveries, and even persons can effect a dramatic change in what seemed like an inexorable progress. Only political pundits, it seems, are immune from the embarrassment of failed prophecy. So, I refrain from any predictions but one.

As I look forward with my now-cataract-less but still astigmatic eyes, I am utterly confident about the fate of my own work and deeply uncertain about scholarship as a whole and in my specific areas of study. My own work will join the great river of forgetfulness that flows into the ocean of oblivion. Perhaps something I said will remain significant for a short period of time in the lives of one or two students. Perhaps in a future generation one of my published opinions will be noticed and exploited. If this is the destiny of even the greatest of scholars, then it is surely mine as well. All the more important, then, that I did my work taking delight in the process rather than in the expectation of success.

Concerning scholarship in the humanities and in New Testament, asking questions rather than making predictions seems the more prudent approach. There seems to be little doubt, for example, that technological change will continue and even accelerate. But what will be its effects on the sort of scholarship that I practiced and taught? Will the dominance of electronic media increase the speed of interaction but also its shallowness? The evidence provided so far by the blogosphere is not encouraging. Will horizontal interconnectivity among students—the hive syndrome—make them more resistant to individual research, to vertical intervention, to independent thinking? In the classroom, will PowerPoint and instruction-through-video reduce the importance of the living instructor and diminish the modeling and imitation of rhetoric and dialectic? Will the study of ancient languages continue to diminish as technology reinforces the perception that the "now" is supremely important and the past has little to teach? Or will the recent stoppage of instruction in cursive writing to the young have the (predictable) effect of blocking access to the entire universe of manuscripts, private correspondence, and diplomatic literature?

Even more pressing questions can be asked concerning the future of scholarship in its institutional and ideological dimensions. The American academy was facing a genuine crisis caused by the cost/benefit disparity even before the coronavirus pandemic of 2020–2021. Can the academy, in the face of technological advances in "distance learning," make a convincing case for education taking place in a specific place and in the company of other bodies? I believe such a case can and must be made, but the appearance that scholarship can be learned and practiced without the need for face-to-face interaction, together with the academy's chronic inability or unwillingness to show how embodiedness is ingredient to true scholarship, will make the case more difficult to argue.

Will the academic institutions that (since the eclipse of monasteries) have served as the natural home of scholarship use their straitened circumstances, as well as political and parental pressure, to continue the trend of supporting research and writing that is demonstrably "useful" in the present, and starving out scholarship that is "nonessential," or "optional"? Here, the question of funding is obviously critical. It has been clear for decades how, in the sciences, external funding has massively directed what gets studied and what does not. The "independence" of academic scholarship—leaving aside corporate scholarship—has already been fundamentally compromised in the sciences. Will it be also in the humanities?

This brings me to the last and most difficult set of questions, which concern scholarship and ideology. As I indicated in the introduction, ideology has never been absent from the study of the humanities, and certainly not from the study of the New Testament. Scholarship that is funded and censored by ecclesiastical bodies is expected to conform to the expectations of the respective churches (as the Catholic *imprimatur* and *nihil obstat* attached to books make obvious).[1] Scholars insisting on the rights of free inquiry within such ideological constraints have had mixed success. But there is nothing particularly iniquitous about such open sponsorship and control. Even if a Roman Catholic scholar like myself is not funded or directed by the church—which has been the case—it is natural that I should work within the framework established by my own deepest life convictions.

Scholars not sharing those convictions are free to challenge me, especially when they suspect that my commitments, rather than the evidence, have dictated my argument.

My concern has more to do with the influence of ideology in less open arrangements, as when scholars convinced of a certain ideological position work to discourage or even block the study of certain subjects, certain periods, or certain writers—not at the behest of an institution, but out of a certain groupthink that exercises the equivalent of institutional pressure. The sort of "cancellation" syndrome that we observe every day in social media had its beginnings in the sort of political correctness that became ever more dominant in American universities and schools of theology over the past several decades.

An anecdote can illustrate. Sometime in the first decade of the new century, I was asked to consult on a Lilly-funded venture involving some of the most notable young theologians in the country on "theological practices." The group had concluded a first round of papers and exchanges and was now considering what they should do next. The suggestion that it study a classic Christian text devoted to practices met quick approval. During a break, I suggested to the leadership that *The Instructor* by Clement of Alexandria (ca. 150–215) offered a perfect opportunity to engage a thinker of the past whose work was totally devoted to "practices" and was unusual for the way in which he treated the genders equally. The leadership liked the idea, but when the proposal was made to the entire group, a profound silence ensued, broken finally by a leading feminist theologian who said, "Isn't Clement overly Platonist?" In code, she meant, isn't Clement, as an ancient male, hopelessly patriarchal, and useless to read? The group offered no resistance, and the reading of Clement was quietly "canceled." It was a remarkable example of how an ideological posture led to a rejection of an invaluable resource from the past, out of (I am sure) pure ignorance. For genuine scholarship, engagement with a figure like Clement—even if he was patriarchal—would be considered all the more important precisely because he did not simply match the predilections of the present age.

The pressure applied by "scholarly consensus" to conform to a specific ideology is as real and powerful as the pressure applied by ecclesiastical bodies or corporate funding agencies. It is possibly even more powerful because it is covert and exercised by a kind of "silencing" that is only with heroic effort resisted. My concern is that—linked to the greater dependence of scholars on electronic/digital communication and the ability to "cancel" differing views almost instantaneously—scholarship in the future will be deeply and adversely affected.

Perhaps my concerns are unfounded. I hope they are. But in the light of what I have experienced and observed, I am even more convinced that in the future, scholars in the humanities will need to cultivate in themselves and encourage in each other true independence of judgment and courage.

NOTES

Introduction

1. A book that covers some of the same ground is the classic by A. D. Sertil-langes, OP, *The Intellectual Life: Its Spirit, Conditions, Methods*, trans. Mary Ryan (Westminster, MD: Newman, 1959), which, despite its many virtues, is both dated and parochial. Closer is James Axtell's *The Pleasures of Academe: A Celebration and Defense of Higher Education* (Lincoln: University of Nebraska Press, 1999). Axtell writes beautifully, but his treatment is almost entirely positive, tends to be defined by the friendly environment of William and Mary, and has a different slant on "becoming" than mine. I have derived much benefit (and enjoyment) also from the memoir of my former colleague at Emory, William M. Chace, *100 Semesters: My Adventures as Student, Professor, and University President, and What I Learned along the Way* (Princeton: Princeton University Press, 2006).

2. *A Greek Concordance to the Greek Testament*, ed. W. F. Moulton and A. S. Geden (Edinburgh: T&T Clark). It was actually Alfred S. Geden who did most of the spadework on the magnificent concordance to which William F. Moulton added his name and assistance; published first in 1897, the work appeared in a fifth edition under the editorship of Harold K. Moulton in 1977. *A Concordance to the Septuagint and the Other Greek Versions of the Old Testament (Including the Apocryphal Books)* appeared in the same year (1897), edited by Edwin Hatch and Henry Redpath (assisted by other scholars). The 1977 Athens edition from Beneficial Books Publishers is a facsimile of the first edition.

3. These monumental lexical works also involved the work of many hands. The first edition of *A Greek-English Lexicon* under the editorship of Henry George

Liddell and Robert Scott in 1843 itself built on many predecessors and benefited from the labor of many scholars. I first used the "revised and augmented" edition by Henry Stuart Jones, with the assistance of Roderick McKenzie (and "with the cooperation of many scholars") in 1968 (Oxford: Clarendon). Charlton Lewis and Charles Short, in turn, based *A Latin Dictionary* on the translation by E. A. Andrews of William Freund's 1850 German version (Oxford: Clarendon, 1962; first ed. 1879). The same incremental gathering of lexical knowledge is evident in *A Greek-English Lexicon of the New Testament and Other Early Christian Literature*. Walter Bauer based his German edition of 1937 on the earlier work of Erwin Preuschen; Bauer's work, in turn, was translated and adapted by William Arndt and F. Wilbur Gingrich in 1957; Gingrich and Frederick Danker continued the project through the University of Chicago Press in 1979.

4. The standard English reference text for all ancient Greek is by Herbert Weir Smyth, *A Greek Grammar for Colleges* (New York: American Book Company, 1920). New Testament scholars also turn regularly to F. Blass and A. Debrunner, *A Greek Grammar of the New Testament and Other Early Christian Literature,* trans. and rev. Robert W. Funk, 9th ed. (Chicago: University of Chicago Press, 1961), as well as C. F. D. Moule's *An Idiom Book of New Testament Greek* (Cambridge: Cambridge University Press, 1953).

5. Started in 1923, this impressive set of literal translations from Greek and Latin authors (facing the original texts) from the Harvard University Press now includes some 530 volumes.

6. Walter Scott, *Hermetica, the Ancient Greek and Latin Writings Which Contain Religious or Philosophic Teachings Ascribed to Hermes Trismegistus,* 3 vols. (Oxford: Clarendon, 1924–1936); a fourth volume, *Testimonia,* was compiled by A. S. Ferguson after the death of Scott in 1925.

7. J. P. Migne, *Patrologiae Cursus Completus, series Latina,* 217 vols. (Paris: Impremerie Catholique, 1841–1855), and *Patrologiae Cursus Completus, series Graeca,* 161 vols. (Paris: Impremerie Catholique, 1857–1866). A prodigy of collocation, editing, and publishing.

8. The late nineteenth-century discovery of a trove of literary and nonliterary fragments from the Greco-Roman period by two young British archaeologists at Oxyrhynchus in Egypt led to a publishing venture that has not yet (at 83 volumes) reached its end; see B. P. Grenfell and A. S. Hunt, *Oxyrhynchus Papyri* (London: Egypt Exploration Fund, 1898–2008).

9. Albert Schweitzer (1875–1965), in addition to his fame as a musicologist and medical doctor, was one of the most significant New Testament scholars of the

early twentieth century, for his landmark work both on Jesus (*The Quest of the Historical Jesus: A Critical Study of Its Progress from Reimarus to Wrede,* trans. W. Montgomery [1906; New York: Macmillan, 1968]) and on Paul (see *Paul and His Interpreters: A Critical History,* trans. W. Montgomery [1911; New York: Schocken Books, 1964] and *The Mysticism of Paul the Apostle,* trans. W. Montgomery [1930; Baltimore: Johns Hopkins University Press, 1998]). Rudolf Bultmann (1884–1976) was the colossus of New Testament studies when I began my studies. He wrote pivotal books on the Gospels (*History of the Synoptic Gospels,* trans. John Marsh [1921; San Francisco: HarperSanFrancisco, 1976]; *The Gospel of John: A Commentary* [1941; Philadelphia: Westminster John Knox, 1971]) and on New Testament theology (*Kerygma and Myth: A Theological Debate* [original essay, 1941; London: SPCK, 1953]; *Theology of the New Testament,* trans. K. Grobel, 2 vols. [New York: Charles Scribner's Sons, 1951–1953]).

10. After publishing two successful popular books with HarperSanFrancisco (in 1996 and 1998), for example, I proposed to John Louden, the editor of those two books, a more substantial scholarly project. He told me that the publisher was not interested in any book that would sell fewer than twenty thousand copies.

11. The most impressive example is the *Thesaurus Linguae Graecae* (*TLG*), begun at the University of California Irvine in 1972, which digitizes all Greek literary texts from Homer to 1453. See also the *Thesaurus Linguae Latinae* (*TLL*), which started in 1894 as a nondigital collection of all Latin texts from 600 BCE to 636 CE, and whose entries are now posted online.

12. See, e.g., A. Von Harnack, *History of Dogma,* 3 vols., English translation by Neil Buchanan from the 3rd ed., appears in 7 vols. or abridged in 4 vols. (1st German ed. 1886–1889; New York: Dover, 1961). When discussing Gnosticism, Harnack did not have available to him the compositions discovered in the twentieth century—such as the Nag Hammadi Library—but only patristic witnesses and a few scattered compositions (such as the *Letter of Ptolemy* and the *Pistis Sophia*), which led him to classify Gnosticism as a specifically Christian phenomenon and "the acute Hellenization of Christianity."

13. For a scathing review of what he calls "Protestant presuppositions" in the study of early Christianity, see J. Z. Smith, *Drudgery Divine: On the Comparison of Early Christianity and the Religions of Late Antiquity* (Chicago: University of Chicago Press, 1994), especially 1–53.

14. I am not indulging in caricature. After a lecture delivered at a Protestant seminary, I was met by a young scholar who introduced herself in just such terms. The exchange went like this: She asked me, "What are you?" and I replied, "Well,

I am a scholar." She responded, "No, I mean, what are you?" When I asked what she meant, she responded with the self-description I report in the text.

15. The full quotation (from *La Femme Pauvre*, 1897) is, "The only real sadness, the only real failure, the only great tragedy in life, is not to become a saint."

16. Based on lectures to young monks at San Anselmo in 1955–1956, Jean Le Clercq's *The Love of Learning and the Desire for God: A Study of Monastic Culture*, 3rd ed. (New York: Fordham University Press, 1982) became a highly influential book for Catholic scholars of my generation.

Chapter One

1. In her novel *Moo*, Jane Smiley has a lovely passage describing the charms of the Flambeau.

2. Some of them were undoubtedly veterans of World War II for whom alcohol served as an anodyne for the (as yet unrecognized) post-traumatic stress disorder (PTSD) they suffered upon return to civilian life.

3. Annie Proulx's *Accordian Crimes* brilliantly portrays the ethnic rivalries among "white" immigrant populations.

4. At confirmation I added Joseph, so my youthful moniker was Timothy Robert Joseph Johnson. The name Luke was added when I made simple vows as a Benedictine monk.

5. The references to morning and evening indicate when the papers arrived on the train, the opposite of their actual publication times.

6. The other was taking the risk of seeking employment in Milwaukee or Chicago.

7. I must rely here on the memories of my older siblings, who are unanimous in their testimony concerning the overt affection that my parents displayed.

8. The arm rubbing seems to be an odd genetic trait, running from my maternal grandmother to my mother, to several of us children.

9. I also remember vividly the sort of mental dissociation I experienced when Father Weber, Pat, and I wended our way to our own house to give communion to my mother in her last days. Ritual and real worlds crashed in my head.

10. These tales, to be sure, frightened as well as entertained. Andersen's "The Little Match Girl" has remained in my imagination as an exercise in pathos unmatched even by Dickens.

11. T. H. White is best known for his *Once and Future King*, which has exercised a broad influence on succeeding fantasy literature, not least the movie *Excalibur*

and the musical *Camelot*. The story of an emotionally isolated child who finds escape from her oppressive warders through involvement with an alternative culture has more than a few points of connection with my own, as we will see.

12. Other favorites included Dorothy Parker's "I would rather fail a Wasserman test, than read a poem by Edgar Guest," and Ogden Nash's classic "On Breaking the Ice," which in its entirety read, "Candy is dandy but liquor is quicker."

13. Another maternal intervention: Ianthe Fandry, mother's rival for the position of town clerk, spotted four of us boys skinny-dipping in the Flambeau, took the clothes we had discarded in the bushes, and called my mother, hoping to embarrass her with our bad behavior. As we huddled in the shelter of the train bridge, Mother showed up with Uncle Art, and gave Ms. Fandry an earful. She was our hero.

14. We didn't entirely lack assignments, of course—I remember in my typical ham-handed way struggling to create a papier-mâché topographical map and making a mess of it. But time at home was mostly free, apart from the mandatory chores all kids had to do. Everyone worked. In that small and impoverished town, there was a complete lack of entitlement.

15. A constant struggle was engaged each freezing day with Skeezix, the school janitor. He would strew ashes on our ice slide, we would refreeze it with fresh water, he would smother it again. A Sisyphean drama.

16. New York: Harper, 1938.

17. New York: Harper, 1940.

18. First appearing in the *New Yorker* (August 31, 1946), it was then published as a book by Alfred A. Knopf in 1946.

Chapter Two

1. Anyone intimately acquainted with the South knows that there is no such thing as a "southern accent"; there are, rather, a variety of regional accents and ethnic distinctions. In the 1950s, white Mississippi kids extended vowels (with way-a-gon [wagon] being three syllables), made strange stresses (*out*side rather than out*side*; *up*stairs instead of up*stairs*), and used odd locutions ("hindcatcher" for the baseball catcher; "hosepipe" for hose). It also takes some time to decode the subtleties that lie within southern locutions. There is a great difference, for example, between "bless your heart" (a form of endearment) and "bless his or her heart" (a form of dismissal).

2. It is a credit to their basic goodness that they so graciously accepted Catholic Yankees whom they had been told since childhood were spawn of the devil.

3. I don't know why, but Mickey seemed constitutionally unable to get us to Mass on time, a source of embarrassment and resentment for boys scheduled as acolytes.

4. Like many of my generation, I can mark the periods of my life by means of music: in the forties and early fifties, classic pop and crooners; in the midfifties, the birth of rock and roll; in the early sixties, folk (the Weavers and Peter, Paul, and Mary); in the midsixties, the Beatles and Bob Dylan; in the late sixties, the supergroups (Creedence Clearwater Revival and the rest); in the seventies, disco and then heavy metal. At the birth of hip hop, I dropped out.

5. This is not altogether true. I do remember how impressed I was by the erotic scenes in Morton Thompson's novel *Not as a Stranger* (1955).

6. Theodore Bilbo (1877–1947) was a two-time governor of the state (1916–1920, 1928–1932) and a US senator (1935–1947). An outspoken member of the Ku Klux Klan, he authored a book entitled *Take Your Choice: Separation or Mongrelization* (1947).

7. *The Tapestry of Mercy—the History of the St. Louis Community of the Sisters of Mercy of the Americas* (2008).

8. Rawley Myers, *This Is the Seminary* (New York: Bruce Publishing Co., 1953).

9. Catholics tended disproportionately to be located, moreover, in riparian towns like Vicksburg and Natchez, or in coastal cities like Gulfport and Biloxi. In the 1950s, the capital city of Jackson had only three parishes (Saint Mary's, Saint Theresa's, and Saint Richard's) in addition to the cathedral parish of Saint Peter's.

10. The "lake" is actually an estuary of the Gulf of Mexico covering some 630 square miles; the causeway is the world's longest span over water.

11. The seminary (and abbey) are actually both named for Saint Joseph, but the post office appellation of "Saint Ben's" is universally used.

12. *The Church's Year of Grace* (Collegeville, MN: Liturgical Press, 1953).

13. Lives of heroic men (Charles de Foucauld, Father Damien), visionaries (Bernadette Soubirous), and virgin-martyrs (Maria Goretti) were typical.

14. Among these petitionary responsive prayers that we recited regularly were the Litany of the Holy Name of Jesus, the Litany of the Most Sacred Heart of Jesus, the Litany of the Blessed Virgin Mary, and—my favorite—the Litany of the Saints.

15. Ember Days were three days of prayer and fasting in each of the four seasons.

16. "Holy Mary, pray for us . . . all you martyrs and confessors, pray for us."

17. My class was the guinea pig for an experimentation in teaching Latin as a spoken language, complete with exercises in recitation using audiotapes in the new language lab. It was fun, but we had a lot of catching up to do when the later curriculum demanded we read Cicero!

18. Especially *The Napoleon of Notting Hill* (1904) and *The Man Who Was Thursday* (1908).

19. For example, *Danton: A Study* (1899); *The Path to Rome* (1902); *Woolsey* (1930); *Characters of the Reformation* (1936).

20. As in Belloc's *The Bad Child's Book of Beasts* (1896) and Chesterton's *Graybeards at Play* (1900), and *Wine, Water, and Song* (1915).

21. Along with Léon Bloy, Charles Péguy—who was killed in World War I—was part of the circle of Parisian intellectuals (including Jacques and Raïssa Maritain) who had a great impact on the Catholic renewal of the twentieth century. I read him in the English translation by Ann and Julien Green in a volume of his verse and prose entitled *Basic Verities* (1943); see R. Maritain, *"We Have Been Friends Together"* and *"Adventures in Grace,"* trans. J. Kernan (South Bend, IN: Saint Augustine's Press, 2016).

22. Augustine, *Confessions* 1.1–2.

23. Available now in Johnson, *Catholic Consciousness: Essays on Scripture, Theology, and the Church* (New York: Paulist, 2021).

24. See M. Adler, *How to Read a Book: The Art of Getting a Liberal Education* (1940).

25. The movie *The Help* is set in that exact time and place, and (with some exaggeration) captures the social dynamics that in an undramatic fashion we all participated in.

26. More precisely, it is God's, but you know what I mean.

Chapter Three

1. The chapter room was used for community meetings, for the recitation of these "little hours" and Compline, and for the weekly "Chapter of Faults," during which monks acknowledged their failings against the community.

2. After the reform, the daily Eucharist was concelebrated by all the priest-monks. The practice of "private masses" ceased.

3. For a sense of how this regimen shaped consciousness, see my two essays "How a Monk Learns Mercy: Thomas Merton and the Rule of Benedict," *Commonweal* 145, no. 16 (2018): 21–24, and "The Rule of Benedict and the Practices of

Ancient Moral Philosophy: The Witness of Monasticism in a Postmodern Age,"
American Benedictine Review 71, no. 2 (2020): 143–79.

4. A sampling: Scheeben, *The Mysteries of Christianity* (1865–1897); Gleason,
Grace (1962); Lubac, *The Drama of Atheistic Humanism* (1949); Congar, *The Mystery of the Temple* (1962); Teilhard de Chardin, *Phenomenon of Man* (1959) and *The Divine Milieu* (1960); Casel, *The Mystery of Christian Worship* (1962).

5. The encyclical reversed the ban on the historical study of the New Testament
and opened the way for the surge of first-rate Catholic biblical study that found
its symbolic expression in *The Jerome Biblical Commentary*, ed. Raymond Brown,
Joseph Fitzmyer, and Roland Murphy (New York: Prentice-Hall, 1968).

6. A sampling: Cerfaux, *Christ in the Theology of Saint Paul* (1954) and *The Church in Pauline Theology* (1962); Dupont, *Gnosis: la Connaissance religieuse dans les epitres de Saint Paul* and *Syn Christo: l'union avec le Christ selon saint Paul* (1952);
Vawter, *A Path through Genesis* (1956); McKenzie, *The Two-Edged Sword: An Interpretation of the Old Testament* (1956); Spicq, *Agape in the New Testament* (1963);
Murphy, *Seven Books of Wisdom* (1960); Ahern, *New Horizons: Studies in Biblical Theology* (1963).

7. A sampling: Ayer, *Language, Truth, and Logic* (1946); Hume, *An Inquiry concerning Human Understanding* (1748); Russell, *Why I Am Not a Christian* (1927);
Bergson, *Creative Evolution* (1907) and *The Two Sources of Morality and Religion*
(1932); Hegel, *Phenomenology of Spirit* (1807) and *Lectures on the Philosophy of History* (1837); Merleau-Ponty, *Phenomenology of Perception* (1945); Proudhon,
What Is Property? (1844); Ortega y Gasset, *What Is Philosophy?* (1907) and *Revolt of the Masses* (1930); Unamuno, *The Tragic Sense of Life* (1912); Berdyaev, *Spirit and Reality* (1946); Sartre, *Nausea* (1938), *No Exit* (1941), and *Being and Nothingness*
(1943); Camus, *The Myth of Sisyphus* (1942); Pascal, *Pensees* (1670); Cassirer, *Essay on Man* (1944); Heidegger, *Introduction to Metaphysics* (1953).

8. What a delight to read him later in life! I especially appreciated his astonishingly pointed (and humorous) aphorisms, as in *Human, All Too Human* (1878).

9. Maximus the Confessor, *The Ascetic Life: The Four Centuries on Charity*, translated and annotated by Polycarp Sherwood, Ancient Christian Writers 21 (Westminster, MD: Newman, 1955).

10. Louis Bouyer was a convert from Protestantism whose *Liturgical Piety*
(1955) was influential at Vatican II; Jean Daniélou was a patristic scholar; his 1988
book on Origen was a pioneering study, and his *Bible and the Liturgy* (1958) likewise was an important resource for the council.

11. Both volumes appeared in the Herder series: *Quaestiones Disputatae; Inspiration* in 1961, and *Theology of Death* in 1965. Already while at Saint Ben's, I had read Rahner's *Encounters with Silence* (1960) as a Lenten exercise.

12. Rahner was a "systematic" theologian who preferred short studies to large monographs. His "transcendental Thomism" provided me with a lasting sense of how anthropology and Christology could be negotiated in terms of embodied spirit. The *Theological Investigations* were collections of such studies that ran to sixteen volumes in all, published between 1954 and 1984.

13. A sampling: Balthasar, *The God Question and Modern Man* (1967); Schoonenberg, *Man and Sin* (1967); Schillebeeckx, *Christ, the Sacrament of Encounter between God and Man* (1963); Haring, *The Law of Christ* (1967); Monden, *Sin, Liberty, and Law* (1965).

14. Founded in 1965 and published five times a year, this hardbound journal featured the essays and studies of all the figures I have named, and many more on the cutting edge of the Catholic theological renewal.

15. During my monastic years, I read short works of Karl Barth (*The Word of God and the Word of Man* [1928] and *Dogmatics in Outline* [1959]); Paul Tillich (*The Shaking of the Foundations* [1948] and *The Courage to Be* [1952]), and Dietrich Bonhoeffer (*The Cost of Discipleship* [1948], *Life Together* [1939], and *Letters and Papers from Prison* [1953]).

16. See *The Gospel according to John, Chapters 1–12*, Anchor Bible 29 (Garden City, NY: Doubleday, 1966).

17. Although I later saw their deficiencies, I was at that point enthralled by Cullmann's *Christ and Time* (1951) and *The Christology of the New Testament* (1959), as well as by Jeremias's *Central Message of the New Testament* (1965), *The Parables of Jesus* (1963), and *The Eucharistic Words of Jesus* (1966).

18. See Erikson, *Childhood and Society* (1950); Kaam, *The Art of Existential Counseling: A New Perspective in Psychotherapy* (1966); Lynch also wrote the brilliant studies *Christ and Apollo* (1963) and *Christ and Prometheus* (1970).

19. R. Otto, *The Idea of the Holy* (1951); G. van der Leeuw, *Religion in Essence and Manifestation* (1933); M. Eliade, *Patterns in Comparative Religion* (1958) and *Myth and Reality* (1963).

20. T. Luckmann and P. Berger, *The Social Construction of Reality: An Essay in the Sociology of Knowledge* (1966), and P. Berger, *The Sacred Canopy: Elements of a Sociological Theory of Religion* (1967).

21. É. Durkheim, *The Elementary Forms of the Religious Life* (1912).

22. *Homo Ludens: A Study of the Play Element in Culture* (1955).

Chapter Four

1. Dahl's doctoral dissertation, *Das Volk Gottes* (1941), written in the face of Nazi ideology, was an act of great intellectual courage; his essays were collected and translated by students: *The Crucified Messiah and Other Essays* (1974); *Jesus in the Memory of the Church* (1976); *Studies in Paul: Theology for the Early Christian Movement* (1977).

2. *The Prophet-King: Moses Traditions and the Johannine Christology*, Supplements to Novum Testamentum 14 (Leiden: Brill, 1967), and "The Man from Heaven in Johannine Sectarianism," *Journal of Biblical Literature* 91 (1972): 44–72.

3. When I arrived at Yale, Malherbe had submitted for publication and then had to wait for years for the appearance of an article that would prove to be widely influential: "Hellenistic Moralists and the New Testament," *Aufstieg und Niedergang der roemischen Welt* II.26.1 (1992): 267–333.

4. English: *The Origin of the Christian Bible* (Tübingen: Mohr, 1968).

Chapter Five

1. As I noted earlier, Yale had no dissertation defense. Readers simply submitted written evaluations, which were kept on file.

2. *Theios Aner: A Critique of the Use of This Category in New Testament Christology*, Society of Biblical Literature Dissertation Series 40 (Missoula, MT: Scholars Press, 1977).

3. In all fairness, it must be said that Yale was not alone in its inability to address chronic illness.

4. *The Literary Function of Possessions in Luke-Acts*, Society of Biblical Literature Dissertation Series 39 (Missoula, MT: Scholars Press, 1977).

5. "On Finding the Lukan Community: A Cautious Cautionary Essay," in *1979 SBL Seminar Papers*, ed. P. Achtemeier (Missoula, MT: Scholars Press, 1979), 87–100.

6. "II Timothy and the Polemic against False Teachers: A Reexamination," *Journal of Religious Studies* 6, no. 7 (1978–1979): 1–26.

7. "The Lukan Kingship Parable (Lk 19:11–27)," *Novum Testamentum* 24 (1982): 139–59.

8. "James 3:13–4:10 and the Topos *Peri Phthonou*," *Novum Testamentum* 25 (1983): 327–47; also on James was "The Use of Leviticus 19 in the Letter of James," *Journal of Biblical Literature* 101 (1982): 391–401.

9. "Romans 3:21–26 and the Faith of Jesus," *Catholic Biblical Quarterly* 44 (1982): 77–90.

10. *Invitation to the New Testament Epistles III: A Commentary on Colossians, Ephesians, 1 Timothy, 2 Timothy, and Titus with Complete Text from the Jerusalem Bible* (Garden City, NY: Doubleday, 1980). The big challenge here was that the commentary was based on the Jerusalem Bible, whose translation was so bad that I constantly had to correct it. A delicate situation.

11. *Some Hard Blessings: Meditations on the Beatitudes in Matthew* (Niles, IL: Argus Communications, 1981).

12. *Sharing Possessions: What Faith Demands* (Grand Rapids: Eerdmans, 2011).

Chapter Six

1. See, e.g., Stephen J. Stein, *The Shaker Experience in America: A History of the United Society of Believers* (New Haven: Yale University Press, 1992); *Jonathan Edward's Writings: Text, Context, Interpretation* (Bloomington: Indiana University Press, 1996), and J. Samuel Preus, *From Shadow to Promise: Old Testament Interpretation from Augustine to the Young Luther* (Cambridge, MA: Harvard University Press, 1969); *Explaining Religion: Criticism and Theory from Bodin to Freud* (New Haven: Yale University Press, 1987).

2. As I recall, our reading included key works by Clifford Geertz, Victor Turner, and Michael Jackson.

3. See H. Penner, *Impasse and Resolution: A Critique of the Study of Religion*, Toronto Studies in Religion (New York: Lang, 1989); J. Z. Smith, *Imagining Religion: From Babylon to Jonestown*, Chicago Studies in the History of Judaism (Chicago: University of Chicago Press, 1988).

4. See, for example, Rudolf Otto, *The Idea of the Holy*, trans. J. W. Harvey (1917; New York: Oxford University Press, 1923); Gerardus van der Leeuw, *Religion in Essence and Manifestation*, Princeton Legacy Library (Princeton: Princeton University Press, 2014); Mircea Eliade, *The Sacred and the Profane: The Nature of Religion* (New York: Harcourt and Brace, 1959); *Patterns in Comparative Religion* (New York: World, 1963).

5. See Jason David Beduhn, *The Manichaean Body in Discipline and Ritual* (Baltimore: Johns Hopkins University Press, 2000).

6. I was astonished to discover, firsthand, that supposedly thoughtful representatives of the media "thought" ethically in terms of narrow professionalism ("get

the story first and get it right") and a defensive appeal to the First Amendment. They seemed incapable of pondering such obvious issues as the financial entanglements of the press or the consequences of exposing private behavior to the public.

7. In fact, the MA did get swallowed up.

8. *The Writings of the New Testament: An Interpretation* (Philadelphia: Fortress, 1986), simultaneously published by SCM Press in London. A second revised edition—with the assistance of Todd Penner, and with greatly expanded bibliographies—appeared in 1999, and a third edition—this one formatted as a textbook, with illustrations, etc.—in 2010.

9. A note on the technological changes in scholarship: for the second edition, the pages of the first were scanned to a disk, and all editing was done electronically, and submitted as an e-mail attachment. The fourteen years between editions had changed scholarly processes completely.

10. In addition to the two articles mentioned in chapter 5, note 8, I published "Friendship with the World and Friendship with God: A Study of Discipleship in James," in *Discipleship in the New Testament*, ed. F. Segovia (Philadelphia: Fortress, 1985), 327–47; "The Mirror of Remembrance (James 1:22–25)," *Catholic Biblical Quarterly* 50 (1998): 632–45; "Taciturnity and True Religion (James 1:26–27)," in *Greeks, Romans, and Christians: Essays in Honor of Abraham J. Malherbe*, ed. D. Balch et al. (Minneapolis: Fortress, 1990), 329–39; "The Social World of James: Literary Analysis and Historical Reconstruction," in *The Social World of the First Christians: Essays in Honor of Wayne A. Meeks*, ed. M. White and L. Yarbrough (Minneapolis: Fortress, 1995), 178–97, as well as "The Letter of James" for the *Dictionary of Biblical Interpretation*, ed. J. Hayes (Nashville: Abingdon, 1988), 560–62.

11. B. Reicke, *The Epistles of James, Peter, and Jude*, Anchor Bible 37 (Garden City, NY: Doubleday, 1964). I do not mean "inadequate" in the sense of incompetent, but only that Reicke could not devote an entire volume to James, which it surely deserved.

12. The results of this research were reported in "Travelling East with James: A Chapter in the History of Biblical Interpretation," in *Lilly Lectures in Religion* (Indiana University, 1989).

13. *Journal of Biblical Literature* 108 (1989): 419–41.

14. This was eventually published as "The Jewish Bible after the Holocaust: A Response to Emil Fackenheim," in *A Shadow of Glory: Reading the New Testament after the Holocaust*, ed. T. Linafelt (New York: Routledge, 2002), 216–32.

15. "Christians and Jews: Staring Over," *Commonweal* 130, no. 2 (January 31, 2003): 15–19.

16. R. C. Tannehill, *The Narrative Unity of Luke-Acts: A Literary Interpretation* (Philadelphia: Fortress, 1986).

Chapter Seven

1. *The Creed: What Christians Believe and Why It Matters* (New York: Doubleday, 2003); *The Revelatory Body: Theology as Inductive Art* (Grand Rapids: Eerdmans, 2015).

2. Carl Holladay, the Old Testament scholar Carol Newsom, and the historian Brooks Holifield, for example, have all been inducted into the American Academy of Arts and Letters. Candler's superb teachers at that time included those three, as well as Don Saliers, Luther Smith, Roberta Bondi, Charles Foster, and Fred Craddock.

3. In New Testament, for example, Richard Hays, John Granger Cook, Steven Kraftchick, Brian Blount, and Gail O'Day are probably the most noteworthy.

4. Next to the hands-on experience of directing dissertations, this sort of training in pedagogy seemed to me to be the indispensable contribution of doctoral faculty to the preparation of the future professoriate.

5. Much anguish attended the demise. As all who have labored in the academy can attest, it is as difficult to drop an educational program, once in place, as it is to cancel governmental initiatives, once begun.

6. "It may be conceded to the mathematicians that four is twice two, But two is not twice one; two is two thousand times one." *The Man Who Was Thursday*.

7. *The Letter of James, a New Translation with Introduction and Notes*, Anchor Bible 37A (New York: Doubleday, 1995).

8. *Letters to Paul's Delegates: A Commentary on 1 Timothy, 2 Timothy, and Titus* (Valley Forge, PA: Trinity Press International, 1996); *Reading Romans: A Literary and Theological Commentary* (New York: Crossroad, 1997).

9. See, for example, A. K. Grieb, *The Story of Romans: A Narrative Defense of God's Righteousness* (Louisville: Westminster John Knox, 2002); V. Nicolet-Anderson, *Constructing the Self: Thinking with Paul and Michel Foucault*, Wissenschaftliche Untersuchungen zum Neuen Testament 2.324 (Tübingen: Mohr Siebeck, 2012).

10. See *"Oikonomia Theou*: The Theological Voice of 1 Timothy from the Perspective of Pauline Authorship" and "Response to Margaret Mitchell," in *Horizons in Biblical Theology* 21, no. 2 (1999): 87–104, 140–44.

11. See "Religious Rights and Christian Texts," in *Religious Human Rights in Global Perspective*, vol. 1, *Religious Perspectives*, ed. J. Witte and J. van der Vyver

(Dordrecht: Martinus Nijhoff, 1995), 65–96; "Proselytism and Witness in Earliest Christianity: A Study in Origins," in *Sharing the Book: Religious Perspectives on the Rights and Wrongs of Proselytism*, ed. J. Witte and R. C. Martin, Religion and Human Rights 4 (Maryknoll, NY: Orbis, 1999), 145–57, 376–84.

12. I also had the opportunity through the Center to work with the brilliant Mark Jordan and contribute as his coauthor an entry on marriage and sexuality to one of Witte's anthologies: "Christianity," in *Sex, Marriage, and Family in World Religions*, ed. D. S. Browning, M. C. Green, and J. Witte (New York: Columbia University Press, 2006), 77–149.

13. M. F. Foskett, *A Virgin Conceived: Mary and Classical Representations of Virginity* (Bloomington: Indiana University Press, 2002).

14. For example, J. Spong's *The Birth of Jesus* and A. N. Wilson's *Jesus: A Life*, in *Christian Century* 110 (1993): 457–58; R. Funk's *The Five Gospels* and J. D. Crossan's *Jesus: A Revoutionary Biography*, in *Philadelphia Inquirer* (1994); and J. P. Meier's *A Marginal Jew* and Crossan's *The Historical Jesus: The Life of a Mediterranean Jewish Peasant*, in *Commonweal*, 1992, 24–26.

15. *Modern Theology* 14, no. 2 (1998): 165–80. The essay appears also in *Theology and Scriptural Imagination*, ed. L. G. Jones and J. J. Buckley, Directions in Modern Theology (Oxford: Blackwell, 1998), 3–18.

16. A collection of these accessible essays appeared in a book that, by my reckoning, no one has read: *The Living Gospel* (London: Continuum, 2004).

Chapter Eight

1. The publication of this volume was the more gratifying, since the vision for the conference was that of a living conversation rather than simply a collection of impressive lectures. But the talks and sermons turned out to be fairly impressive. *The Vocation of Theology: Inquiry, Dialogue, Adoration*, ed. R. Matthews (Nashville: Foundry Books, 2017).

2. *Prophetic Jesus, Prophetic Church: The Challenge of Luke-Acts to Contemporary Christians* (Grand Rapids: Eerdmans, 2011). As the subtitle indicates, this treatment of Luke-Acts deliberately turned its prophetic vision of Jesus and the early church into a set of challenges to the contemporary church. I was therefore particularly pleased when I was asked to respond to five reviews of the book at a panel for the Society of Pentecostal Studies at the SBL meeting in 2012.

3. For example, "Debate and Discernment/Scripture and the Spirit," in "Disputed Questions: Homosexuality," *Commonweal* 121, no. 2 (1994): 11–13 (reprinted

in *Virtues and Practices in the Christian Tradition*, ed. N. Murphy et al. [Harrisburg, PA: Trinity International Press, 1997], 215–20); "Homosexuality, Marriage and the Church: A Conversation with Luke Johnson, David Matzko, and Max Stackhouse," *Christian Century* 115, no. 19 (1998): 181–84; "Sex, Women, and the Church," *Commonweal* 130 (2003): 11–17; "Homosexuality and the Church: Scripture and Experience," *Commonweal* 134, no. 12 (2007): 14–17. Later, I wrote "The Church and Transgender Identity: Some Cautions, Some Possibilities," *Commonweal* 144, no. 5 (2017): 19–23.

4. For example, "Sex and American Catholics" (Currie Lecture in Law and Religion, Emory, 2002); "The Complex Witness of the New Testament on Sex, Marriage, and the Family" (International Conference on Sex, Marriage, and the Family, Emory, 2003); "Matthew on Marriage and Divorce" (McDonald Lecture on Jesus and Culture, Emory, 2012); "Sexuality and the Life of Faith" (Sacred Worth, Candler School of Theology, 2000); "Scripture and Homosexuality: A Workshop" (Episcopal Diocese of Birmingham, Alabama, 2000); "Sexuality and the Holiness of the Church" (Covenant Network Convention, Chicago, 2004); "Word Made Flesh: Homosexuality and Scripture" (New Ways Ministry Symposium, Minneapolis, 2007); "Doing the Truth in Love: Eros and Maturity in Christ" (New Ways Ministry Symposium, Baltimore, 2012); "Thinking about Homosexuality" (Faithful and Fortunate Families, Atlanta, 2020).

5. "The Apostle Paul," "Early Christianity: Experience of the Divine," "Jesus and the Gospels," "The Story of the Bible," "Practical Philosophy: The Ancient Moralists," "Mysticism in Judaism, Christianity and Islam," "Christianity" (for the Great World Religions course), and "The History of Christianity up to the Reformation."

6. Far more than I was probably willing to acknowledge, the influence of Kierkegaard and Barth affected my approach to preaching.

7. And they sometimes were simply satisfying in themselves. In 2002, I delivered the Marquette Lecture at Marquette University, "Septuagintal Midrash in the Speeches of Acts," which was published as a small book later that same year by Marquette University Press. The exercise did not lead anywhere further, but it offered me the chance to scratch an old itch.

8. *The First and Second Letter to Timothy: A New Translation with Introduction and Notes*, Anchor Bible 35A (New York: Doubleday, 2001).

9. Anchor Bible 35 (1990). Although he was able to provide a commentary only on Titus, Quinn in his introduction sketched his overall sense of all three letters.

10. "Transformation of the Mind and Moral Discernment in Paul," in *Early Christianity and Classical Culture: Comparative Studies in Honor of Abraham J. Mal-*

herbe, ed. J. T. Fitzgerald et al., Supplements to Novum Testamentum 110 (Leiden: Brill, 2003), 215–36; "Life-Giving Spirit: The Ontological Implications of Resurrection in 1 Corinthians," *Stone Campbell Journal* 15, no. 1 (2012); "The Body in Question: The Social Complexities of Resurrection in 1 Corinthians," in *Unity and Diversity in the New Testament: Studies in the Synoptics and Paul*, ed. C. W. Skinner and K. R. Iverson (Atlanta: SBL Press, 2012); "God Was in Christ: Second Corinthians and Mythic Language," in *Myth and Scripture: Contemporary Perspectives on Religion, Language, and Imagination*, ed. D. E. Callender, Society of Biblical Literature Resources for Biblical Study (Atlanta: SBL Press, 2014), 201–12.

11. "The Paul of the Letters: A Catholic Perspective," in *Four Views on the Apostle Paul*, ed. M. Bird (Grand Rapids: Zondervan, 2012), 65–96; included are "Response to Thomas Schreiner" (48–52), "Response to Douglas Campbell" (149–52), and "Response to Mark Nanos" (200–203).

12. *L'Epitre aux Hebreux*, 2 vols., Etudes Bibliques (Paris: J. Gabalda, 1952–1953).

13. This influence was mediated especially by the great Benedictine spiritual teacher Dom Columba Marmion, in books such as *Christ the Ideal of the Monk*, trans. Mother Mary Thomas (1926; Ridgefield, CT: Roman Catholic Books, ca. 2005).

14. As with my original lecture, the book generated a very mixed response, a glimpse of which is available in my responsive essay "Conversation, Conversion, and Construction," *Nova et Vetera* 4, no. 1 (2006): 172–85, which also contains the critical essays to which I respond.

15. See, e.g., D. Leder, *The Absent Body* (Chicago: University of Chicago Press, 1990).

16. Like others before me, I came to love Nietzsche the epigrammatist with penetrating psychological insight.

17. Not surprisingly, this book also generated a mixed response. Robert Louis Wilken wrote a completely hostile review in the journal *First Things* ("The Christian Difference," May 2010), while Robin Darling wrote a much more qualified critique, to which I wrote a reply; see R. Darling, "Among the Gentiles: Greco-Roman Religion and Christianity; A Review Essay and Response," *Conversations in Religion and Theology* 8, no. 2 (2010): 107–19.

Chapter Nine

1. "How a Monk Learns Mercy: Thomas Merton and the Rule of Benedict," *Commonweal* 145, no. 16 (2018): 21–24; earlier, I wrote "The Myth, the Monk, the Man: Reading and Rereading Thomas Merton," *Commonweal* 142 (2015): 22–24.

2. "Can We Still Believe in Miracles?," *Commonweal* 146, no. 4 (2019).

3. *Canonical Paul*, vol. 1, *Constructing Paul* (2020); vol. 2, *Interpreting Paul* (2021).

4. One day I idly listed the names of the scholars with whom, over my academic career, I had engaged in dispute either orally or in writing. The list is so lengthy that it surprised even me. And I did not include the more than two hundred book reviews I had written!

5. A selection of my scholarly articles appeared as *Contested Issues in Christian Origins and the New Testament: Collected Essays*, Supplements to Novum Testamentum 146 (Leiden: Brill, 2013).

Chapter Ten

1. It should be clear that I have no patience with that form of degrading egalitarianism that thinks "excellence" is an elitist term that should be canceled.

2. The point is worth stressing: scholarly curiosity tends to grow with the acquisition of new knowledge, rather than diminish. There is always something more to learn about the subject one is studying, and that subject connects to others in the context of which the present subject needs to be seen, and so forth.

3. An analogy to breakfast cereals is apt. Publishers love commentary series in the same way that Kellogg's loves new versions of corn flakes; no matter how inferior, every cereal has some market share—so do mediocre commentaries.

4. For the respective profiles, see Johnson, *The Real Jesus* (1996).

5. See my review of N. T. Wright's *The New Testament and the People of God* (Minneapolis: Fortress, 1992), in *Journal of Biblical Literature* 113 (1994): 536–38. Wright seeks to portray Judaism at the time of Christianity's birth but pays virtually no attention to Judaism in the diaspora.

6. See D. B. Hart, *The New Testament: A Translation* (New Haven: Yale University Press, 2017); see also my review in *Commonweal*, March 7, 2018.

7. See W. C. van Unnik, *De Aphthonia van God in de oudchristelijke Literatuur* (1973).

8. See Johnson, "James 3:13–4:10 and the *Topos* PERI PHTHONOU," *Novum Testamentum* 25 (1983): 327–47.

9. This self-restriction of focus is surely connected to the notion of a "special revelation" that is thought to be contained within the pages of the Bible alone—nothing "revelatory" can be expected from the Greco-Roman world, or even from a Judaism outside of Palestine.

10. The reader may remember that when a doctoral student at Yale, I had been recruited to respond to an oral presentation by Koester of this proposed book. See H. Koester, *Introduction to the New Testament*, vol. 1, *History, Culture, and Religion in the Hellenistic Age*; vol. 2, *History and Literature of Early Christianity* (Boston: de Gruyter, 1982).

11. To object that each of these areas is so vast and complicated that other aspects of the symbolic world must be bracketed for responsible work to be done on any one of them is legitimate only if, in fact, one's field of study is one of these areas, and not the New Testament!

12. As I say, perhaps, or probably, naïve; but the deeper truth is that "method" should be so fitted to the subject studied that it *should* appear as something "natural" rather than as something imposed upon the text. The best use of method has no need to call attention to itself, precisely because it works so well.

13. See "Glossolalia and the Embarrassments of Experience," *Princeton Seminary Bulletin* 18 (1997): 113–34.

14. G. K. Chesterton, *Saint Francis of Assisi* (London: Hodder & Stoughton, 1923).

Chapter Eleven

1. His discussion of courage is in the *Nicomachean Ethics* 3.6–9.

2. It eventually dawned on me that the majority opinion was not in an insignificant degree influenced by doctrinal considerations (ideology, if you will). Scholars in the Reformation tradition "saw" the ambiguous genitive construction *pistis Christou* (or *pistis Iesou*) as "faith in Christ" or "faith in Jesus" even when the grammar and syntax of Paul's sentences demanded the subjective translation, "Christ's faith" or "the faith of Jesus."

3. A Greek Synopsis lays out the three gospels of Matthew, Mark, and Luke in parallel columns, so that similarities and differences can easily be tracked, if less easily accounted for.

4. Only once did I review a book written by someone I thought of as a friend, and the effort to remain utterly fair in my judgment was excruciating.

5. And found it strange to be on a panel with Smith and Wendy Doniger at the American Academy of Religion Conference in 2011, responding to Robert Bellah's *Religion in Human Evolution: From the Neolithic to the Axial Age* (2011).

6. Perhaps the most impressive contemporary example within my field of New Testament studies is John P. Meier's exhaustive study of the historical Jesus, *A Marginal Jew*, whose five volumes extend from 1991 to 2016, with a sixth volume still in view.

7. My foundation here is Marcel, *Being and Having*.

8. See *Images of Hope*.

Epilogue

1. *Nihil Obstat* = "Nothing hinders"; *Imprimatur* = "Let it be printed." I have never sought either of these ecclesiastical stamps of approval.

INDEX

ABC, 148

Abilene Christian Seminary, 97

Abingdon Press, 145

academese, 206

academy, the, 3–4, 12, 14–15, 98, 104, 111, 121, 137, 143, 148, 183, 205, 206, 222–23, 229, 230

Ackerman, James, 118

Adams, Alice, 206

Adler, Mortimer, 49, 50, 239

Aelius Aristides, 81, 171

Ahern, Barnabas, 61, 166, 240

Alexandria (VA), 162

Alice in Wonderland (Carroll), 31

Alice through the Looking-Glass (Carroll), 31

almsgiving, 82

ambition, 22, 213–14, 218

American Benedictine Review, 70, 175, 240

Amis, Kingsley, 162

Anchor Bible, 125, 126, 145, 165, 217

anger, 103, 210

Anglican Church, 79

anthropology, 64, 118, 136, 190, 197, 200, 201

anti-Semitism, 126, 194

apocalyptic, 197

Apophthegmata Patrum, 60

Aristotle, 62, 187, 189, 201, 210, 222

Arndt, William, 8, 234

Ascent of Mt. Carmel (John of the Cross), 49

Asclepius, 171

Asia, 157

Atlanta, 132, 133, 135, 141, 153, 169

Atlanta (magazine), 148

Augustine, Saint, 48, 59, 167, 239

Australia, 157, 168

avarice, 220

Avot of Rabbi Nathan, 79, 198

Axtell, James, 233

Ayer, A. J., 63, 240

Ayres, Lewis, 154

Balch, David, 79, 91

Balthasar, Hans Urs von, 67, 241

Bammel, Ernst, 97

Bangkok, 157

Barnett, Joby, 114, 134

Barnett, Kimberly, 114

Barnett, Mary, 92, 114

Barnett, Ross, 36

Barth, Karl, 241, 247

Bauer, Walter, 234

Baumann, Hugh, 49

Baumann, Paul, 127

Baur, F. C., 8

Beardslee, William, 88

Becnel, Andrew, 59

Beduhn, Jason, 121, 243

Being and Having (Marcel), 63

Bellah, Robert, 251

Belloc, Hilaire, 48, 239

Berdyaev, Nikolai, 63, 240

Berger, Peter, 69, 81, 101, 201, 241

Bergson, Henri, 63, 240

Berling, Judith, 118

Bernanos, Georges, 49

Berrigan, Daniel, 127

Bilbo, Theodore, 40, 238

Bird, Michael, 166

Bismark (ND), 153

Black, Clifton, 167

Black Panther Party, 76

Blass, F., 8, 234

Bloomington (IN), 68, 113, 114–16, 131, 133, 134, 135, 169

Blount, Brian, 245

Bloy, Leon, 14, 236, 239

Boers, Hendrikus, 131, 138

Bondi, Roberta, 245

Bonhoeffer, Dietrich, 241

Boone, Joanne, 40

Borg, Marcus, 148

Boston, 76, 157

Boston College, 143

Boston University, 143

Bouyer, Louis, 67, 240

Boylan, Eugene, 48

Brewster, Kingman, 78

Brooks, Cleanthe, 64

Brown, Dee, 58

Brown, Raymond, 68, 107, 132

Buddhism, 118

Bultmann, Rudolf, 9, 68, 69, 78, 168, 201, 214, 235

Bury My Heart at Wounded Knee (Brown), 58

By Light, Light (Goodenough), 204

Callan, Terry, 78, 91

Cambridge University, 97

Campany, Rob, 119

Campbell, Douglas, 248

Campenhausen, Hans von, 80

Camus, Albert, 63, 264

Canada, 157

Candler School of Theology, 112, 131, 137, 144, 156, 159, 161, 164, 200; centennial of, 160, 172; faculty, 132, 137, 138, 140, 173; library, 145

Carr, Ephraim, 67

Carter, Jimmy, 136

Casel, Odo, 61

Cassian, John, 60; *Conferences*, 60; *Institutes*, 60

Cassirer, Ernst, 63, 240

Catholic Biblical Association, 107, 144, 152, 167, 175, 191

Catholic Biblical Quarterly, 123

Catholicism, 19, 21, 37, 41, 42, 69, 73, 92, 97, 100, 107, 118, 169, 182, 230; charismatic, 73, 77, 82, 100, 167; identity, 14–15; of Kennedy, 51, 56; in Louisiana, 43; in Mississippi, 41, 43; parishes, 38, 39, 52, 77, 135, 169, 238; practices of, 26, 28, 115, 135; prayer in, 27; religious orders, 10; sacraments of, 27, 40, 66, 73, 83, 84, 100, 115, 153; scholarship, 73–74, 152, 167, 191, 230; scholastic philosophy in, 62; tradition in, 152, 182

Catholic University, 67

Catholic Worker, 50

CBS, 148

Center for Biblical and Literary Criticism, 118

Centre College, 151

Cerfaux, Lucien, 61, 214

Chace, William, 137, 143, 144, 158, 161, 233

character, 187

charismatic movement, 72, 77, 82, 83

Chatham, Josiah, 52, 54

Cheever, John, 130

Chesterton, G. K., 45, 62, 127, 142, 203, 219, 250

children, 99–100

Childs, Brevard, 79, 124

Chinese religion, 118

Christian Century, 127, 152, 182

Christianity, 119, 148, 153, 181

Christian mysticism, 119

Christian origins, 117, 125, 152, 165, 170, 171, 181, 182, 187, 190, 197, 198, 201, 217, 218, 226

Christology, 98

church, 148, 150, 168, 183, 225

Church of Christ, 78, 97

Claremont McKenna College, 151

clarity and cogency, 205–8

Clement of Alexandria, Saint, 231

clinical pastoral education, 140

Clinton, Hillary, 164

CNN, 148

Cody, Aelred, 68

College of William and Mary, 233

Colwin, Laurie, 206

committees, 111, 218, 223, 227

Commonweal, 127, 153, 161, 175, 182

Communist Manifesto (Marx), 63

comparative religion, 73, 119

competing loyalties, 218

Concept of Anxiety, The (Kierkegaard), 63

Concilium, 67

Concluding Unscientific Postscript (Kierkegaard), 63

Confessions (Augustine), 48

Congar, Yves, 61, 67, 191

Congregationalist, 154

Conspirata (Harris), 202

Constantine, 172, 198

contentment, 220–22

contextual education, 141, 144

Cook, John Granger, 245

Coomarswamy, Ananda, 62

Cooper, Alan, 79

Copleston, Frederick, 62, 216

coronavirus pandemic, 174, 230

courage, 210–12, 218, 225, 232

Covington (LA), 35, 42, 73

Cox, Harvey, 57

Craddock, Fred, 138, 245

Crawfordsville (IN), 144

Creative Fidelity (Marcel), 63

Creative Ministry (Nouwen), 68

Crossan, John Dominic, 147, 148, 246

Cry, the Beloved Country (Paton), 49

Cullmann, Oscar, 68, 241

curiosity, 188–92, 198, 218, 225

curriculum, 104, 105, 122–23, 144, 154, 161

Dahl, Nils, 15, 78, 81, 85, 86, 87, 96, 179, 242

D'Angelo, Mary Rose, 79

Daniélou, Jean, 67, 191, 240

Danker, Frederick, 8, 234

Danner, Victor, 118

Darien (CT), 98

Darling, Robin, 248

Day, Dorothy, 50, 127

Dead Sea Scrolls, 197

Death of Ivan Ilych, The (Tolstoy), 70

Debrunner, A., 8, 234

deconstruction, 103, 197, 204

DeRosier, Paul, 153

detachment, 218–20

Dialogues (Plato), 178

Diary of Anne Frank, The (Frank), 162

Dibelius, Martin, 103, 107, 181, 214

Dickens, Charles, 130

Dickinson, Emily, 198, 206

Didache, 198

Dio Chrysostom, 81

Diogenes Laertius, 62

Dionysius the Areopagite, 198

discernment, 130–31, 145, 167

discipline, 214–16, 217, 218

dissertations, 138, 143, 146, 158, 213, 228

Dittes, James, 96

Doniger, Wendy, 251

Drane, Lance, 41

Dublin, 157

Duke Divinity School, 154

Duke University, 131, 143, 154, 157

Dulles, Avery, 127

Dunn, James, 147

Dupont, Jacques, 61, 240

Duquesne University, 72, 168

Dura Europos, 204

Durham (NC), 154

Durkheim, Émile, 69, 81, 201, 241

ecclesial hermeneutics, 168, 182

Eilberg-Schwartz, Howard, 119

Either/Or (Kierkegaard), 63

Eliade, Mircea, 69, 121, 241, 243

Eliot, T. S., 48

Emory University, 5, 97, 98, 101, 102, 112, 125, 129, 131, 134–54, 155–73, 179, 180, 213; Center for Law and Religion, 146

Encyclopedia Americana, 108

England, 157, 168

Entre Nous, 51

Epictetus, 48, 81, 107, 121, 171, 198, 214

Epicureans, 82, 171, 190

epistemology, 62, 182, 203

epochē, 219

Erikson, Erik, 68, 241

ethics, 118, 136, 161

Europe, 157

evangelical, 154, 158, 166

Evers, Medgar, 35

Ewing, Lucia, 102

excellence, 187

exegesis, 102, 103, 104, 139, 143, 193, 211, 215

existential, 190, 203

experience, 100, 102, 103, 131, 141, 167, 168, 170, 182, 190, 217, 227, 228; religious, 101, 110, 152, 177, 181, 217

Fabiola (Wiseman), 41

Fackenheim, Emil, 118, 126, 244

Farmer, William, 211–12

Fascher, Erich, 80

Faulkner, William, 49, 64

Fear and Trembling (Kierkegaard), 63

feminism, 12, 103, 112, 197, 231

Ferguson, A. S., 234

Ferguson, Everett, 78

fiction, 199, 201, 202

Fifield (WI), 19–20, 22, 25, 26, 31–33, 34

Fifield News, 25, 51

Fine, Lawrence, 11

Fiore, Ben, 101

First Urban Christians, The (Meeks), 78

Fischel, Henry, 69, 70

Fitzgerald, F. Scott, 49

Fitzgerald, John, 101

Fitzmyer, Joseph, 152

Flambeau River, 20

Fordham University, 67

Fortress Press, 108, 109, 110, 124, 152

Foskett, Mary, 146, 147, 246

Foster, Charles, 245

Four Views on the Apostle Paul (Bird), 166

Fowl, Stephen, 145

Fox, Bill, 158–59

Francis of Assisi, Saint, 203

Frankl, Victor, 68

Freedman, David Noel, 125

Frost, Robert, 206

Frye, Billy, 132, 136, 137

Frye, Northrop, 201

fundamentalism, 149, 196

Funk, Robert, 8, 147, 246

Furman University, 151

Geden, A. S., 8, 233

Geertz, Clifford, 201, 243

gender roles, 10–11

Gennep, Arnold van, 201

Georgetown University, 91, 92

Germany, 157

Gerow, Richard, 39, 42, 53

Gilson, Étienne, 62

Gingrich, Wilbur F., 8, 234

Glazier, Michael, 126

glossolalia, 201

Gnosticism, 69, 121, 197, 235

Goldin, Judah, 79, 82

Gonzaga University, 87, 95, 143

Good, Deirdre, 149

Goodenough, Erwin, 78, 203

Grabert, Colman, 67

grace, 85, 92, 179

Graduate Division of Religion (Emory), 138, 141–42

Graduate Theological Union, 74

Grawemeyer Award, 172

Greco-Roman, 81, 85, 86, 101, 126, 143, 152, 160, 170, 177, 187, 192, 194, 197, 198, 214, 218

Greece, 157

Greene, Graham, 49

Greer, Rowan, 79, 86, 96

Gregorian chant, 44, 46, 72

Gregory the Great, Saint, 59; *Life of Benedict*, 60

Grenfell, B. P., 234

Grieb, A. K., 245

Guest, Edgar, 237

Gustafson, James, 136

Haddad, Michael, 50

Hadrian's Memoirs (Youncenour), 202

Hahn, Hilary, 213

Hamm, Dennis, 82

Haring, Bernard, 67, 241

Harnack, A. von, 235

HarperSanFrancisco, 147, 150, 235

Harrington, Daniel, 126

Harrington, Michael, 127

Harris, Robert, 202

Hart, David Bentley, 249

Hart, James, 118

Harvard University, 78, 81, 90, 113, 121, 136, 143, 159, 196

Hasidism, 203

Hatch, Edwin, 8, 233

Hauerwas, Stanley, 154

Hays, Richard, 112, 147, 148, 245

Hebrews, Letter to the, 166–67

Hegel, G. W. F., 63, 240

Heidegger, Martin, 63, 240

Heifetz, Jascha, 213

Heim, David, 127

Hemingway, Ernest, 49

heretics, 48

Hermetica (Scott), 8, 198

Hersey, John, 33

Hertzberg, Arthur, 68

Hildebrand, Dietrich von, 62

Hiroshima, 33

historical-critical method, 11, 66, 78, 80, 102, 103, 149, 152, 167, 181, 191–92, 193

historical Jesus, 103, 145, 148, 169, 189, 193, 217

History of Philosophy (Copleston), 62, 216

Hitchens, Christopher, 176

Hock, Ronald, 79, 91

Holifield, Brooks, 245

Holladay, Carl, x, 97, 98, 99, 101, 105, 110, 112, 129, 131, 132, 136, 138, 139, 142, 143, 146, 157, 180, 245

Holladay, Donna, 97, 98, 99, 136

Hollar, John, 108

Holocaust, 126

homosexuality, 104

Homo Viator (Marcel), 63

Hope Is the Thing with Feathers, 50

Huckleberry Finn (Twain), 49

Huizinga, Johan, 73

Humanae vitae, 72

humanities, 95, 106, 120, 124, 187, 192, 195, 197, 198, 199, 203, 210, 229, 230

Hume, David, 63, 240

Hunt, A. S., 234

Hunter, Gordon, 153

Hunter, McKenzie, 153–54

Hynes, James, 162

hyperspecialization, 11, 196, 199

hypotheses/theory, 193, 197, 198, 199, 200, 207

ideology, 12–14, 82, 85, 103, 111, 119, 194, 219, 230, 231

Ignatius of Antioch, Saint, 69

Iliad (Homer), 162

Images of Hope (Lynch), 68

imagination, 167, 176, 193, 202–5, 218

Imitation of Christ (Kempis), 44

Imperium (Harris), 202

Indiana, 43, 122, 127

Indianapolis, 115, 122, 144

Indiana University, 5, 68, 72, 98, 102, 113, 114–29, 134, 145, 162, 170, 179, 200

Indian religion, 118

Inferno (Dante), 162

Inspiration in the Bible (Rahner), 67

Instructor, The (Clement of Alexandria), 231

Israel, 157

Italy, 157

intellectual freedom, 127

intelligence, 188

Interpretation, 123

Intimacy (Nouwen), 68

Introduction to the New Testament (Koester), 196

Introduction to the Devout Life (Sales), 44

Islam, 119

Jackson, Michael, 243

Jackson (MS), 34, 35, 36, 37, 38, 40, 42, 52, 237, 238

James, Letter of, 103, 107, 124, 126, 127, 145, 161, 165–66, 181, 194, 196, 217

James, William, 170

Jane Eyre (Brontë), 49

Jeremias, Joachim, 68, 241

Jerome, Saint, 59

Jesuits, 82

Jesus at 2000, 149

Jesus Seminar, 147

Jewish Bible after the Holocaust, The (Fackenheim), 126

Jim Crow, 33, 36

John XXIII, 51, 56

John of the Cross, 49

Johnson, Joy Randazzo (wife), 45, 73, 82–85, 87, 89, 90, 92, 97, 98, 99, 100, 112, 114, 115, 131, 132, 133, 134, 136, 144, 153, 154, 155–57, 163, 167, 168, 172, 174, 177, 179, 183

Johnson, Luke Timothy, career: articles of, 107, 127; book reviews of, 107, 108, 123, 127, 147, 153, 199, 208, 211; as chair of Emory University Faculty Council, 143; commentaries of, 106, 125–26, 127–29, 145, 146, 166, 167, 217; and committee work, 14, 104, 105, 121–23, 141–44, 156, 158–60; as a contrarian, 180, 181; and counseling, 102, 130; and depression, 88, 90, 92; dispensation from vows, 84, 89, 92; and dissertation(s), 82, 86–91, 96, 106, 108, 128, 158, 161, 166, 174, 191, 200, 217; as editor, 51, 123; excommunicated status of, 84, 92; as faculty member, 5, 95, 96, 97, 104–5, 117–19, 121–23, 136–38, 140–43, 156, 158, 160, 173, 223;

faculty service, 104–5, 121–24, 139–45, 180, 227; grading papers, 120, 139, 153, 157, 173, 227; Internet debate, 149; job search, 110; jobs of work, 106, 108, 164, 166, 175; letters of recommendation, 75, 121–22, 227; literary criticism, 64, 80, 86, 88, 90, 103, 107, 199, 200; lectures (public), 151, 163–64, 174–75, 207; and the media, 150–51; monastic life, 57–59, 61, 86, 179, 209 (*see also* monasticism [Benedictine]); office hours, 140, 156; and peer review, 107, 118, 123, 124; Phi Beta Kappa lectures, 151–52, 170, 218; and preaching, 71, 84, 110, 127, 156, 163, 207; and promotion, 104, 110, 131, 143, 214; reading life of, 30, 33, 39, 47, 60–63, 188, 198–202, 209, 215–16; recruitment, 41, 104, 130, 138, 158, 159, 213, 223; and religious studies, 11, 13, 68, 96, 113, 138, 141, 170, 181; and religious studies department at Emory, 129, 138; and religious studies department at Indiana University, 117–19, 121, 200, 218; and research, 25, 103, 105–7, 124–29, 139, 145–52, 180, 188, 189, 193, 199, 215, 224–25, 227, 228; retirement, 172–73, 174–84; and role of dean, 144, 214; teaching assistants of, 101, 139–40; and tenure, 91, 96, 105, 106, 110, 130, 143, 214, 218; travel, lack of, 157; university senate service, 123, 143; works of love, 106, 108, 167, 175; writing (publishing), 25, 51, 102, 105, 138, 143, 145–52, 157, 164–72, 175–78, 183, 187, 188, 216, 224

Johnson, Luke Timothy, family of, 145, 179, 225, 226; ancestry, 21, 26; father, 20, 22, 23, 28; mother, 20, 22, 23–24, 28, 31, 32, 34, 36, 37, 38, 179

Johnson, Luke Timothy, personal life: and anger, 180; and faith, life of, 14–15, 26, 38, 54, 65, 89, 100, 102, 115, 136, 145, 175, 180, 181, 228; at Fifield Grade School, 32–33; finances, 97–99, 131, 136, 154, 156, 163, 164, 172, 180, 219; and forensics competition, 33; and medical issues, 99, 136; and memory, 89, 188, 199; and music, 28–29, 39, 45–46, 50, 52, 54, 56, 65, 71, 83, 179; and sense of God's presence, 15, 28, 167, 168, 175, 176; at St. Peter's Parochial School, 39–41, 50; surgeries, 173, 174

Johnson, Luke Timothy, siblings of: LaNelle, 34, 35, 37, 39, 52; Margaret, 22, 23, 26, 34; Mary Jane, 22, 23, 24; Mickey, 22, 23, 27, 34, 35, 37, 39, 41, 52; Nancy, 22, 23, 26, 34; Pat, 22–25, 26, 31, 32, 35, 37, 38, 39, 42, 51, 53, 169; traits of siblings, 25–31; Warren, 34

Johnson, Luke Timothy, works of: *Among the Gentiles*, 152, 172, 180, 181, 218; *Brother of Jesus, Friend of God*, 165; *Canonical Paul*, 177, 181; *Constructing Paul*, 204; *The Creed*, 63, 136, 169, 182; *Decision Making in the Church*, 109, 130; *Faith's Freedom*, 131, 168, 183; *The First and Second Letter to Timothy*, 165; *The Future of Catholic Biblical Scholarship* (with William Kurz), 182; *Living Jesus*, 150, 218; *Miracles*, 175, 218; *Prophetic Jesus, Prophetic Church*, 217; *The Real Jesus*, 146, 149,

151, 177, 218; *Religious Experience in
Earliest Christianity*, 152, 170, 218; *The
Revelatory Body*, 136, 168, 183, 217;
Scripture and Discernment, 145, 167,
183, 217; *Sharing Possessions*, 108, 168,
183, 217; *Some Hard Blessings*, 108;
Teaching Religion to Undergraduates,
87; *Theology of the New Testament*, 68,
177; *Writings of the New Testament*, 9,
124, 167, 168, 183, 217, 244

Johnson, Tiffany (daughter), 89, 90,
100, 114, 115, 116, 134, 153

Jones, Gregory, 145, 154

Jones, Henry S., 233

Jordan, Mark, 246

Josephus, 194, 204

Journal of American Academy of Religion,
123

Journal of Biblical Literature, 123, 126

Joyce, James, 162

Judaism, 66, 81, 85, 101, 119, 171, 177, 187,
190, 198; background, 143; dialogue
with, 68, 126, 127; Gnosticism, 70;
Hellenistic, 78, 97, 194, 195, 197, 204;
midrash, 80; mysticism, 118, 119, 197,
198, 203; polemics, 126; rabbinic, 69,
79, 82, 86, 197; synagogue, 66, 204;
Talmud, 69

Juel, Don, 79, 91

Julian (Vidal), 202

Justice, Elaine, 148

Kaam, Adrian van, 68, 241

kabbalah, 203

Kant, Emmanuel, 63

Karris, Robert, 81

Kavanagh, Aidan, 66

Keck, Leander, 130

Kee, Howard Clark, 147

Kempis, Thomas à, 51

Kent Fellowship, 86, 90

Kermode, Frank, 118

Kierkegaard, Søren, 63, 64, 135, 247

Kimmelman, Reuven, 79

King, Martin Luther, Jr., 56

Knight, Bobby, 113, 117

Koester, Helmut, 90, 196, 250

Kraftchick, Steven, 112, 142, 245

Kümmel, Werner, 214

Küng, Hans, 108

Kurz, William, 74, 75, 80, 81, 82, 89, 167,
182

LaGree, Kevin, 131, 132

Laney, James, 132

Laney Graduate School, 158

languages, 5–6, 188, 229; Aramaic, 5;
French, 6, 47, 74, 85; German, 6, 74,
79, 85; Greek, 5, 47, 61, 66, 67, 82, 85,
89, 91, 102, 128, 160, 167, 187, 195, 196,
204; Hebrew, 5, 74, 79, 80, 81, 85, 196;
Latin, 5, 26, 40, 46, 47, 55, 62, 66, 72,
206, 239

Larkin, Philip, 206

Larmann, Marian, 54

Law, Bernard, 52

LeClercq, Jean, 15, 236

lectio divina, 58

Leder, Drew, 168, 248

Lee, Richard, 76

Leeuw, Gerhardus van der, 69, 121, 241,
243

Leo, Saint, 59

Leo XIII, 62

Leonard, Elmore, 206

Lewis, Charlton, 8, 234

LGBQT, 161

Liddell, Henry, 8, 107, 233–34

Lightfoot, John, 61

Lilly Foundation, 122, 125, 144, 231

Live from Nazareth (Vidal), 202

Lodge, David, 162

Loeb Classical Library, 8

Long Day's Journey into Night (O'Neill), 162

Long Island Sound, 98

Long Loneliness, The (Day), 50

Louden, John, 147, 149, 235

Louisville Presbyterian Seminary, 154

Love, Jan, 160

Loyola University of Baltimore, 154

Loyola University of New Orleans, 143

Lubac, Henri de, 67, 191

Lucian of Samosata, 81

Luckman, Thomas, 69, 101, 201, 241

Luke-Acts, 68, 82, 86, 87, 88, 90, 107, 109, 118, 121, 126, 127–28, 161, 165, 182, 200, 201, 217, 246

Luther, Martin, 125

Lynch, William, 68, 222, 241, 251

MacDonald, Dennis, 113, 240

Madison (CT), 98

Major Trends in Jewish Mysticism (Scholem), 203

Malherbe, Abraham J., 78, 79, 80, 81, 86, 87, 92, 96, 97, 107, 110, 179, 242

Man against Mass Society (Marcel), 63

Manichaeism, 121

Man's Search for Meaning (Frankl), 68

Marcel, Gabriel, 63, 64, 108, 201, 251

Marcus Aurelius, 48, 121

Maritain, Jacques, 62, 63, 239

Maritain, Raïssa, 239

Marks, Herbert, 118

Marmion, Columba, 60, 248

Marquette University, 247

Martino, D. J., 168

mastery of the subject, 195–98

Matzko, David, 247

Marx, Karl, 63

Marxism, 68

Mauriac, François, 49

Maurin, Peter, 50

Mauss, Marcel, 201

Maximus the Confessor, 66, 240

May, William, 69, 75, 119, 121

McDonald, Alonzo, 158–59

McGuire, Anne, 101

McKenzie, John, 61

McKenzie, Roderick, 234

MDiv degree, 105, 137, 139, 140

Meeks, Wayne, 69, 74, 75, 78, 81, 82, 85, 86, 87, 88, 91, 96, 119, 120, 159, 179, 180

Meier, John P., 152, 246, 251

Melançon, David, 54, 55, 64

Merleau-Ponty, Maurice, 63, 240

Merton, Robert, 82

Merton, Thomas, 48, 60, 127, 175, 249

Metz, Johannes Baptist, 68

Metzger, Bruce, 214

Migne, J. P., 8, 234

Milwaukee, 19, 20, 22

Milwaukee Braves, 25

Index

Milwaukee Journal, 22, 25

Milwaukee Sentinel, 22

Mina, Denise, 206

Minear, Paul, 78

Minot (ND), 153

miracles, 175–76, 182

Mistress Masham's Repose (White), 31

Mitchell, Alan, 101

Mitchell, Margaret, 146, 245

Mitchell, Nathan, 67, 69, 70

modernity, 175, 182

Modern Theology, 152

monasticism (Benedictine), 35, 54, 107, 175, 179, 226; liturgical life, 45, 46, 55, 56, 57, 59; novitiate, 55, 57; St. Joseph Abbey, 43, 55, 70–74, 84, 166, 173; St. Meinrad Archabbey, 43, 56, 65–71; tensions, 71–72, 183

Monden, Louis, 67, 241

Moses, Robert, 76

Moule, C. F. D., 8, 97, 234

Moulton, Harold K., 8, 233

Moulton, William F., 233

Mount Holyoke College, 151

Moxnes, Halvor, 82

multitasking, 222

Murder in the Cathedral (Eliot), 50

Murphy, Roland, 61, 240

Myers, Rawley, 238

Mystery of Being, The (Marcel), 63

mystery religion, 204

mysticism, 205

myth, mythology, 176, 201

Nag Hammadi, 80, 197

Nanos, Mark, 248

narrative, 88, 109, 191–92, 197, 201, 202

Nash, Ogden, 237

Nashville, 112, 145

Natchez-Jackson, Diocese of, 35, 54

Native Son (Wright), 33

Needham, Joseph, 216

neo-Thomism, 62

Neumann, Matthias, 67

new atheists, 176, 182

New Canaan (CT), 98

New Haven (CT), 74, 75–77, 82, 87, 92, 98, 131

New Orleans, 42, 43, 61, 72, 97, 143

New Orleans Times-Picayune, 51

New Revised Standard Version, 195

Newsom, Carol, 245

Newsweek, 148

New Testament in Human Transformation, The (Wink), 88, 103

New Testament introduction, 97, 101, 105, 109, 124, 129, 139–40, 180, 189–91, 214

New York City, 76, 98

New Yorker, 237

New York State, 92

New York Times, 148

Neyrey, Jerome, 82, 101

Nicolet-Anderson, Valerie, 245

Nicomachean Ethics (Aristotle), 187, 250

Nietzsche, Friedrich, 63, 86, 135, 169, 248

Nock, Arthur Darby, 78, 214

Noonan, John, 159

North Carolina, 91

Norwalk (CT), 98

No Time for Sergeants, 50

Notre Dame Seminary, 43, 61–64
Notre Dame University, 67, 72
Nouwen, Henri, 68
novels, ancient, 121

Oakes, Paulinus, 40, 41
Oates, Joyce Carol, 130
Oberlin College, 142
O'Connell, Edwin, 49
O'Day, Gail, 138, 245
Odyssey, The (Homer), 162
Oedipus Rex (Sophocles), 162
Ojibwa, 21
Olivelle, Patrick, 118, 122
On Superstition (Plutarch), 171
On the Theology of Death (Rahner), 67
Opus Dei (prayer), 55, 56, 58, 59
Origen, 126, 167, 168, 240
Orphic strand, 171
Orsi, Robert, 119
Ortega y Gasset, José, 63, 201, 240
orthodoxy, 48
Otto, Rudolf, 69, 121, 241, 243
Oxford University, 157
Oxyrynchus Papyri, 8

Parker, Dorothy, 237
Park Falls (WI), 19, 21, 22, 26, 31
Parsch, Pius, 44, 51
Pascal, Blaise, 63, 240
passionate detachment, 210, 218
Passionists, 66
Pastoral Letters, 146, 165–66
Paton, Alan, 49
Patrologia Graeca, 8, 125
Patrologia Latina, 8, 125
Paul, apostle, 161, 162, 165, 166, 176–78,

181, 189, 194, 196; authorship of, of NT
books, 204–5; school of, 204; theol-
ogy of, 177–78
Paul VI, 72
peer review, 124
Péguy, Charles, 48, 239
Pelikan, Jaroslav, 159
Penner, Hans, 119, 243
Penner, Todd, 243
perfectionism, 220–21
Perry, Anne, 202
persistence, 216–18
PhD programs, 78–91, 122, 129, 132, 138,
141–43, 144, 158, 213
phenomenology, 121, 168, 169, 170, 200,
217, 219
Phenomenology of the Body, The (Mar-
tino), 168
Philadelphia, 110
Philo, 121, 194, 204
Philoctetes (Sophocles), 162, 212
Philosophical Fragments (Kierkegaard),
63
philosophical religion, 118
philosophy, 43, 47, 48, 61–64, 80, 83, 136,
187, 188, 201; Hellenistic, 69, 197, 218
Philosophy of Existence, The (Marcel), 63
Pirke Avot, 198
Pitts, Mark, 125
Pius XII, 61; *Divini afflante Spiritu*, 61
Plato, 177, 178
Platonism, 178
Plotinus, 189
Plutarch, 81, 121, 171, 198
poetry, 47, 67, 202, 205, 239
Poimandres, 69, 171

Index

polemics, 126

Pompeii (Harris), 202

Pontchartrain, Lake, 42, 43, 61

possessions, 82, 85, 87, 90, 103, 121, 191, 200

postcolonialism, 12, 103, 194, 197

Powell, Colin, 164

Powers, J. F., 49

President's Advisory Council (Emory), 143

Preus, Sam, 118, 122, 243

Preuschen, Edwin, 234

Pride and Prejudice (Austen), 49

priesthood, 55, 58, 61, 70, 84, 163

Priests and People, 153, 182

Princeton Theological Seminary, 142, 152, 167

Princeton University, 97

professional assessment, 140

Prophetes (Fascher), 80

Protestant, 67, 98, 99, 127, 152, 163, 169

Protestant Faculty of Paris, 143

Proudhon, Pierre Joseph, 63, 240

Proulx, Annie, 206, 236

psychology, 64, 68, 83, 103, 136, 197, 200

Pythagorean, 82, 171

Quinn, Jerome, 165, 247

Qumran, 69, 82, 86

Rahner, Karl, 67, 191, 241

Random House, 169, 170

Ransom, John Crowe, 64, 206

Red Badge of Courage (Crane), 162

Redpath, Henry, 8, 233

Reicke, Bo, 125, 244

religion, 170–72, 188, 197, 218

Religious Studies Review, 123

reputation, 218

Resonance, 70

respect for evidence, 192–95, 218

resurrection, 101, 150, 176, 217

Richardson, Ralph, 162

Richey, Russell, 159–60

Robbins, Vernon, 129, 138

Robert W. Woodruff Distinguished Chair of New Testament and Christian Origins, 131–32, 134, 136, 137, 144, 145, 146, 154, 172

Rome, 157, 190

Rule of Benedict, 54, 56, 173, 175

Russell, Bertrand, 63, 240

Russia, 157

Russo, Richard, 162, 206

Sacra Pagina, 126, 217

Sacred Canopy (Berger), 69

Saint Andrews University, 143

Saint Joseph Seminary ("Saint Ben's"), 42, 43–51, 52, 53, 54, 70–74, 95, 119, 200, 217

Saint Meinrad School of Theology, 65–71, 72, 95, 114, 166, 179, 224

Saint Thomas Aquinas (Chesterton), 62

Saliers, Don, 245

Sanders, David, 153

Sartre, Jean-Paul, 63, 240

Scheeben, Matthias, 61, 240

Schein, Bruce, 79

Schillebeeckx, Edward, 67, 191, 241

Schoekel, Luis Alonso, 88

scholarship, 96, 143, 180, 188, 220; becoming and being a scholar, 95, 209;

and capacity to compartmentalize, 157; and celebrity, 150–51, 163; and concentration, 106, 209; definition of, 2–4; excellence in, 187, 188, 195, 202; as game, 14, 219–20, 222; and leadership, 138; and memory, 89, 106, 209; and multitasking, 106; New Testament, 5–6, 70, 73, 74, 80, 103, 106, 117, 118, 125, 130, 139, 142, 164, 165–67, 191, 193, 196, 199, 211, 226, 228–32; Old Testament, 73, 74, 118, 138, 196; persistence in, 157, 216–18; public, 156; and real life, 100, 145, 155–57, 227; virtues (intellectual), 187–208, 209; virtues (moral), 208, 209–25

Scholem, Gershom, 69, 203

Schoonenberg, Piet, 67, 241

Schopen, Gregory, 119

Schreiner, Thomas, 248

Schweitzer, Albert, 9, 234

Science and Civilization in China (Needham), 216

Scott, Robert, 8, 107, 233

Scott, Walter, 234

Scripture, 67, 68, 102, 108, 109, 115, 139, 161, 167–70, 175–76, 177, 182, 183, 190, 194, 196, 200, 209

Seale, Bobby, 75

Seattle, 167

Secular City, The (Cox), 57

Segal, Alan, 79

Seltser, Barry, 118

seminary, 13, 35, 41, 42, 209

Seneca, 81

Sentences of Pseudo-Phocylides, 198

Sentences of Sextus, 198

Septuagint, 81

Sertillanges, A. D., 233

Seven Storey Mountain (Merton), 48

sexuality, 57, 103, 104, 127, 161, 183

Shakespeare, William, 130

Shapiro, Karl, 206

Sheen on the Silk, The (Perry), 202

Sherwood, Polycarp, 66, 240

Short, Charles, 8, 234

Sickness unto Death, The (Kierkegaard), 63

Sifre on Deuteronomy, 79, 198

Simon, Yves, 62

Sisters of Mercy, 40

Smiley, Jane, 236

Smith, David, 113, 118, 122, 130

Smith, Jonathan Z., 78, 119, 152, 214, 235, 243, 251

Smith, Luther, 245

Smyth, Herbert, 8, 234

Snow, C. P., 162

Social Construction of Reality (Berger and Luckman), 69

Society for Values in Higher Education, 87

Society of Biblical Literature, 13, 91, 106, 107, 144, 146, 148, 149, 222, 246

sociology, 11–13, 64, 81, 103, 165, 197, 200, 201, 229

sociology of knowledge, 69, 81, 190

Socrates, 189

Songy, Benedict, 73

South Korea, 157

Spicq, Ceslas, 61, 166, 240

Spong, John, 246

Stackhouse, Max, 247

Index

Stanford University, 131

Stein, Steve, 118, 243

Sternberg, Meier, 118

Stetson University, 151

stoicism, 171

Stone Lectures, 152, 218

strategic planning, 143, 159

structuralism, 103

Studzinski, Raymond, 67, 70

Sufism, 118, 119

Superior (WI), 33

supersessionism, 127

supervised ministry, 140

symbolic world, 101, 182, 190, 197

synopsis, Greek, 250

Synoptic Problem, The (Farmer), 211–12

Tannehill, Robert, 127, 244

Taoism, 118

Tapestry of Mercy, The, 237

Tassin, Anthony, 64

Tate, Allen, 64

Taylor, Vincent, 61

teaching, 5, 70, 73, 87, 89, 97, 100–104, 105, 106, 118, 119–21, 127, 136, 138–45, 156, 160, 163, 180, 183, 187, 215, 224, 227, 228

teaching assistants, 224

Teaching Company, 162–64

technology, 7–11, 222–23, 229, 244; print, 7–8, 244; digital, 9–10, 232, 244

Teilhard de Chardin, Pierre, 61

tenure, 13, 104

Teresa of Ávila, 49

Theological Investigations (Rahner), 67, 241

Theological Studies, 123

theology, 43, 47, 61, 65–70, 80, 83, 104, 127, 143, 160, 167–70, 176, 181, 188, 192, 200; inductive, 141, 192; narrative, 145, 192; pastoral, 130–31, 140–41; political, 68; public, 178

Thiering, Barbara, 147

Thomas, Dylan, 48

Thomas Aquinas, Saint, 62, 70; *Commentary on the Gospel of John*, 70; *Summa theologiae*, 70

Thompson, Morton, 237

Till, Emmett, 35

Tillich, Paul, 241

Time, 148

Tirosh-Rothschild, Hava, 119

Tolbert, Mary Ann, 112

Tolstoy, Leo, 70

Too Late the Phalarope (Paton), 49

translation, 195

Tremendous Lover, The (Boylan), 48

Turner, Victor, 201, 243

Tutu, Desmond, 164

Tyler, Anne, 206

Unamuno, Miguel de, 63, 240

Uncle Tom's Children (Wright), 33, 36

undergraduates, 95

Union Theological Seminary, 132

United Methodist Church, 137, 160

University of Chicago, 143, 146, 152, 159

University of Detroit, 91

University of Iowa, 74

University of Michigan, 137

Unnik, W. C. van, 249

US News and World Report, 148

Vanderbilt University, 112, 129

Vatican Council I, 70

Vatican Council II, 56, 65, 66, 68, 108, 183, 191

Vawter, Bruce, 61, 240

Vico, Gianbattista, 6

Vidal, Gore, 202

Vietnam War, 56

virtue, 187

Voltaire, 221

Wabash Center, 144

Wagner, James, 158

Wainwright, Arthur, 138

Waiting for Godot (Beckett), 162

Wake Forest University, 143, 151

Warren, Robert Penn, 64

Wasteland, The (Eliot), 48, 162

Way of Perfection, The (Teresa), 49

Weaver, Mary Jo, 118

Wellesley College, 86

Westminster John Knox Press, 175

White, Michael, 101

White, T. H., 31, 236

White Citizens Council, 36

Wikenhauser, Alfred, 214

Wilken, Robert Louis, 248

William B. Eerdmans Publishing Co., 165, 176

Williams, Jackie, 101

Wills, Garry, 159

Wilson, A. N., 246

Wilton (CT), 98

Wink, Walter, 88, 103, 149

Wisconsin, 35, 36, 38, 43, 54, 80

Wisse, Frederick, 80, 81

wit (and humor), 22, 30, 39, 51, 54, 83, 202

Witt, Gregory de, 44

Witte, John, 146

Wodehouse, P. G., 48

Woods, Jimmy, 50

Worley, David, 101

Wright, N. T., 147, 149, 249

Wright, Richard, 33, 36

Xavier-Rynne (Francis X. Murphy), 58

Xenophon, 190

Yale Divinity School, 78, 92, 95–113, 117, 124, 125, 127, 130, 144, 159, 165, 179, 200

Yale University, 5, 74, 75, 77, 82, 91, 97, 98, 100, 110, 113, 143, 191; benefits, 98; compared to Indiana University, 117, 118; health plan, 98, 99; library, 7–8, 77; PhD program, 17, 78, 81, 85, 89, 90, 91, 179, 242

Yale University Press, 172

Yarbro Collins, Adela, 149

Yarbrough, Larry, 101

Youncecour, Margarite, 202

Zeller, Hubert van, 60

Zuckerman, Bruce, 79